THE
WOODWORK
BOOK

Editor
Piers Dudgeon
Main editorial consultants
John Makepeace   Robert Ingham
Dennis Gray   Richard Starr (U.S.A.)
B. C. Hopking

Art director
Mike Ricketts
Design assistant
Martin Atcherley
Illustrators
Rob Shone   Stephen Attalides
Andrew Farmer   Nick May
Original photography
Rod Shone

Craftsmen
Fred Baier   Richard La Trobe Bateman   Norman Beverton
Ashley Cartwright   Wendell Castle   John Hardy
James Krenov   Sam Maloof   Richard Raffan
Howard Raybould   Bob Stocksdale

We would like to thank all the craftsmen for contributing the designs which are the core of the book, their advice and the spirit in which it was given. We also owe much to the encouragement of John Kelsey, editor of the American based *Fine Woodworking* magazine, and Ann Hartree, whose *Prescote Gallery* in England provides one of the country's most important showplaces for the work of Britain's finest craftsmen. Our thanks too to The Timber Research and Development Council and the British Home Timber Merchants Association.

The quotes by George Nakashima on pages 8 and 18, the quotes by Professor Bruce Hoadley (pages 12 and 16), and those by Robert Foncanon on pages 162/3 are all reprinted by kind permission of *Fine Woodworking* magazine, as too is the U.S.A. and Canada listing of hardwood merchants. Copyright © 1979, 1980 The Taunton Press Inc.

Conceived and produced by Pilot Productions Ltd.

First published in Great Britain in 1980 by
Pan Books Limited

This edition published in 1988 by
Treasure Press
59 Grosvenor Street
London W1

Copyright © 1980 Pilot Productions Ltd

ISBN 1 85051 271 X

Printed in Hong Kong

THE WOODWORK BOOK

Introduced by
John Makepeace

TREASURE PRESS

Contents

Introduction

Part one: WOOD

Part two: PLANS

Projects have been accorded one to four asterisks
as a progressive measure of the technical ability
required to make them.

Part three: TOOLS & TECHNIQUES

Notice

In the light of recent findings regarding the inflammable properties of foam-filled furniture, the publishers advise against using foam for the items of furniture on pages 58 and 85.

Introduction by John Makepeace

When the idea of a book about woodworking for the amateur was first mooted, I recoiled intuitively. After years of receiving countless letters from enthusiasts about particular problems, the prospect of writing a book on the subject was more than I could contemplate at the time. However, the need for a more penetrating book was quite obvious.

As we talked about the idea, it became clear that the book should not focus on technical information alone. The decision reflected one that I had made twelve months earlier in establishing the *School for Craftsmen in Wood* at Parnham House. Then, I was determined that we should provide a course which would help integrate students into society as self-employed designers and craftsmen. Had we emphasised technique to the exclusion of other important aspects, at best we would have produced graduates with super-high standards of manual skill without aesthetic sensitivity – a trait all too common amongst woodworkers.

While this book has not been designed to cover all aspects of the Parnham course – we make a point of teaching business management and marketing, for example – there remains a link between the idea of the school and the aims and intentions behind the book's composition.

Many of the contributors have lectured and run seminars at Parnham. All have practical and commercial experience as professional craftsmen, and can speak with clarity and the authority which comes from first-hand experience and the continuous struggle in the early years of starting a business. The Timber and Tools sections have been compiled under the direction of Robert Ingham, Principal of the School, a superb craftsman and very able designer.

Intentions

We are constantly reminded that today we enjoy increased leisure time. That may seem an illusion because a large proportion of Western civilization takes its hobbies and sport so seriously that spare time as such is always at a premium.

In almost all cases, those recreational activities provide opportunities for personal fulfilment and development often denied individuals in this technological age.

The improved equipment available for small-scale woodworking, the growing interest in our homes, together with the high cost of good products distributed through the retail trade, have combined to generate increased interest in making things of quality and individuality at home.

The purpose of the book, therefore, is to encourage individual craftsmanship by example, by instruction, and by demonstrating the sometimes contrasting attitudes of those who have established themselves as successful designers and workers in wood.

The word "craftsman" is over-used – particularly by unions and advertising copywriters!

Craftsmanship, as I understand it, means not only a facility with materials and skills, but also a dedication to excellence in every aspect of a product.

For many of us, the very act of making things well is an expression of optimism, a belief in a future that puts our past in perspective, even a desire to leave for future generations a more challenging starting point than we have inherited. That motivation is not restricted to the professional craftsman.

Instead of showing industrially-made artefacts, commonly the source of inspiration for the amateur, our selection of some of the best-known makers – of different ages, philosophies, and from various parts of the world – makes available to an international audience design ideas and attitudes which will enable the amateur to become more personally involved in every aspect of his own creations. Whilst many will be happy to use the given plans as they stand – they have been purposely "graded" to appeal to all woodworkers whatever their technical abilities – others will no doubt wish to adjust, modify, and improve upon them, according to their particular circumstances.

The response of all the contributors to the idea of sharing their ideas has been remarkably generous. Without exception, their work is increasingly prized not only as functional objects, but because they demonstrate an unusual combination of skill and creativity. Yet professional designers are not normally prepared to make their work so explicit. For whatever reasons, there are traditions of secrecy which here have given way to an openness that permits us all a unique opportunity to learn how to make splendid things in wood.

Why wood?

It is probably true that most people choose to work with wood because they were taught to make things with it at school. Typically, woodwork classes and do-it-yourself books for the amateur are aimed at imparting woodworking techniques (the science of the subject). It is an efficiency-based training frequently concerned with short-cuts and labour-saving devices designed to enable the student to *cope* with the inherent problems of wood, and move as effortlessly as possible to making functional objects. This book is different in that real practising professional craftsmen have produced plans to provoke the imagination of the amateur woodworker, and the advice they impart is grounded in methods sensitive to the nature of the materials which they use.

Much of what results from the usual educational process might arguably be better made out of metal, plastic or some other artificial material.

"Many evening classes merely provide facilities with very little real educational value. The objects offered to the amateur for him to make are so banal in design that there is very little to attract his imagination."
John Makepeace

Lost in the approach is an acknowledgement of the natural idiosyncracies of wood and their potential in designing objects which have more to recommend themselves than that they are functional.

The natural characteristics of wood
When we talk about the characteristics of wood, we mean its hardness, softness, weight, colour, stability, texture, figure, grain pattern, workability and durability. Endlessly varied qualities (no trees are the same, even within the same species) determine what we can do with it. Selection is based upon whether we want to turn it, carve it, mould it, build outdoor furniture with it, produce surfaces on which to work or for display.

"Wood is a quite extraordinary material which covers a wide spectrum of weight, colour, strength, grain and other characteristics. If you make a wise selection, according to your requirements, virtually anything is possible."
Howard Raybould

The importance of this message – that the characteristics of wood have an essential bearing upon what we do with it – is recognised by all the craftsmen here. What does vary is the degree of 'respect' which they accord the material as a *starting point* for design. Some allow the wood to *dictate* the form of a finished object. This is the reason why Richard La Trobe Bateman admits enjoying working with wet wood. Others, like Wendell Castle, are concerned with imposing forms on the material. But these forms are designed and constructed within boundaries imposed by the nature of the material. Whichever school of contemporary furniture design we agree with, it remains a fact that wood – the material – provides unique 'problems to solve', challenges which when met in an

imaginative fashion can be translated into design decisions of an extremely individual kind.

"The enjoyment is in coping with the technical restraints of wood. That's the fun of being your own designer. You respond to whatever the technical restraints happen to be. Nor do you just cope with them. You can positively use them in your favour. That's the creative aspect of it."
Richard La Trobe Bateman

Wood – an opportunity for personal expression
"People are beginning to look for something to do where they can say the things that they cannot say in the bank or at the office, to people who haven't got the time to listen."
James Krenov

There are very many superb woodworkers who have very little talent for design as such. That is almost certainly true, but does not necessarily deny these 'superb woodworkers' the opportunity to create individual pieces of furniture through a) not accepting, without understanding, so-called rules layed down by an efficiency-based training; and b) becoming more curious about the qualities of wood in relation to the job in hand.

In the end, if one thousand people made all the pieces of furniture in this book and followed the instructions to the letter, you would be amazed how different the results would be. A lot of each individual would get into those pieces whether they liked it or not. By giving clues as to how these individual differences may be *intentionally* directed towards each piece of furniture, it may become clear that originality, in the sense of individuality, is not an inexplicable God-given talent.

"In the past, this originality thing has been primarily a visual message. Craft knowledge – the methods – have been taught in such a way that anyone can produce the objects they need with the minimum amount of effort and the maximum amount of efficiency. Then, if you're original, the object is original. That's the training ... But many students are not satisfied that that's what it is about. There's this big question mark. Maybe there's another kind of originality – the finger prints of the person who made the thing."
James Krenov

More is said on page 140 about Krenov's exposition of design as a retrospective judgement of really good craftsmanship. But what leads on from the quote above is that the result, which we are all after, is not dependent upon outside rules which enable us to get to it in the easiest possible fashion, but upon decisions which each of us takes – decisions with regard to selecting wood (page 22), marking out at preparation stage (page 32), choosing how to joint wood (page 174), selecting tools for each part of the job based upon an understanding of how tools operate on the material (pages 144 to 173), and selecting one's own method of

finishing (page 182). If the process is personal enough in this way, then that personal expression will show in the result. Suddenly 'Look what I have done!' reflects a whole host of decisions which you alone have taken – decisions which underline the unimaginative nature of so much mass-produced furniture today.

Taking time and learning to see
There are two conditions which apply to this approach. First, that the job has to take the time that it needs. As an amateur it is leisure time we are talking about – arguably *the* most important time. Which makes it all the more important that it be spent to best advantage. The amateur benefits in this respect since, unlike the professional, he is not bound to time in a competitive sense. The second condition is that we develop an awareness of the potential of our materials and not be senselessly hidebound by rules presented by others as irrefutable. For example, grain is invariably characterised as a problem. Our attention is drawn time and again to the difficulties in working across it. How often are its positive aspects highlighted? "Grain," states Krenov, "is part of the *graphics* of wood." He goes on to demonstrate how grain patterns on two book-matched rectangular cupboard doors create an illusion of a more interesting, 'friendly', oval shape. On page 177 his book-matched cabinet doors provide a good example of grain used to visual advantage. There are many other ways in which it can be exploited to 'change' or accentuate shape. If he had reversed these doors, the grain patterns would have accentuated the corners and hardened the shape of the cabinet. Time spent experimenting in this way convinces that grain patterns, colour, shadings and lines can all be harnessed to make the form of a piece more individual.

You might decide to not ignore wood's irregularities but incorporate them into a table top or whatever. George Nakashima believes that *"lumber with the most interest poses the most difficult problems, and so often the best figuring is accompanied by knots, areas of worm holes, deep openings, cracks . . ."* On investigation you may learn that sapwood is not *de facto* useless for furniture. Strength differences between sapwood and heartwood are usually insignificant. The point about sapwood is that it is less decay-resistant. You may also notice the subtle colour shift between sap and heart. Could you use it to advantage?

As we begin to really look at it, we can begin to understand why wood has been described as 'an extraordinary material'. *"When we get close enough to it, then what we are about to do is transformed,"* concludes Krenov.

Finally, then, it is in the surprises that wood has to offer, the endless possibilities which it affords the curious craftsman as he studies it in relation to the job in hand, the enjoyment which results from developing one's own individual logic in relation to its characteristics... it is in all these things that lies the answer to our question, 'Why wood?'

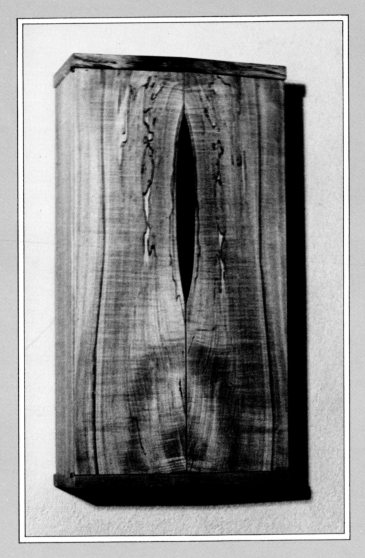

A small wall cabinet made by
James Krenov. "This wood has
both pattern and rhythm. The
opening, where the doors meet,
was prompted by the edge of the
later resawn plank."

"I always think of wood being alive. I grew up in primitive places in the North where there were many legends and the supposition that some objects were animated and alive with a spirit of their own." James Krenov

Wood structure

"A tree is made up of a myriad of cells, all of which were alive when they were formed, some of which are still alive, but most of which (in the wood of the tree) are dead ... The thin cambium layer, which is the growing interface between bark and wood, is composed of living cells. Cambium cells divide to produce new bark (the outer coating of the tree which affords protection) and wood cells (which become sapwood). As the newly divided cambial cells differentiate and transform into various specialised wood cells, they remain alive for several days – long enough to assume their final shape and to develop the full cell-wall thickness.

"In newly matured sapwood, only a few cells (roughly 10%) remain alive. They are called parenchyma cells. By retaining their living contents they are able to assimilate and store carbohydrates ... The non-living cells may still participate in the tree's life functions by providing means of sap conduction through their now empty cavities (vessels in hardwoods, tracheids in softwoods), or they may simply strengthen and support the tree according to their relative cell-wall thickness.

"As sapwood eventually becomes heartwood, the parenchyma cells also die. Heartwood is all dead cells. No sap conduction takes place in heartwood."
Professor Bruce Hoadley

How does a tree feed itself?

Sap consists of water and dissolved mineral salts. Rapid evaporation from leaf surfaces draws the sap up through roots and numerous tiny vessels in the tree itself.

Carbon dioxide, as a constituent of air, is breathed in through tiny leaf pores known as stomata.

Chlorophyll (the green pigment in leaves) catalyses a complex chemical reaction (known as photosynthesis) between carbon dioxide, water and sunlight to produce sugars and starches on which a tree lives.

When photosynthesis has converted the sap into essential foods, the nutrients traverse the tree via the bast and thence into the inner tree via capillaries called medullary rays, which run radially across the trunk section.

How does a tree breathe?

Trees need oxygen just as animals do. Respiration takes place through tiny pores in the leaves known as stomata and air is suffused through the tree. During daylight, when photosynthesis is taking place, carbon dioxide is absorbed in the process, and any excess oxygen is expelled. At night, when photosynthesis stops, very little air is taken in by the leaves. During this period any excess carbon dioxide is exhaled through the stomata. In this way, forests are responsible for maintaining the delicate balance of oxygen and carbon dioxide in the atmosphere.

Does a tree continue to breathe when cut down?

When a tree is cut down its life support system comes to a halt. Even the parenchyma sapwood cells gradually die as the wood is dried. In no sense can wood be said to breathe after it is dead. The shrinking and swelling of wood in response to variations in atmospheric humidity is the result of wood fibre acting like a sponge soaking up moisture in an effort to maintain itself in a sympathetic state with its environs. Nor, incidentally, does wood feed itself when dead – feeding wood with wax or other finishes is a figure of speech. No finish nourishes wood.

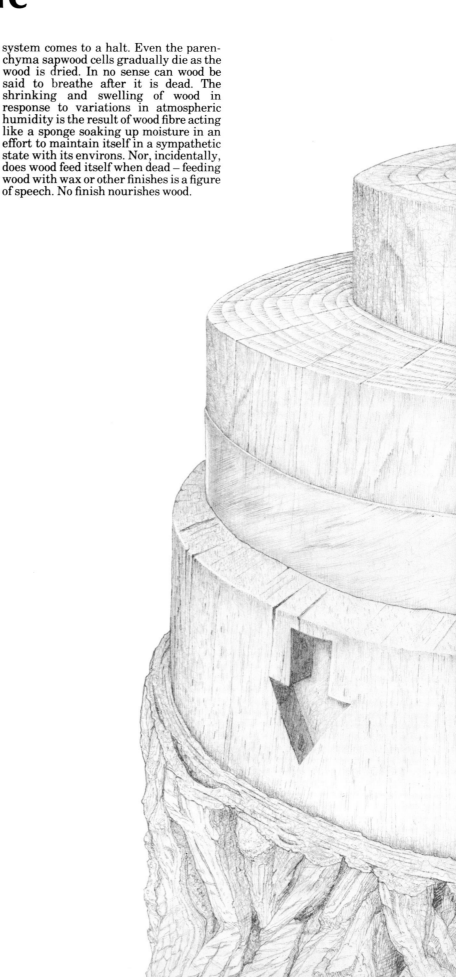

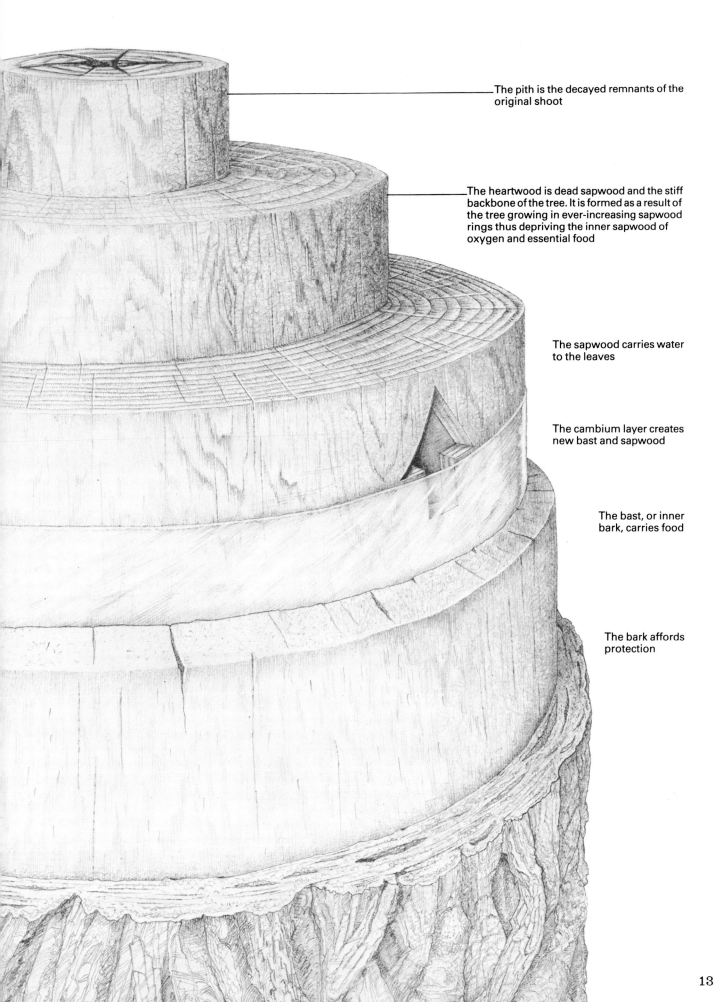

The pith is the decayed remnants of the original shoot

The heartwood is dead sapwood and the stiff backbone of the tree. It is formed as a result of the tree growing in ever-increasing sapwood rings thus depriving the inner sapwood of oxygen and essential food

The sapwood carries water to the leaves

The cambium layer creates new bast and sapwood

The bast, or inner bark, carries food

The bark affords protection

13

From forest to wood yard

Characteristics of hardwoods and softwoods

The distinction between hardwoods and softwoods is a distinction between two groups of trees. Softwoods come from coniferous (cone-bearing) trees – hardwoods come from broad-leaved, usually deciduous trees, which shed leaves in autumn.

*Within this general classification, it should be noted that, despite the terminology, some softwoods are actually harder than many hardwoods – yew for example; and there are some hardwoods, like balsa which are very soft.

*Softwoods are generally cheaper than hardwoods because they tend to be grown in forests of one variety, which clearly facilitates felling and transportation; hardwoods grow in temperate regions and take longer to mature than softwoods; softwoods tend to grow long straight trunks, and are thus commonly available in cheaper, longer boards.

*While it is often stated that hardwoods are more difficult to work than softwoods and make cutting edges blunt more quickly, there is no *certain* rule. Many softwoods, e.g. yew, Columbian pine, 'knotty pine' are very difficult to plane, whereas ash, sycamore, even elm can be easy to plane. A great deal depends on the individual piece.

* For outdoor use, wood should be selected for its durability and rot-resistance. Most softwoods deteriorate fast outdoors.

*Characteristically, many hardwoods are more decorative than softwoods. Consequently, where appearance is important, as in furniture making, hardwoods are preferable.

*Since there are many more varieties of hardwoods than softwoods there is more choice.

*Hardwoods are more resistant to surface marking and their closer grain formation makes them better for surfaces which will come into contact with food.

*Hardwoods tend to be more durable and have a longer lifespan than softwoods.

Felling

Generally speaking the process is for the trade buyer to negotiate purchasing trees standing on a given tract of land within a forest area. He will negotiate on the basis of an approximate cubic footage of a particular species. There he may find a number of prime examples of timber alongside lower grade timber which is not as valuable; and lastly there may even be species of timber unfamiliar in world market terms. Sometimes, particularly fine timbers attract a separate negotiation within the area which is the overall subject of negotiation. As we shall see the veneer market increasingly takes the finest hardwood timbers.

In Central and South America, Asia and Africa, rain forest hardwoods often grow in very tall straight, cylindrical bowls. Elsewhere, trees tend to display a main trunk length to a point where the trunk forks in two directions. If the wood after this fork is usable – it does tend to be of a lower quality than the main trunk wood (more defects and less heartwood) – then the whole tree will be felled at once. But boughs are rarely used for furniture since once converted they will be much more likely to 'move' (i.e. shrink or swell) than the main trunk. The reason for this is that there is proportionately less heartwood and the annual ring formation encourages shrinkage.

Should you be involved in felling your own trees, it is worth noting that some are protected and there is an onus on you to contact the Forestry Commission before doing so. There is a relatively inexpensive chain saw on the market, the

Plain-sawn log
Most logs are sawn through and through to yield the maximum amount of useful wood.

Boughwood

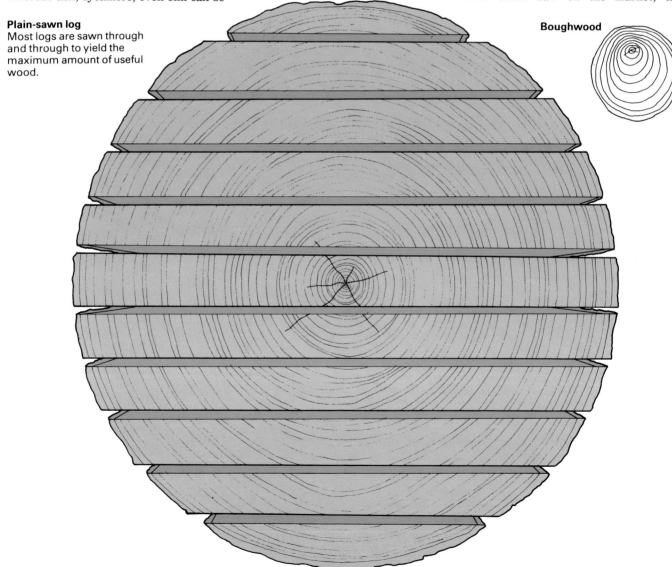

14

Alaskan Chain Saw, which has been produced for cutting logs into planks. A distinct advantage of choosing your tree, felling it, flitch-cutting it (cutting it in longitudinal sections) and re-sawing the fine thick planks when dry and as you need them, is that the wood will always be of more interest to you, more personal to you – your work will certainly not suffer as a result! More practically, you may restrict your gathering of wood to odd pieces of drift wood or such like. Take it home and retrieve a selection for carving or turning.

The saw mill
The next stage is to convert the felled log into planks. A log may be cut at the saw mill in two ways. It may be that the sawyer will actually revise his decision as to how to cut the log as he works through it and discovers its figure (decorative characteristics) through the structure. He will be thinking of the requirements of his customers and also how to derive the most value from the cutting. It is one of the most important jobs in the saw mill.

The plain-sawn flitch-cut log
Usually saw mills will cut their logs 'through and through' as shown in the illustration. Planks cut this way produce end grain which displays the log's annual rings running from edge to edge.

The quarter-sawn log

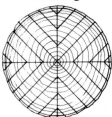

Years ago, in order to cut logs so that the sawn boards would display maximum figure, logs would be cut radially from the centre (see illustration). The problem with this was the amount of waste. But, if you did cut wood in this way, it would be very much harder wearing as the cuts follow the lines of cleavage. Nowadays, saw mills get as near as they can to radial cuttings with minimum waste and maximum figure (see illustration).

You will notice by looking at both illustrations of plain-sawn and quarter-sawn logs that the middle planks of the plain-sawn log are in fact quarter cut and thus more likely to reveal an attractive figure inside the log.

One very real difference between plain-sawn and quarter-sawn logs concerns their future behaviour. As we shall see in the section on seasoning (page 16) quarter-sawn boards are likely to move (i.e. shrink, swell or cup) less when drying out than plain-sawn boards. It follows, therefore, that mid-tree boards in a plain-sawn log will be less likely to be problematic later than those cut from elsewhere.

British grown hardwoods are rarely stripped of their bark at the saw mill, and once cut into planks the bark can help to protect the timber from the effects of too fast drying. Fast drying can lead to cracked or split wood. Most imported timbers, however, are debarked before shipping because bark is a breeding ground for insects and decay. There are some exceptions to this – we found some French beech and oak that had come in with bark. But in general, imported timber is stripped of its bark and exported square-edged. It will also have been partially dried at source to a 25% moisture level which is, incidently, 5% the wrong side of the dry rot safety line.

Quarter-sawn log
A log cut as close to the natural lines of cleavage as cost permits.

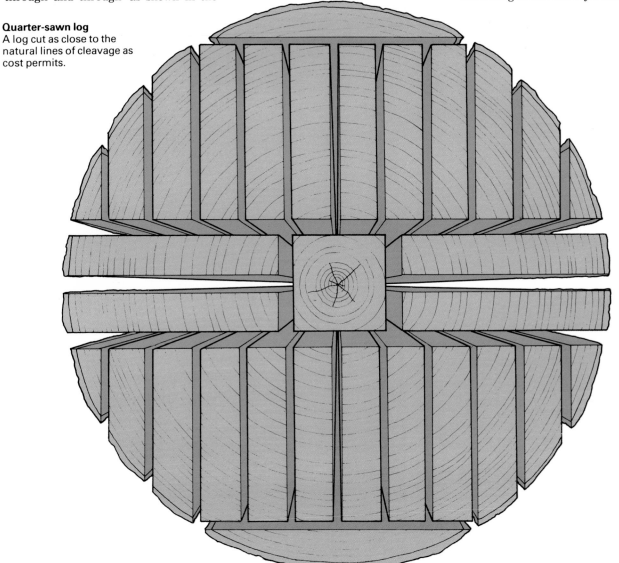

Seasoning and movement

Seasoning refers to the reduction of moisture content in wood. The word probably derived originally from those seasons in the year when natural drying could be most efficiently carried out. The object of seasoning wood, and thus reducing its water content, is to minimise the problem of discolouration and fungus, and render it less likely to shrink and generally distort. As soon as the tree is felled it begins to dry out naturally.

"A sopping wet sponge, just pulled from a pail of water, is analogous to wood in a living tree to the extent that the cell walls are fully saturated and swollen, and cell cavities are partially-to-completely filled with water.
"Now imagine wringing out a wet sponge until no further liquid water is evident. The sponge remains full-size, fully flexible and damp to the touch. In wood the comparable condition is called the fibre saturation point, wherein although the cell cavities are emptied of water, the cell walls are fully saturated and fully swollen, and therefore in their weakest condition. The water remaining in the cell walls is called bound water. *Just as a sponge would have to be left to dry (and shrink and harden) so will the bound water slowly leave a piece of wood if placed in a relatively dry atmosphere."*
Professor Bruce Hoadley

The fibre saturation point of wood is usually 30% moisture content. Once wood has reached this point the process of drying will be greatly slowed down, although it will continue to dry out until its moisture content is *in balance with the humidity of its surrounding atmosphere.*

Moisture content levels
Fungus in wood can only arise when the moisture content exceeds a figure of approximately 20% in an atmosphere with inadequate ventilation. What follows is a rough advisory guide of recommended moisture content levels.

Recommended percentage moisture content levels:	
16%	UK outdoor furniture
12/14%	Occasionally heated rooms
11/13%	Normally heated rooms
9/11%	Continuously centrally heated rooms and general level for southern and coastal regions of USA
8%	Most northern and central regions of USA
6/8%	Radiator shelves and arid south west of USA

See page 23, **Is it seasoned?**

Methods of seasoning
The unending dispute amongst professionals as to whether converted timber should be air dried or kiln dried is of little more than academic interest to the amateur unless he is sensitive to the consequences of steam kiln drying.

"Can it be that we are forgetting the feel of air-dried wood under our own tools, and no longer notice how the kiln-dried wood is less alive, even in shavings? It actually sounds different – listen as you work. And the colours: notice that a kiln-dried Italian walnut hasn't the clarity it had before; the soft tints of pink and grey are gone. After all, kiln-dried wood has been steamed, almost cooked."
James Krenov

The answer to the dispute may lie in the qualification that not all kiln-dried timber is dried properly, and poorly air-dried timber can be equally useless.

Kiln drying
Timber is stacked in kilns where hot air and steam are pumped across all surfaces of the wood. What can cause damage is the creation of an excessively dry atmosphere in the kiln which dries the timber too quickly. Also, kiln drying is the most expensive process. The advantages of kiln drying are the speed of the process over air drying, and the ability to attain moisture content levels in timber lower than is possible outside.

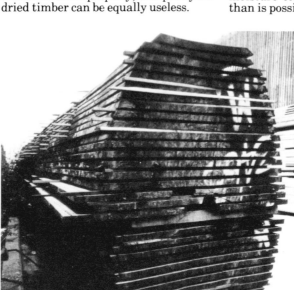

Left:
Air drying stacks should be supported well off the ground to prevent excess moisture gathering at the bottom. Each course of boards is separated by narrow strips of dry wood called stickers placed at the ends of each board and no more than 460mm (18in) apart. Outdoor stacks should be covered with waste boards or old roofing against exposure to rain and sun.

Below:
A commercial kiln.

Air drying

Timber is stickered (see illustration) so that air can pass across all surfaces of the wood, but should be protected from the degrading effects of direct sun and rain. The ideal position is on a hillside, the stack exposed to a good drying wind, and its top protected by a lean-to roof.

Mr. A. W. Denby of Specialist Wood Services, Stourbridge, West Midlands, DY7 6LR, explains a new development:

"It is now possible to create and maintain ideal drying conditions in a boxed off part of one's own workshop or yard, and to dry one's own timber gently to the required moisture content with little or no degrade. An air-conditioning unit is enclosed, along with properly stickered timber, in a heat-insulated and vapour-proof box. "Within the box, air is drawn by a fan over a hot compressor. The resultant warm air circulates through the timber stack and picks up moisture from the wood. This warm, and now moist air passes over the cooling section of the unit, condenses, and drops into a tray, running out of the box via a pipe. The dried air is then re-heated over the compressor and recirculated to repeat the process.
"This heat-pump action is so remarkably efficient that smaller units run on as little as 300 watts (the power of three electric light bulbs). The smallest unit costs around £350 and will dry from 20 to 60 cu. ft. at a time."

How do changing humidity levels affect wood?

You will never be able to predict future movement in a piece of wood or a piece of furniture other than in a fairly general fashion. Wood is not a homogeneous solid and, unlike our hitherto analogous sponge, it will not shrink or swell similarly in all directions.

There are three main principles of movement of wood:

1. Timber moves most along the line of its annual rings. As a log dries out the circumference of the log will decrease in size.

2. The amount of movement between the rings is approximately half that along the length of the rings.

3. Timber is generally stable (i.e. does not move) along its length, regardless of humidity variation in the atmosphere.

The plain-sawn plank
According to the above principles, the plank will tend to move most across its width. It will move approximately half as much through its thickness.

The quarter-sawn plank
Again, on the above principles, most movement will be in its thickness.

Warping and distortion
A further distinction occurs between the plain-sawn and quarter-sawn plank when we consider the problem of distortion as they dry. The annual rings in the

The felled log
As a log dries out, its circumference shrinks most along the line of its annual rings.

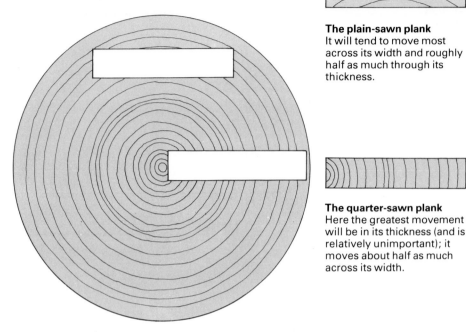

Annual rings tend to become less curved when drying. There is a greater tendency towards distortion in a plain-sawn plank than in a quarter-sawn.

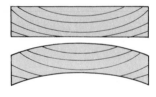

The plain-sawn plank
It will tend to move most across its width and roughly half as much through its thickness.

The quarter-sawn plank
Here the greatest movement will be in its thickness (and is relatively unimportant); it moves about half as much across its width.

quarter-sawn plank are roughly the same length, whereas the annual rings in the plain-sawn plank vary greatly in length. There is a tendency for the wood to pull away from the smallest ring on the plain-sawn plank and thus bend away from the heart of the tree. There is virtually no tendency to distortion in a quarter-sawn plank. Further and worse havoc is created when the grain direction is irregular as we have already noted in relation to bough wood (see page 14).

Movement in timber after purchase
Once you have got your wood home there is of course no reason for it to stop swelling and shrinking in sympathy with the humidity of its environment.

The first thing to do is to reassure yourself as to the actual moisture content of your wood. The traditional method, known as the oven method, is to take a small block of wood from the plank (it is a good idea to take it from the centre of the plank rather than the end as the end is likely to be unrepresentatively dry), note its weight and then put it in a low heat oven until its weight fails to drop following intermittent weighing tests. At this stage its weight is called its *dry weight*. The difference between its original weight and its dry weight is known as its lost weight. Its percentage moisture content can be worked out by the following equation:

$$\text{MOISTURE CONTENT PERCENTAGE} = \frac{\text{LOST WEIGHT} \times 100}{\text{DRY WEIGHT}}$$

If the moisture content level is way above the requisite level then you have no alternative but to let it air dry in stick. Bear in mind that wood stored under cover but exposed to the open air in Great Britain is unlikely to dry below a percentage moisture content of 15% during a dry season or around 20% in fairly humid conditions. This figure will of course vary with the humidity level in your area. Professor Hoadley makes the point that in central New England, U.S.A., the relative humidity averages around 77% and air-dried lumber will have a moisture content of 13/14%. See also page 16.

Once you have satisfied yourself that the wood is near the percentage moisture content level that you require for the surroundings in which it will be placed, stand the wood in the room in which it will be used for two or three weeks prior to building.

And remember that if you are *not* building in the room in which it will stand, a knowledge of the humidity in your workshop, and possibly an adjustment of it is essential. Atmospheric humidity can be measured by means of hygrometers, and atmospheric humidity can be adjusted by (de) humidifiers.

In addition to taking these precautions against wood movement (which can otherwise play havoc with your designs) there are, as we shall see in the Plans, various design measures which can be taken when you are actually building the piece.

Irregularities and defects

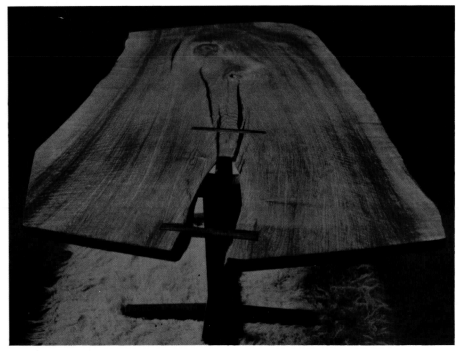

Live knot
Dead knot

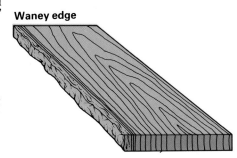

Waney edge

Many craftsmen take pains to point out that irregularities in a finished piece can add character, a personal touch, something which goes part of the way to making a piece more individual.

George Nakashima, as evidence of his basic philosophy of design, takes a fairly revolutionary attitude towards natural irregularities in wood. For him, as we have seen, knots, cracks, any so-called natural defects, far from posing problems may even be potential avenues of hope. *"Just short of being worthless,"* says Nakashima, *"A board often has the most potential."* He has spent forty years making contact with timber merchants across the world. He will seek old forgotten trees and breathe new life into them, fashioning gnarled extravagant burls, giving them a full second life as extremely individual pieces of furniture. The wood, however irregular, dictates the

form. A plank split in two down a third of its length is prevented from cracking apart completely by a butterfly key being worked across the widest point of that crack. Thus this apparent 'reject' is fashioned into a fine 3ft×7ft single board walnut table.

A maverick perhaps, but a thoroughly successful craftsman nonetheless, whose example makes a mockery of accepted principles by suggesting that 'problem' wood can be worked to advantage.

Recognising irregularities

"Investigate your wood; remember that it is seldom just what it appears to be ... knots play strange tricks, sometimes appearing almost out of nowhere, or, when you imagine they must go deep in the wood – they are in reality only on the surface, and quickly fade."
James Krenov

Plugging a hole left by a knot

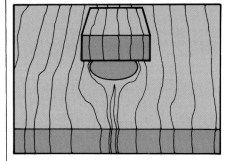

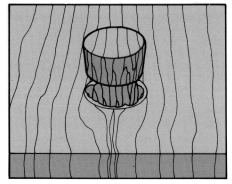

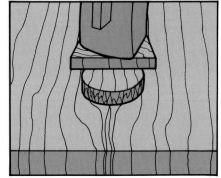

1. Select a piece of patch wood with a similar figure and grain pattern to the board wood.

2. Decide the size and shape of the patch, make the patch wood accordingly and with your chisel, pare it down so that it tapers all the way round into a sort of plug.

3. Place the shaped plug over the defect and scribe a pencil mark onto the board wood equal to the size and shape of the base of the plug (i.e. its smallest surface area).

4. With a scribing gouge of a suitable profile pare down the knot hole to the mark you have made.

5. Glue the plug, place a piece of softwood over it and with a mallet tap it into the hole.

6. Finish with a sharp plane, then a scraper, if necessary finally with abrasive paper.

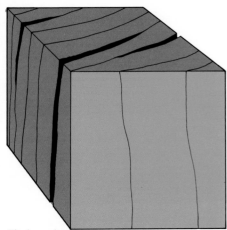

Pitch pockets

Burr wood

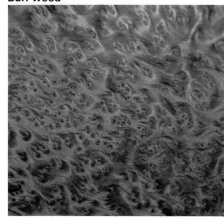

Knots

There are two kinds of knot. A live knot (which is sound, tight and slightly tacky with resin) is the ingrown basal position of a cleanly pruned living branch. A dead knot is loose (will probably fall out if included in a piece of furniture) and is the result of a mature branch having broken off, leaving a dead stump encased in the tree.

It is true to say that *all* knots weaken timber.

Waney edges

Waney edge refers to the outer edge of a board, which may display bark. When it is removed, a board is square-edged. Waney edges are susceptible to decay and insect invasion.

Pitch (or resin) pockets

The trouble with pitch pockets is that they very often remain hidden below the surface of the wood and only later develop into a serious structural defect. You cannot hope to find all of them, but you can learn to look for them. Remove the resin from the pockets and patch as for replacing a dead knot.

Burrs (or burls)

Burrs are growths which may be caused by fungal or insect invasion. Some are very valuable pieces of timber. They usually occur at the base of a trunk.

Shakes

Heart and star shakes develop along the medullary rays; cup and ring shakes along the plane of the annual rings. Decay, weather, felling, badly controlled drying can variously produce shakes, or splits as they are sometimes known.

Some defects due to seasoning

Cupping, Bowing and stick marks

We have already seen how in the drying process wood can move and warp. Badly arranged sticks (when planks are air drying) can also cause cupping or bowing of boards (see illustration), and badly stacked timber sometimes betrays permanent and ingrained marks caused by water collecting around the sticks. This latter problem, a reflection of atmospheric conditions, may mislead an unwary purchaser as to the age of the wood. A truly old log drying in stick may well look dirty but discolouration due to age can be planed to reveal the log's original appearance. You can ask a merchant whether he will do this for you, but will have to accept that it may delay your order a day or two.

Honeycombing

Honeycombing is the result of timber being poorly dried. Often too fast kiln drying is to blame. There is no way that you can reverse the process and it does severely affect the structural strength of timber. Too rapid kiln drying can also lead to the collapse of wood cells – in effect the moisture has been withdrawn too fast from the wood for it to be replaced by air, and the result is extensive shrinking and warping.

Other seasoning defects:
Surface checks

Surface checks or splits occur when a board is dried too quickly or if air-dried timber is exposed to direct sunlight or heavy rainfall. Unlike honeycombing, surface checks are visible in unplaned boards. Honeycombing is visible only if a board has been cross cut since seasoning.

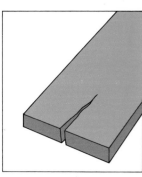

End checks

End checks, or small splits in the end of a board, may occur however fastidious is the seasoning process. Larger checks can occur during seasoning because board ends are the first and fastest to dry out. Make allowance for these before marking out.

Shakes

Bowing and cupping

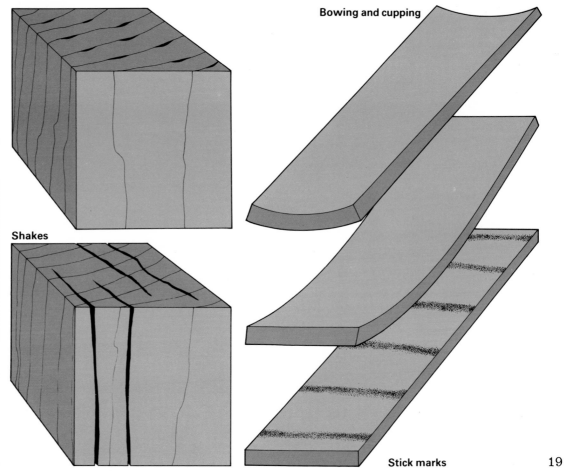

Stick marks

19

Man-made sheet materials

The manufacture of veneer

The manufacture of veneer is a highly specialised business. First, the log must be prepared. This involves immersing it in boiling water or subjecting it to steam (both operations designed to soften the wood) until it has reached precisely the optimum temperature for clean cutting. The cutting is no simple process either. The log must be set at the correct angle to the knife or saw, and the thickness and rate of cutting judged by experience. Furthermore, because cutting is always done across the grain there is always the possibility of tearing up wood fibres (as, for example, can happen when hand planing across the grain).

Below:
Rotary peeling
Right:
Slicing
Far right: 3-ply, 5-ply & multi-ply sheets

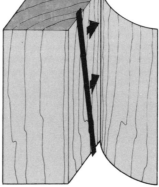

and moved up and down against a fixed knife set diagonally to the log. The knife can be geared to cut extremely fine face veneers. Each downwards motion of the log automatically feeds the knife forward according to its pre-adjusted setting.

If a whole cylindrical log section is cut, the initial cutting will produce a cleaner and more decorative veneer than later as the knife cuts against the rings, when it tends to produce a more woolly result. Most consistently decorative results are produced by slicing quarter-sawn log sections.

Plywood – a balanced construction

Plywood is made by bonding veneers with

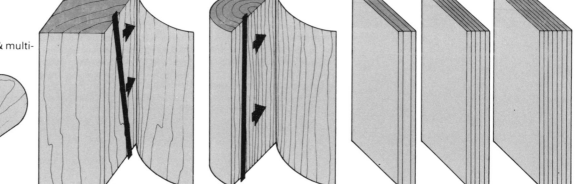

veneer on either side. Blockboard can be made from hardwood strips and is in same tropical and sub-tropical countries, e.g. Malaya. The grain direction in the face veneers runs at right angles to the grain of the softwood strips. A more expensive and superior kind of blockboard has two additional veneers whose grain direction runs parallel to that of the core veneers.

Blockboard is available in large sheets and is particularly noted for its rigidity. It is suitable for stout carcase-work, and table tops, doors, partitions, etc. If there is a particular drawback to the range of blockboard readily available through timber merchants and D.I.Y. stores, it is

Cutting methods

Years ago, all veneer cutting was done by enormous circular saws (and even earlier by hand). The problem with these methods is that however finely set are the saw teeth, the saw's cutting action produces a great deal of sawdust waste. Nowadays circular saws are still used for some particularly difficult hardwoods and, wasteful as their action is, they can produce veneers of high quality since these saws are less likely to cause damage to wood fibres than the more popularly used fixed veneer knife. Circular saws are also used in cutting some highly figured veneers from irregular outgrowths or branches.

There are two sorts of veneer cutting by knife.

Rotary peeling

Following their preparation, logs are cut to size and mounted on huge 'lathes'. The cutting knife is fixed to feed itself towards the lengths as it rotates on the 'lathe'. Rotation rates increase as soon as the length of log has been cut to a pure cylindrical shape. This cutting action produces a large continuous sheet of veneer which is later trimmed, cut, dried and graded.

Slicing

Rotary peeling is only used for cutting certain species of veneer. Common hardwoods with clear cylindrical boles and grain patterns peel with least wastage and tearing of wood fibres. These species are in fact suitable mainly for plywood manufacture and for corestock (the inner veneers) in expensive plywood.

Slicing, on the other hand, produces a finer, more decorative veneer. The log, or log section, is set in a vertical position

their grain alternately at right angles to one another. An odd number of veneers glued in this way prevents a structural imbalance in the ply, each outer veneer of a 3-ply board producing an even pull around the central core.

Plywood can be bought 3-ply, 5-ply or multi-ply an indication of the number of veneers used. Remember, if you are facing any wood material with sheets of veneer, there should always be an odd number of veneers giving an even pull around the central core. Thin as one extra face veneer may be, it can cause the central core to distort.

The central core in a sheet of plywood may sometimes be thicker and made of less dense wood than its balancing veneers, but generally each veneer is of the same thickness and is cut from the same (or at least similar) species of wood. This ensures equal stiffness in the lateral and perpendicular direction to the grain of the face veneers. Plywood veneers are not made too thick, as their tendency to distort can overcome the bonding adhesive designed to counteract such movement. Multi-ply, therefore, should be built up on both faces of the sheet, bearing these facts in mind.

Sizes of plywood sheets are always quoted with the length of the face grain given first. W.B.P. on the label of British made plywoods indicates that the veneers are bonded together with phenolic resin glue which is water and boil proof, and thus ideal for outdoor conditions. Ashley Cartwright uses marine quality plywood in his large garden table for precisely this reason.

Blockboard

Blockboard is constructed from parallel softwood strips faced with a hardwood

the inconsistency of manufacturing standards. Too often, cheaper blockboard displays loose softwood strips or untidy or peeling veneers.

Chipboard

It is essential to understand the construction of chipboard in working it or designing things to be made with it. Sheets are composed of wood chips and a synthetic resin glue pressed together into rigid units. Complete plants are set up to utilize whole trees in its fabrication, particularly trees of lower quality and smaller size.

Chipboard is marketed in several different forms. It may be sold plain, veneered, or with a plastic surface. Flooring chipboard is the same density all the way through – basically a sort of reconstituted solid wood. There are lower density chipboards for general purpose carcase-work. And there are special furniture-boards which have been developed to display the finest woodchips at the sheet's surface, presenting an ideal surface for veneering. Invariably, the wood chips will have been carefully pressed to lie parallel to the sheet surface as shown in the illustration. In less fine chipboard the chips may be at right angles to the surface and as a result, sheets are less stable and less strong when bent.

Working properties

All man-made sheets are very stable.

They can, like solid timber, be cut or planed (though planing to thickness is bound to create problems – sanding is advisable when necessary), drilled, or routered, although they will soon dull the cutting edge of hand tools. Allow for the effect of glue present in all man-made sheets by keeping cutting edges sharp, fitting tungsten-carbide bits to drill or router, and using tungsten-carbide cutting edges on your power saw.

Special chipboard screws are available with specially designed threads, since nails and screws are not generally as effective as in solid timber. The absence of end grain in chipboard can actually facilitate angled butt joints, nothing other than glue being necessary to complete the construction.

Plywood is the best man-made material for bending; its ability to bend is related to the species of wood, the thickness of each veneer (and the overall thickness of the plywood sheet), and the type of adhesive used to bond the veneers.

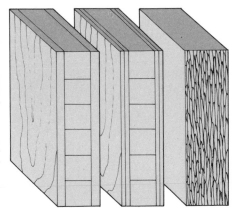

The value of man-made sheet materials

"I cannot agree with the premise that man-made boards are cheap and nasty. Some very fine antiques, even some Georgian pieces, were made out of home-made plyboards. They used thicker plys, but would glue them just like plywood today to stop 'movement'. The fact is that whenever you have got large areas of wood, 'movement' can really mess you about. You have to design around such problems when you use solid timber – it actually limits you."
Fred Baier

Solid timber – its disadvantages for the furniture maker

"Certainly there is a good deal of prejudice about man-made sheet materials made out of wood. This is not surprising in view of the low quality of some of the plywoods made in the early days when the adhesive was particularly attractive to woodworm. Some of the adhesives were not water resistant either, so they were inclined to fall apart in damp conditions. Nowadays there are very much better glues.

"In assessing the value of plywoods, blockboard, chipboard and other sheet materials made out of timber, it is important to understand the inherent problems of solid timber. Once you understand these problems, sheet materials can be presented as a viable alternative . . ."
John Makepeace

Solid timber is inclined to split along the grain. It is thus not practical in large load-bearing widths.

Unseasoned solid timber is unstable.

Its preparation can be difficult and time-consuming.

Working with solid timber can be extremely wasteful.

The quality of solid timber may vary even within a plank.

Man-made sheets – a functional solution

"When we take thin slices of wood and lay one on top of the other in alternate directions, we get all the benefits of strength combined with stability."
John Makepeace

"The first thing is that plywood stays flat, and because the veneers are glued with their grain at right angles to one another, plywood doesn't expand or contract. The top of my desk (see Plans) cannot afford to expand or contract."
Fred Baier

All prefabricated timber is stable. It is also available in large sheets already prepared to uniform thicknesses. This saves an enormous amount of time and preparation, *and* the quality is consistent.

The cost of hardwoods and plywoods varies considerably within their respective species and grades. Some plywood is actually much more expensive than some solid timber, but even then its availability in large sheets or uniform proportions can save a great deal of wastage and make a mockery of any imagined saving.

Finally, you can finish man-made boards in veneer without the preparation necessary in veneering solid timber.

"The point is that the nicest looking timbers are often so difficult to work that you might well avoid them anyway.

Timber with an attractive rippled figure is frequently impossible to plane because the grain is going in every direction, and the plane just rips it up. You could spend months scraping it down. Why not save money and time by using such attractive timber as veneer on man-made boards?"
Fred Baier

Man-made sheets – an aesthetic solution

"It is also important to point out the aesthetic qualities of sheet materials. Some sheet materials can be positively attractive although the commercial world normally tries to conceal the fact that the product which they are selling is not made of solid wood."
John Makepeace

"If you forget for a moment how they are promoted as cheap substitutes and take these materials for themselves, then you change the ballgame straight away."
Richard La Trobe Bateman

John Makepeace explains how he used both the technical and aesthetic characteristic of birch ply in this pivoted storage unit comprising twelve trefoil drawers which fan out from a central stem. The piece is currently on display at London's Victoria & Albert Museum.

"Plywood is of course made in many qualities. But, at its best, it is a superb material, difficult to work but clearly expressive of its two-dimensional stability. In designing the storage unit I was looking for a way of cantilevering for strength from the stainless steel column outwards, and not only outwards but laterally as well. Plywood is capable of achieving strength in both directions and on its edge, giving a highly decorative expression to the construction."
John Makepeace

Buying wood

How to buy softwoods

Generally speaking, the wood that you buy already planed is softwood. It is stocked in timber yards up and down the country as a planed item. It may be referred to as PAR, which means planed all round the plank, or PBS, which means planed both sides.

The sizes the timber merchant will quote, however, will be the sizes of sawn and not planed softwood. You should know, therefore, that planing removes approximately 3mm (1/8in) from each side of the plank. Either make the necessary adjustment to your order, or make it clear that you are referring to planed or 'finished' measurements, as they are professionally known.

Whenever you are purchasing wood, allow a little extra on the length measurement for waste due to cutting, and dirty or cracked ends.

Buying hardwoods

The truth is that hardwood suppliers are notoriously inconsistent. But take heart in the fact that it *is* possible to find merchants who are happy to supply the amateur and perform other services. Much will depend, however, on where you go and how you go about the business of getting what you need.

Where to go

At the end of the book there is a list of hardwood and softwood suppliers and sawmillers. But get out and about. Several people have reported surprise purchasing facilities specifically aimed at fostering the growing amateur market for hardwoods.

Accept the fact that as an amateur you are unlikely to be the merchant's best customer. If you take the trouble to build a rapport with him he is much more likely to do you the odd favour.

Both John Hardy and Norman Beverton strongly recommend that you seek out country saw mills, positioned as they are on the doorstep of home-grown forests. The people who run them very often have generations of experience behind them, with the same love for what they are doing as the craftsmen whose designs are in this book. Unlike the large city merchant, who may be most interested in removing bulk stock from timber yard to lorries and thence to build-ing and construction companies or other industries, the country saw mills are frequently run by people who are prepared to impart information because it is part of their lives. They have a personal interest and are far more likely to sell in small quantities to the amateur than are city merchants.

The attitude of most saw mill proprietors seems to be that they are prepared to service most orders. They are in the market to sell to timber merchants, to construction firms, and to the public.

Be aware of *all* the outlets in and about your area. Don't be afraid to compare costs, for in the end there are no rules. When John Hardy was adviser to the West Riding Education Authority for Handicrafts, he came upon an ideal outlet for his particular needs in the shape of local veneer saw mills. He explains:

"We still go to veneer cutters today to buy the boards that are left after the veneers have been taken (veneer backing boards). Eventually, when the veneer knife can peel no more from a log section because it has cut right down to the clamps which are holding the log, what is left would surprise you. There is a veneering place near Design Workshop that actually packs veneers in these off-cuts. In fact, this so-called waste comprises superb pieces of English oak! Whenever I go there and see a piece I just pick it up. They don't want it! We used to get in touch with the veneer saw mills on an official basis and buy their whole production of packing boards. We would take them to a central place and the schools would come round at purchasing time and collect them."

Go prepared

Before you go, make a drawing – proper plans and elevated sections – so that you have a clear idea of how much wood you need. You would do well to decide everything, even the joints you are going to cut, before you negotiate the purchase. Allow at least twenty-five per cent more wood than your measurements show. Sawing, planing, spoilt ends, and waney edges (present on virtually all English hardwoods) have to be taken into account. Imported timbers generally come into the country square-edged.

Selecting your wood

The first thing is to identify your chosen species of wood. As Robert Ingham points out in his section on The Preparation of Timber, it helps if all the pieces come from one source – if possible the same tree.

You should ask for the thickness you require, but do not necessarily expect the merchant to supply you only the amount of wood that you want. He is unlikely to split up large planks of wood for you. But he may agree to cut the planks to your specifications, and charge you.

Before Ashley Cartwright had fully equipped his Northamptonshire workshop, much of his cutting was done by a local saw mill. Arguably, if the merchant is prepared to machine cut and plane your wood, the extra cost far outweighs time consumed later in preparing the boards yourself. On the other hand if you wait until you get it home, then you can at least decide which bits you want for which parts of the furniture. If the merchant cuts it for you, you will not necessarily get the most advantageous cut. In any case, deciding what to use where, is really part of the art of the thing.

Once you have decided upon the species, look at the various logs lying in stick and notice how they are stacked. More often than not, if the stacks are untidy they will have been sorted through. Those left may be rejects. Also look for marks around the sticks – it can be a sign of badly stacked timber. If water has collected around those sticks for any length of time, the chances are that you will never be able to plane the marks away. General dirtiness may also be a sign of age in which case the dirt can be planed away to reveal the original tone of the wood beneath. That log could be a prime target. But do not be misled. Dirtiness is really only a *sure* sign of atmospheric conditions and may be misleading in terms of age.

Think about the wood in relation to what you are going to make. Try and imagine the various parts of the plank in your piece of furniture. Play with the possibilities. Unplaned wood may at first glance look like so much firewood but persevere and you will determine at least the surface figure and grain pattern. How might that be used in your piece? Look also at the wood's irregularities, and decide whether they will impede or

possibly stimulate your design. Above all, don't feel pressured to make up your mind – take the time to look and choose. Don't be bullied into taking the planks that the merchant suggests.

Is it seasoned?
It may not be essenial to ascertain whether the timber you are choosing has been air-dried or kiln-dried – it's up to you (see page 16). But it is important to get some idea of its moisture content.

"As a general rule, timber merchants talk of timber being dry when it has been in stick for only a few months. A timber merchant's remark about dryness of timber should invariably be regarded with suspicion, unless he specifies the moisture content. He will only be able to do this with any certainty if he has kilned the timber, or if he has measured its moisture content with a meter while you are there. To be fair, it would be impossible for a timber merchant to keep a constant record of the dryness of every log in his yard."
John Makepeace

Moisture meter
Moisture meters (see illustration) work on the principle that wood is a bad conductor of electricity, whereas moisture is a good conductor. The measure of resistance to an electric current passing between two electrodes is expressed by the meter as a percentage of moisture present in relation to the total bulk of the

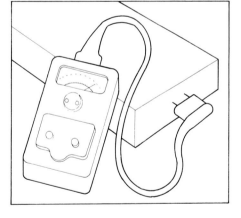

wood. If you or the merchant is able to measure moisture content at point of purchase, recall the moisture content table on page 16 and judge how practical it is for you to buy that plank.

Generally, however, the merchant will simply tell you how long a log has been lying in stick. As a rough guide, air-dried hardwoods need twelve months per 25mm (1in) thickness to reach a state of equipoise with the atmosphere; a 25mm (1in) thickness of softwood needs six months to become so seasoned.

In conclusion, much of your success in buying hardwood timber will rest upon your ability to turn the realities of the business to your advantage. You may be encouraged by the fact that not all professional craftsmen have what Richard La Trobe Bateman refers to as 'gumption' – an ability to succeed in these down-to-earth practical areas.

"I always get done. It's tremendous fun buying timber, going to country sawmills for home-grown wood. I often go to a place which only used to deal with the trade, but now they have a section for the general public. They suddenly discovered the huge market for people who just like making things. But although I am a professional, I am totally intimidated by these guys. They won't let you choose. I am sure you will be all right if you know what you are looking for, but I never seem to have the gall to crawl over the wood with my nose right next to it, turn over every plank and go through the whole tree. It's a talent of persuading people – you either have it or you don't."

Two other tips are worth bearing in mind. Recently converted timber is much cheaper than seasoned timber. If you have the facility and time to air-dry it yourself, you have a clear advantage. Secondly, unfamiliar timbers constantly appear on the market. They will be cheaper for a while – for as long as they remain an unknown quantity – but are not necessarily poor quality. Utile is one timber which was ignored when it first appeared on the market, but today it is very much in demand for furniture and its price reflects this demand.

Wood chart

The following list is by no means complete but gives brief notes on many of the available hardwood species. Much of this information has been taken from data made available by the Forest Products Research Laboratory and the Timber Research and Development Association, Buckinghamshire, England.

As there are hundreds of known hardwoods our coverage has been restricted to those which are best known for their suitability for furniture making, turning and decorative veneer, coupled with availability. Availability will vary greatly from place to place, and we return to this subject later.

Being of the plant kingdom, each tree, and therefore each log, varies from the next. The nature of the wood, its appearance and physical properties will depend on a number of factors and while knowing the species tells us much about the wood, other agencies in its growing life make it unique. Amongst these are:

1. The type and quality of soil on which it is grown. This affects size and inclusion of minerals taken from the soil into the wood. Colouring can also be introduced in this way.

2. The continued or interrupted availability of rainfall and sunlight affects growth and the evenness of texture.

3. Exposure to tropical storms. This can cause thunder shakes or cross-grain

fractures due to the tree being bent to such an extent that alternate stretching and compression cause the fibres to break in places.

4. Fungal and insect attack. The latter can be the cause of such abnormal figure as masur birch, a product of larvae workings. Fungus can alter the colour and strength of wood.

Knots of course occur in all trees bearing branches, and can, thanks to the grain movement around them, be used to good effect.

Anyone buying timber in small quantities or wishing to obtain a piece of solid timber with a particular figure, will experience problems. It will help to look at the general structure of the business.

The importers of decorative hardwoods are, in the main, located near international ports where logs or lumber are received, cut, kiln dried or air seasoned as is the practice. Timber importing of solid wood, plywoods, or veneers is a wholesale operation. Importers supply in bulk to inland merchants, furniture manufacturers, joinery makers and other wood-using industries. It is not often that an importer will have the facility to satisfy requests for odd pieces of hardwood, but there are possibilities.

This leads us to one of the importer's customers – the merchant, who may have a limited choice, or the manufacturer who may be willing to sell falling pieces or

off-cuts at his works to those who will not involve him in labour costs.

Veneer slicing will yield backing boards or veneer remains as they are called. This is the slab of 25mm (1in) to 40mm (1½in) thickness which remains after as much veneer as is saleable has been sliced from the log. Being decorative, these are clearly very good value and can be stored in stick to season before use.

Kiln drying, the modern method of seasoning wood using air circulation, humidity and temperature in a controlled situation, offers the chance to obtain kiln test pieces. Each kiln charge which is often 1,000 cu ft (approximately 28m³) has at least four test pieces which are weighed at regular intervals during the drying process. They are generally between 0.5 and 1.0 metre long with the thickness and width of whatever stock was being dried at the time. For wood turning and small furniture pieces these can be the answer. Kiln drying is often carried out by the importer, sometimes by the end user.

For native hardwoods the small country sawmill will be prepared to show an interested craftsman what is available, but do not expect him to take numerous logs out of stick in a search for one figured board. While most of those employed in the timber industry are only too pleased to assist the craftsman and offer advice, the cost of labour limits time and handling in the yard.

Commercial European hardwoods and related species from elsewhere

Alder *Alnus spp* **T. P.**
Black alder, *A. glutmosa*, and grey alder, *A. incana*.
Pale darkening to light brown, sap not distinguishable from heartwood. Lustreless surface with some dark streaking. Density light to medium. Not as strong as beech, works fairly well with fine sharp cutting edges. Turns and peels.

Apple *Malus spp* **T.**
Pale to pinkish brown wood which turns extremely well. As with pear the wood improves and mellows with age as demonstrated by some very fine examples of small antique pieces of French and English furniture.
American apple wood T. Is as strong, hard and compact, and again suitable for turnery.

Ash *Fraxinus spp* **F. T. DV. P.**
Brownish white sap/heart sometimes streaked with darker markings that provide the more decorative olive ash. Straight grained. Fairly coarse texture. Tough, strong, flexible. Works well to a good finish.
Tamo Japanese ash *F. mandshurica* **F. DV. P.** Light brown heartwood, lighter in weight than European ash. Not to be confused with sen (*Kalopanax pictus*) which looks similar but lacks tamo's characteristic qualities.
American ash *F. nigra, F. pennsylvanica, F. americana* are principal species. **F.** (soft grades) Mainly joinery

and heavy construction.
Softer grades more suitable for furniture.
The **White ash** *F. americana* offers the larger cutting sizes – white to grey-brown colour.

Beech *Fagus spp* **F. T. P.**
White to light red/brown sap/heart, sometimes darker red heart. Straight grained. Fine, uniform texture. Strong, but density variable. Variable working properties but generally fairly easy. Finishes well. Non durable. Turns pink if steamed in drying process.
American beech *F. grandifolia* **F. T.** Is generally coarser and heavier than European beech.
Japanese beech (*F. crenata*). Much as European beech.

Birch *Betula spp* **F. T. DV. P.**
Two forms – silver and common. White to yellow brown sap/heart. Fairly straight grained. Darker markings and grain disturbances occasion masur birch, a highly decorative wood. Very strong and tough but works fairly easily and finishes well.
North American birch F. T. (Yellow birch only). There are more than nine species of *Betula* in North America. Paper birch *B. papyrifera* and Yellow birch *B. alleghaniensis* being the most important.

Cherry *Prunus spp* **F. T. DV. P.**
Unlike ash, beech, birch, there's a well-defined colour difference between heartwood (pale pinky brown) and sapwood (which is lighter). Fine textured wood.

Mostly straight grain. Tough and strong. Works well except when cross-grained when it may tear. A fine decorative hardwood which finishes well. When polished turns to a rich warm colour.
North American cherry F. T. Sometimes known as black cherry *P. serotina*. Larger tree but marginally lighter than European cherry.
Japanese cherry F. T. Known as yama-zakura.

Chestnut *Castanea spp* **F. T.**
Spanish or sweet chestnut has distinct heart/sap colours, heartwood resembling oak in its yellowy brown colour. Very often spiral grain figure. Softer and weaker than oak. Works well and takes a fine finish. Watch that it has been dried carefully as it tends to collapse or honeycomb in drying, unless treated with care.
American chestnut *C. dentata* **F.** Blighted by fungus, supplies limited.

Chestnut (Horse chestnut) *Aesculus spp* **T.**
Cream to yellow brown not to be compared with Spanish/sweet chestnut. Only suitable for low quality turnery.

Elm *Ulmus spp* **F. T. DV.**
Easily defined heart and sapwood. Dutch elm stronger than common English (red) elm, and being of straighter grain is easier to work. Heartwood light to dark brown with light green streaks sometimes being present. Attractive clusters of small pip knots often occurring. Very attractive figure due to cross-grain and irregular growth rings. Coarse texture,

finer on the Continent. Needs care in working as grain likely to pick up.

North American elm Rock elm *U. thomasii* **F.** Is used particularly for chair rockers and in its light brown colour, its lack of distinction between heartwood and sapwood, its straight grain and fine texture, it is notably different in appearance from slipper elm (*U. fulva*) and white elm (*U. americana*).

Very little North American elm is being exported to Europe at the present time because trees have been severely affected by elm disease.

Indian elm *U. integrifolia.* Is light yellow in colour and used for cheap furniture amongst other things.

Holly *Ilex aquifolium* **T. DV.**
No clear distinction between heart and sap – a whitish colour with a detectable green cast. A dense wood but with a fairly even texture. Fairly difficult to saw on account of irregular grain pattern, but it is hard and works cleanly. Is best air seasoned in fairly small dimensions.

Hornbeam *Carpinus spp* **T.**
Dull white with some grey streaks on the quarter sawn faces. Sap not distinguishable from heartwood. Cold to touch. Often cross-grained but with fine even texture, fairly dense. Dries readily but shrinkage to be expected in the process. Turns well, good resistance to wear. Used for piano parts and butchers' blocks.

Lime *Tilia spp* **T.**
No clear distinction between heart and sap. Pale brown in colour after exposure, with little figure but a fine texture. Softish wood with a straight grain and fair degree of strength. Ideal for carving. White to yellow colour when first sawn.

Maple *Acer spp* **T. DV.**
Properties similar to sycamore, fine textured and full of lustre, but not as white and rather softer.

North American maple **F. T. DV. P.**
Produces hard and soft species. Rock maple *A. saccharum/nigrum* is hard and more difficult to work than soft maple. (Silver maple, *A. saccharinum*. Red maple, *A. rubrum*).

The hard rock maple is cream to light brown with darker staining in heartwood. Very fine textured grain. Good resistance to wear.

(Figured forms of maple include bird's eye maple, fiddle-back maple, blister and curly maple. Very attractive and available in veneer form.)

Oak *Quercus spp* **F. T. DV.**
Yellowy brown heartwood displaying bold silver flash in quarter-sawn boards. Its toughness depends upon where it is grown (the Central European oak is slower grown and milder) and this tends to determine its ease of working. Cutting tools need to be keen especially when tackling the most decorative surfaces. Oak is very strong. Careful drying essential.

North American oak (Red oak, *Q. Rubra/falcata/shumardii* and white oak, *Q. alba*) **F. T. DV.**
These are the main species. Colour variable. Red oak from pink to pale reddish brown; white oak from yellowy brown to pale reddish brown. White oak displays a more attractive figure.

Japanese oak otherwise known as ohnara, *Q. mongolica* **F. T. DV.**
Paler than European oak or American white oak. Attractive figure. Milder and easier to work than European or North American oak.

Pear *Pyrus communis* **T.**
The wild pear tree has pinkish brown wood, little figure but fine even texture and displays a fine lustrous finish. Clean working.

Plane *Platanus spp* **F. DV.**
Distinct heart/sap colouring with heartwood resembling colour of beech. But large broad rays give quarter-sawn surfaces a fleck figure (known then as lacewood). Strong timber which works well, although care in planing (with keen blade) is needed to avoid damaging figure. Mostly used for decorative work.
American plane *P. occidentalis* **DV.**
Is also known as sycamore or buttonwood.

Poplar *Populus spp* **F. P.** (generally only for framing and drawers).
Soft, fine textured wood, whitish in colour. Uniform in appearance and straight grained. Relatively strong for its weight. Woolly grain can tend to bind on sawing, sanding recommended after planing.
North American poplar is available as Canadian aspen, *P. tremuloides*, black cottonwood, *P. trichocarpa*, Eastern cottonwood, *P. deltoides*, Canadian poplar, *P. balsamifera*.

Sycamore *Acer spp* **F. T. DV.**
Heart and sap similar whitish colour. Straight to wavy grain. It may be fairly plain in colour but quarter sawn surfaces display a silky lustre and it's a good wood to colour. As strong as oak. Difficult to work when grain is wavy. Watch out for drying defects – sticks can stain it if dried too slowly. It is best end-racked under cover to maintain an even light colour while drying. Logs with a fiddle-back figure are sought after for veneer.

Walnut *Juglans spp* **F. T. DV.**
Colour varies, from creamy to black streaked, greyish brown heartwood with lighter sap. One of the most attractive timbers but variable as to country of origin. Go for English, French or Italian walnut. Usually coarse textured and wavy grained. Works fairly easily. The straighter the grain the more flexible. Takes a good polish.
North American walnut otherwise known as Black walnut, *J. nigra* **F. T. DV.**
Has a purple black heartwood, with creamy sap.

Key:
F.	Used for furniture
T.	Used for turning
DV.	Used in decorative veneer
P.	Used in man-made sheets

Commercial Australasian hardwoods

Southern hemisphere beech, *Nothofagus spp*, is available as:
Tasmanian myrtle *N. cunninghamii* **F. T. P.**
Otherwise known as myrtle beech, myrtle, or Tasmanian beech.

Sap and heart separated by intermediate zone of lighter coloured wood. True heart is reddish brown. Comparable to European beech (*Fagus spp*).
Silver beech *N. menziesii* **F. T.**
Otherwise known as Southland beech, red beech, or hard beech.

Darker than European beech and lacks its figure on quarter sawn surfaces. It is probably rather easier to work. Uniform pink-brown colour.

White beech *Gmelina spp* **F. T. P.**
Completely unrelated to true beech. It is a relative of teak and sometimes known as grey teak. No distinction between sap and heart. Works well.

White birch *Schizomeria ovata* **T. P.**
Pale brown heartwood. Straight grain and fine texture. Strong and easy to work.

Black bean *Castanospermum australe* **F. DV.**
Streaked brown in colour with a coarse texture. Generally straight grain. Hard and strong and not too difficult to work although care should be taken when planing over those lighter coloured streaks which may crumble under blunt blades. Capable of a fine finish.

Australian blackwood *Acacia melanoxylon* **F. T. DV.**
Otherwise known as black wattle. Colour variable in heartwood from light to reddish to dark brown. Although the grain is usually straight, an attractive figure is often displayed by more irregular patterns. Medium fine texture. Strong and tough. Works fairly easily depending on grain pattern. Polishes well.

Australian cedar *Toona australis* and *Cedrela Toona* **F.**
Related to South American cedar, *Cedrela spp*, and not to be confused with *Cedrus*, the softwood cedar. Rich red brown heartwood streaked with darker rays. Close uneven texture but fairly straight grain. It's a rather weak wood and tends to be woolly.

Coachwood *Ceratopetalum apelatum* **F. T. P.**
Otherwise known as scented satinwood. No clear distinction between heart and sap, although former a darker brown. Its main attribute is a delicate fleck figure displayed on quarter sawn surfaces. The grain is fairly straight and together with a fine even texture its workability and appearance are ideal, in selected stock, for furniture and cabinet making.

Queensland maple *Flindersia spp* **F. DV. P.**
Unrelated to and distinct in appearance from true maple (*Acer spp*). It looks more

Apple

North American elm

Plane

Ash

Holly

Poplar

Beech

Lime

Sycamore

Birch

Maple

Walnut

Cherry

Oak

North American walnut

North American cherry

North American oak

Tasmanian myrtle (beech)

Chestnut

Japanese oak

Silver beech

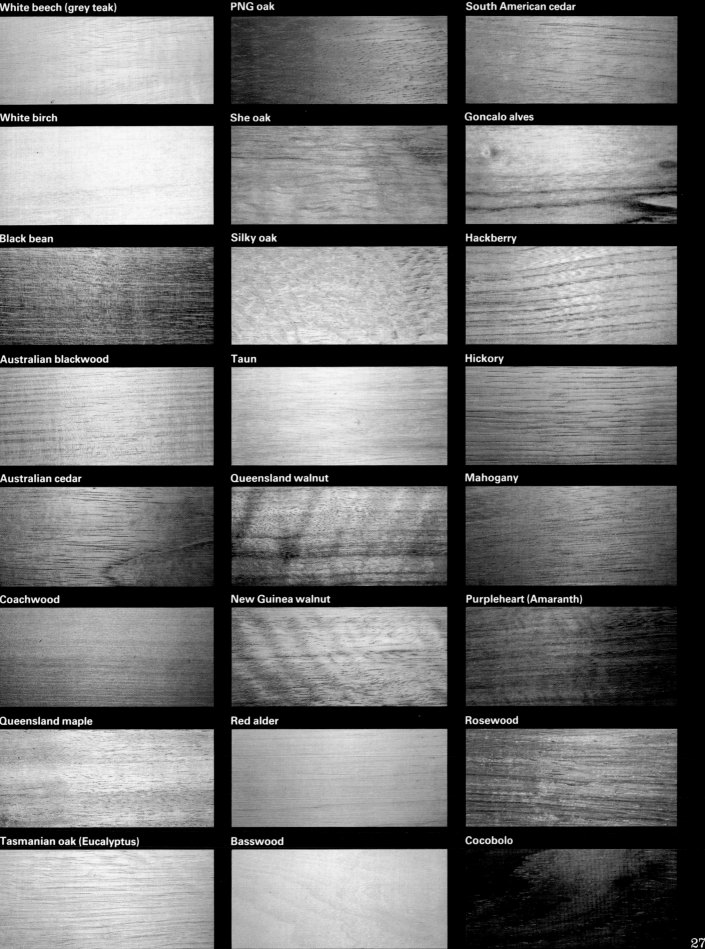

White beech (grey teak)

PNG oak

South American cedar

White birch

She oak

Goncalo alves

Black bean

Silky oak

Hackberry

Australian blackwood

Taun

Hickory

Australian cedar

Queensland walnut

Mahogany

Coachwood

New Guinea walnut

Purpleheart (Amaranth)

Queensland maple

Red alder

Rosewood

Tasmanian oak (Eucalyptus)

Basswood

Cocobolo

27

Wood chart 3

like African mahogany. Light brown with a shiny figure when quarter sawn due to wavy interlocked grain. Very strong. Although the grain may pick up when planing, it generally works well.

Queensland maple is one, albeit the most important, of a variety of botanically improperly named timbers produced by the *Flindersia* species. Others are described as ash, teak and maple.

Tasmanian oak *Eucalyptus spp* **F. P.**
Botanically incorrect name for a form of eucalyptus. Pale wood. Straight grain. Open texture. Tough and strong. Not easy to dry successfully but works quite well and produces a smooth finish. Uniform colour with some fine gum veins apparent on surface.

PNG oak *Castanopsis acuminatissima* **F. DV. P.**
A relative of true oak, *Quercus*, and sweet chestnut, *Castanea*, which explains why it is sometimes known as Indonesian chestnut. Pale brown wood displaying a slight fleck figure in quarter sawn boards. Works fairly well.

She oak *Casuarina spp* **F. T. DV.** from selected logs.
Again, unrelated to true oak. Variable in colour – yellow to fairly dark red. Shiny with mottled figure. Straight grain and fine open texture. A very attractive wood which needs to be dried with care.

Silky oak *Grevillea spp* – *Cardwellia spp* **F.DV.**
Both species similar in appearance but unrelated to true oak. *Grevillea* has been introduced to Africa where it is known as African silky oak. Reddish brown with silver streaks which produce its attractive figure. Straight grain except where the grain passes around the rays – in which areas it is not easy to plane, although in general it works well and produces a reasonable finish.

Taun *Pometia pinnata* **T. DV. P.** from selected logs.
Pale brown with pink tinge in the heartwood. Occasional wavy grain and a coarse uneven texture. Strong. Works well.

Queensland walnut *Endiandra palmerstonii* **F. DV.**
Otherwise known as Australian walnut. Unrelated to European walnut, *Juglans*, but of similar appearance. Brown colour with marked streaks which together with its wavy grain and shiny look produces a very attractive figure particularly on quarter-sawn surfaces. Its strength is more similar to European oak than true walnut, and although all-in-all it is not an easy timber to work, it can produce a good finish.

New Guinea walnut *Dracontomelum spp* **F. DV.**
Known also as Pacific or Papua walnut. Paldao, *D. dao*, is a related species and is found in the Philippines. Yellow brown with slight red tinge. It displays an attractive figure in selected stock due to wavy grain pattern. Fairly fine texture. Works quite well although it has a dulling effect on cutting edges.

Commercial American hardwoods
(See also above)

Red alder *Alnus spp* **F. T. P. DV.** from selected logs.
Yellow to reddish brown in colour, Red alder displays a straight grain and even texture. A softish weak wood.

Basswood *Tilia americana* **T. P.**
This creamy brown, fine textured, straight-grained timber is notably easy to work, but like poplar is not suitably strong for furniture. It is often known as American lime.

South American cedar *Cedrela spp* **F.**
Similar reddish brown to Honduras mahogany though perhaps lighter. Fairly strong and easy to work. Medium to coarse textured and normally straight-grained. In behaviour and in its attractive appearance, it is a very useful wood. Also known as 'cigar box cedar', but not to be confused with *Cedrus spp.*

Courbaril *Hymenae spp* **F. T.**
Also known as yatoba. Pale coloured sap with reddish brown heartwood of uneven shades giving striped effect. Medium to coarse texture. Has a warm glow when surface is planed. Turns well.

Goncalo alves *Astronium spp* **F. T.**
Known also as zebrawood in the U.K., and tigerwood in the U.S.A.
Reddish brown timber mottled with darker spots and streaks. Its irregular grain and tendency to warp and check in drying does not facilitate its working properties, but it finishes well.

Hackberry *Celtis spp* **F.**
Linked with *Ulma* (the elm family) in North America, but has greyish sap and heart. Its irregular grain makes it quite difficult to work, but it is tough, strong and fairly hard, and has a moderately fine texture. In Africa, *Celtis spp* is also found and has been used successfully as a substitute for Ash.

Hickory *Carya spp* **F.** (mainly chairs) **T.**
Not unlike ash in general appearance, though not as decorative. Coarse textured, generally fairly straight grained, but reddish brown in colour and if anything stronger and tougher than *Fraxinus spp.* It is a particularly dense wood and thus fairly hard on cutting tools.

Imbuya *Phoebe porosa* **F. T. DV.**
Also known as embuia and 'Brazil walnut'. Heartwood yellow to olive to chocolate brown. Fine texture and easy to work, with a distinctive spicy odour when first cut.

Lapacho *Tabebuia spp* **F. T.**
The heartwood is often tripey with colours of yellow-olive to greenish brown. The colour restrictions and very irregular grain make the wood attractive. Not easy to work, needs to be sanded or scraped after planing. Fine texture.

Mahogany *Swietenia spp* **F. DV. P.**
Sold according to country of origin –

Brazilian, Honduras, Peruvian, etc. See also African mahogany, a related species. Medium to deep red brown. In selected logs irregular grain patterns produce a very attractive figure. Works well to an excellent finish.

Purpleheart *Peltogyne spp* **F. T. DV.**
Also known as amaranth.
Very attractive figure due to fairly irregular grain pattern, well-defined violet-purple heartwood and a natural lustre. It is strong, dense and you will need to keep your cutting tools sharp.

Rosewood *Dalbergia nigra* **F. DV.**
Known as Rio rosewood in the U.K.
A very attractive hard and heavy wood, darkish purple in colour with black streaks and oily in appearance. Tends to dull tools and its oiliness does not facilitate a high polish. Distinct white sapwood. No longer readily available other than in veneer. (See Asian woods.)
    Cocobolo *D. retusa* **T.**
Similar to *D. nigra* but with a definite reddish tinge to the heartwood. When planed it has the feel of cold marble. Excellent for small decorative items and turnery. Unsuitable for gluing.
    Kingwood *D. cearensis* **T.**
Also known as Violet Wood.
A shiny violet-brown timber with darker streaks. Hard, heavy, capable of a fine finish, but restricted to inlay work and turnery due to small stature of trees.

Satinwood *Fagara flava* **F. T.**
Otherwise known as Jamaica satinwood or San Domingan satinwood. Very attractive timber used preferably to *F. Macrophylla* from Africa. Neither to be confused with Ceylon satinwood (below).
A fine yellowy, creamy coloured wood with variable grain but frequently a mottled figure. Works fairly well, turns and finishes excellently.

Virola *Virola spp* **F.** (Heavy Virola) **P.** (Light Virola).
Both heart and sap a pinky golden brown. A straight-grained, fairly coarse textured wood not noted for its strength properties, but one of Brazil's most important general-purpose export timbers. Works well.

American whitewood *Liriodendron tulipifera* **F.** (but mainly joinery) **P.**
Also known as yellow or tulip poplar, and outside America as tulip tree or canary whitewood. Not to be confused with *Populus spp.* A green/yellow or brown wood which displays little figure except for a streaked colour alternately green, black, brown or red. It's a soft, fairly weak timber, and straight grained. Fairly easy to work.

Commercial Asian hardwoods
See below for: **Amboyna** (see Padauk)

Ebony *Diospyros spp* **F. T.**
A heavy. brittle wood none too easy to work but finishes very well. Its familiar jet-black colour, fine even texture and frequently wavy grain provides an attractive figure. Since trees are small, its use usually confined to small objects.

Indian laurel *Terminalia spp* **F. T. DV.**
Light or dark brown with darker stripes. Coarse even texture with generally straight grain. Superficially not unlike walnut. Hard strong and tough to work but finishes well.

White chuglam *Terminalia bialata* **F.**
Also known as Indian silver-grey wood. Generally both heart and sap a uniform silver-grey colour, but selected logs display an attractive appearance due to a light or olive brown colour streaked with darker markings. As strong as oak, but stiffer. Works fairly well and takes a good finish. Limited availability.

Meranti *Shorea spp* **F. P.**
The genus produces three timbers suitable for furniture making – light red M., white M., and yellow M. are distinguished as their names suggest by their heartwood colour. Fairly coarse but even textured. Wavy grain. All work quite well.

Ramin *Gonystylus spp* **F. T. DV. P.**
Straw coloured heart and sap. Fine even texture and generally straight grain. Virtually as strong as beech, but will not bend readily – altogether a lighter wood. Works well but has a tendency to split.

Indian rosewood *Dalbergia latifolia* **F. T. DV.**
Dark purple/red brown with dark streaking giving a very attractive appearance. Sap yellow to white, heartwood not as black as the South American or Rio rosewood, but density and working properties are much the same. Available in logs or sawn lumber.

Ceylon satinwood *Chloroxylon Swietenia* **F. T. DV.**
Golden yellow in colour, frequently with an exceptional figure. Fine, shiny texture. Very strong and quite difficult to work. Finishes well.

Teak *Tectona grandis* **F. T. DV. P.**
One of the best known and best all-round timbers, teak occurs in many tropical zones such as India, Burma, Thailand, and has been planted in West Africa and the West Indies. An oily dark wood which displays both straight and irregular grain, and a coarse uneven texture. Almost as strong as oak, but lighter. It works well, but is severe on cutting tools.

Commercial African hardwoods
(See also Asian, American, Australian hardwoods)

Abura *Mitragyna ciliata* **F. T. P.**
A palish brown wood, sap and heart of similar colour – sometimes streaked. Fine texture, generally straight grain. Good utility wood.

Afara *Terminalia superbia* **F. DV.**
Similar yellowish-brown colour to oak, but Dark afara displays grey marked figure and more valuable as veneer. Works easily and takes a good finish.

Afrormosia *Pericopsis elata* **F. DV.**
Similar in appearance to teak, but without its oily appearance. Strong, works

well and takes a good finish.

Afzelia *Afzelia spp* **F. DV.**
Light to reddish brown heartwood often with mottled figure. Coarse texture and irregular grain. Strong, but not easy to work. Very stable.

Agba *Gossweilerodendron balsamiferum* **F. P.**
Similar grain figure to mahogany. Cream to brown heartwood and slightly lighter sapwood. Close even texture, works well though a fairly hard and brittle wood. Takes a good finish.

Aningeria *Aningeria spp* **F. DV.**
There are various species whose colours vary from pale to pale brown. The grain is sometimes wavy and quarter-sawn boards display a surprisingly decorative figure. Quite difficult to work.

Berlinea *Berlinea spp* **F.**
Light to dark reddish brown with dark streaks. Coarse texture and often irregular grain. Strong and tough, but works quite well. Although it does not bend well, it can be used in place of oak.

African blackwood *Dalbergia melanoxylon* **T.**
A hard, straight-grained, fine-textured wood, much denser than *Dalbergia nigra* (rosewood) – both are part of the same family, *Leguminosae*. Used mainly for making wind instruments, but good for turning if tools kept keen. Purple brown to black.

Cordia *Cordia spp* **F.**
Golden brown to fawn with dark streaks and particularly attractive in quarter sawn boards which display a mottled figure. Medium texture and generally straight grain. Works quite well.

Gaboon *Aucoumea klaineana* **F. P.**
Resembles African mahogany to look at, but unrelated. Generally straight grained with no marked figure.

Guarea *Guarea spp* **F. T.**
There is black G. and white G., the former having a better colour – a paler mahogany, the latter displaying a better figure and having a cedar-like scent. Both strong and fairly easy to work.

Idigbo *Terminalia ivorensis* **F. P.**
Similar to oak in appearance, with a characteristic growth-ring figure. Irregular grain pattern and a coarse uneven figure. Yellow with faint green tinge.

African mahogany *Khaya spp* **F. T. DV. P.**
From the same family as American mahogany (see above) – *Meliaceae*, but distinct.
Reddish brown wood, coarser and more resistant to splitting than American mahogany. Attractive striped figure due to interlocking grain.

Makore *Tieghemella heckelii* **F. T. DV. P.**
Light to deep red in colour, occasionally

with darker streaks. Appreciably stronger and finer than mahogany, but difficult to work.

Mansonia *Mansonia altissima* **F. T.**
Similar in appearance to American walnut, having a purplish tinge, but its colour varies greatly. It is tough and strong like walnut, works fairly easily and gives an excellent finish. Colour fades.

Muninga *Pterocarpus angolensis* **F. T.**
Similar to padauk, another species of *Pterocarpus (see below)*. Yellowy brown to dark brown with darker markings. Grain varies. Not as strong as padauk, but more durable and easy to work.

Obeche *Triplochiton scleroxylon* **F.**
A fine textured, white-cream wood with little distinction between sap and heart. Very light but quite strong for its weight. Works easily and produces an excellent finish.

Olive (East African) *Olea spp* **F. T.** (particularly)
Beige coloured streaked with grey and darker markings to produce an attractive irregular figure. Fine textured, but a hard, heavy and very strong wood. Not easy to work.

Padauk (African) *Pterocarpus spp* **F. T. DV.**
Fairly dark brown in colour with reddish tinge and darker markings. Variable grain. Coarse in texture, stronger than oak, heavy, but good working properties. All-in-all a very attractive timber. Vivid red when first cut.

Sapele *Entandrophragma cylindricum* **F. DV.**
Not unlike mahogany in colour but displays a notable regular stripe especially on quarter-sawn surfaces. Hard, heavy and strong. Close textured. Works quite well but interlocked grain can be a problem. Finishes well.

Utile *Entandrophragma utile* **F. DV.**
Similar to sapele in colour (reddish brown) and uses. Grain more irregular but less attractive figure. Works and finishes well.

African walnut *Lovoa klaineana* **F. DV.**
Related to mahogany (*Meliaceae* family) but derives name of walnut from black veins. Its similarity to African mahogany is especially strong in terms of its striped figure due to interlocking grain. Works fairly easily. Golden brown.

Wenge *Millettia Stuhlmannii* **F. T. DV.**
Also known as panga panga.
Very dark brown heartwood with a yellow sap. Alternate bands of dark and lighter tissue give a decorative figure. Straight grained coarse texture. Heavy and stable.

Zebrano *Brachystegia fleuryana* **DV.**
Also known as zebra wood, and rarely seen in the solid.
Pale brown in colour with narrow streaks of dark brown or black.

Wood chart 4

Satinwood

Teak

African blackwood

Virola

Abura

Cordia

American whitewood

Afara

Guarea

Ebony

Afrormosia

Idigbo

Indian laurel

Afzelia

African mahogany

Meranti

Agba

Makore

Ramin

Aningeria

Mansonia

Ceylon satinwood

Berlinea

Muninga

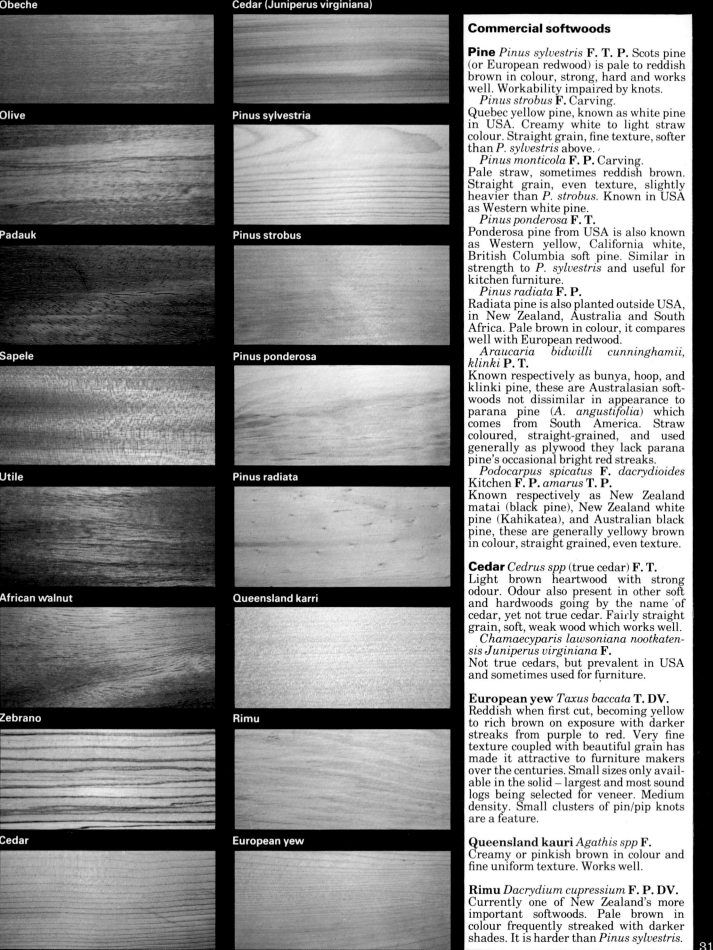

Obeche

Olive

Padauk

Sapele

Utile

African walnut

Zebrano

Cedar

Cedar (Juniperus virginiana)

Pinus sylvestria

Pinus strobus

Pinus ponderosa

Pinus radiata

Queensland karri

Rimu

European yew

Commercial softwoods

Pine *Pinus sylvestris* **F. T. P.** Scots pine (or European redwood) is pale to reddish brown in colour, strong, hard and works well. Workability impaired by knots.
  Pinus strobus **F.** Carving.
Quebec yellow pine, known as white pine in USA. Creamy white to light straw colour. Straight grain, fine texture, softer than *P. sylvestris* above.
  Pinus monticola **F. P.** Carving.
Pale straw, sometimes reddish brown. Straight grain, even texture, slightly heavier than *P. strobus*. Known in USA as Western white pine.
  Pinus ponderosa **F. T.**
Ponderosa pine from USA is also known as Western yellow, California white, British Columbia soft pine. Similar in strength to *P. sylvestris* and useful for kitchen furniture.
  Pinus radiata **F. P.**
Radiata pine is also planted outside USA, in New Zealand, Australia and South Africa. Pale brown in colour, it compares well with European redwood.
  Araucaria bidwilli cunninghamii, klinki **P. T.**
Known respectively as bunya, hoop, and klinki pine, these are Australasian softwoods not dissimilar in appearance to parana pine (*A. angustifolia*) which comes from South America. Straw coloured, straight-grained, and used generally as plywood they lack parana pine's occasional bright red streaks.
  Podocarpus spicatus **F.** *dacrydioides* Kitchen **F. P.** *amarus* **T. P.**
Known respectively as New Zealand matai (black pine), New Zealand white pine (Kahikatea), and Australian black pine, these are generally yellowy brown in colour, straight grained, even texture.

Cedar *Cedrus spp* (true cedar) **F. T.**
Light brown heartwood with strong odour. Odour also present in other soft and hardwoods going by the name of cedar, yet not true cedar. Fairly straight grain, soft, weak wood which works well.
  Chamaecyparis lawsoniana nootkatensis Juniperus virginiana **F.**
Not true cedars, but prevalent in USA and sometimes used for furniture.

European yew *Taxus baccata* **T. DV.**
Reddish when first cut, becoming yellow to rich brown on exposure with darker streaks from purple to red. Very fine texture coupled with beautiful grain has made it attractive to furniture makers over the centuries. Small sizes only available in the solid – largest and most sound logs being selected for veneer. Medium density. Small clusters of pin/pip knots are a feature.

Queensland kauri *Agathis spp* **F.**
Creamy or pinkish brown in colour and fine uniform texture. Works well.

Rimu *Dacrydium cupressium* **F. P. DV.**
Currently one of New Zealand's more important softwoods. Pale brown in colour frequently streaked with darker shades. It is harder than *Pinus sylvestris*.

Board preparation

Preparation from rough-sawn boards to accurate surfaces

Most craftsmen would agree that extreme care in preparing timber prior to marking out for joint positions can pave the way to an easy passage in the construction of a piece of woodwork.

Having spent some time studying how best to use the timber of your choice, both aesthetically and economically, mark out the various components with a soft black pencil. Make an allowance for preliminary sawing and subsequent planing. As a general rule, add 12mm (½in) to the finished length, 6mm (¼in) to the finished width and 3mm (⅛in) to the finished thickness. See illustration for laying out.

It helps to identify the pieces, by name or a number, and in this way relate them to the drawing or cutting list from which you are working.

Try wherever possible to get all the timber selected and prepared in one go so that the work has progression and is not held up. Ideally, all the pieces will come from one source, if possible from the same tree.

Having marked out the pieces on the board, saw them out using a crosscut to saw across the grain and a rip saw to saw with the grain.

Planing. Accurate preparation of surfaces

This is an aspect of woodwork that puts some people off. It can be slow and laborious and it often reminds one of early, perhaps less successful attempts at school. A well sharpened and finely tuned jack or fore plane makes all the difference. Even if you have managed to have your timber machine planed at the saw mill, it may require some adjustment by hand. The description that follows assumes rough sawn boards as the starting point. Though not as much work is involved, it can also be implemented to adjust machined surfaces should they require it.

Planing the face side

Start by planing the face side. This is usually the surface of a piece of wood that is selected for its best qualities and will be the surface that shows in the finished piece. Constant checking of the surface with a straight-edge is essential. After some time your eye will become trained and the frequency of checking will be reduced. The final check of the face side should be carried out to ensure flatness lengthways along the board, across its width, and diagonally. When you are satisfied that the surface will stand all the checks, identify the surface with a face mark. The accuracy of the remaining surfaces will depend largely on the accuracy of the face side.

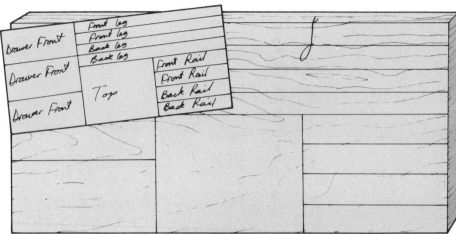

Above:
A typical example of preliminary selection and positioning of pieces.
Right:
An example of a cutting list showing finished sizes. When marking out, add 12mm (½in) to lengths, 6mm (¼in) to widths, 3mm (⅛in) to thicknesses.

Qty	Name	Length	Width	Thickness	Thickness	Thickness
3	Drawer Fronts	16½"	6¼"	¾"	¾"	1½"
2	Front Rails	18"	2"	¾"	¾"	½"
2	Back Rails	18"	2"	¾"	¾"	
1	Top	17"	15"	¾"	¾"	2

Planing the face edge

Next, plane the face edge. Again the choice of this edge should be related to the position that the piece of wood will occupy in the finished construction. Check for accuracy along the length of the planed edge with a straight-edge. With a try-square, check that the edge is square to the face side. Always make sure that the inside face of the stock of the try-square is held against the face side when checking the squareness of the face edge. The try-square and straight-edge form a close partnership in this exercise. When you are satisfied that the face edge is true, identify it with a face mark. Look upon these marks as your guarantee that the surfaces have been checked and have passed the required standards – a form of hallmark. Later when you come to do the marking out, the face marks will form valuable reference points.

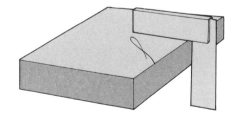

Planing to width

Now, plane the piece to width. To do this set a marking gauge to the required dimension and gauge a line on both the face side and the opposite and as yet unplaned surface. Make sure that the stock of the marking gauge is held against the face edge, this will give you two lines that are perfectly parallel to the face edge. All that remains is to plane down to the two lines and the piece of wood is prepared to width.

Planing to thickness

Finally, set the marking gauge to the thickness required. With the stock of the marking gauge against the face side, gauge lines on both edges and, on wide boards, along the ends as well. Plane the surface timber away until you reach the gauge lines. Bear in mind that a gauge line is in fact a fine V-shaped groove running along the grain. You should stop planing when you have halved this 'V'. If you remove the 'V' completely, the wood will be too thin, and if subsequently it has to fit into a slot, groove or opening of some kind, it will be loose. Always think about the part that the piece of wood will eventually play in the construction and try to react accordingly. Do not forget that final cleaning up could reduce the width or thickness still further.

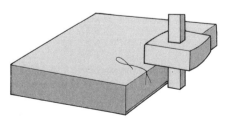

These general guidelines apply whether the pieces are small or large. Where several pieces are to be prepared to the same width and thickness, obvious economies of time and effort can be made by planing all the face sides first, followed by all the face edges, with one gauge

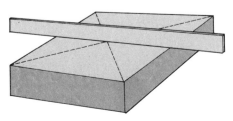

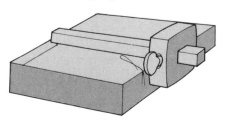

setting mark all the pieces to width. Do the same with the thickness.

Planing can be a very satisfying aspect of making anything in wood, but constant attention to the cutting edge is essential. As soon as the edge shows signs of dullness, sharpen it and enjoy its new lease of life. To carry on with a dull edge will not save time. Rub candle wax on the sole of the plane as a form of lubrication and you will be amazed how much easier it is.

During this stage in the surface preparation of pieces, some speed is essential. Try to get the pieces planed in as short a time as possible. It is not a question of hurrying the work. Try and set aside a period of time to do the planing without too many breaks in continuity, for timber, as you will discover, can be a very perverse material. Problems can be minimised by getting it planed and assembled quickly, and locking it into the construction as soon as is practical.

Another consideration is to store it carefully. When you purchased your boards from the timber merchant they were kept apart by sticks during the seasoning process. If you continue to do this until they are finally assembled and glued together, all the surfaces will remain free to react to humidity and temperature changes and will stand a better chance of staying flat and stable. Get into the habit, therefore, of putting the wood you are working with in stick, even if you plan only to leave them for short periods – even overnight. In any case, it makes for a tidy and orderly workshop.

This takes care of surface preparation. A final word about accuracy. Be honest with yourself when checking surfaces with straight-edges and try-squares. On narrow surfaces there should be little doubt. On wide surfaces, overall accuracy should be aimed at, bearing in mind that the jack plane blade has a cambered edge which will produce a slightly wavy surface.

Marking out and cutting to length
This stage follows surface preparation; in fact it is no bad idea to complete the entire process of marking out, even marking out the joints, at this stage.

One part of the process, often vital to the success of a project, deserves to be given special consideration – squaring ends. Where possible work on more than one piece of wood at the same time. Take, for example, a chest of drawers. The top and bottom pieces of the carcase and the front rails need to be exactly the same length. So, when marking out for length, bind them together either in a vice or with cramps.

Any other features common to more than one piece – such as shoulder lines and joint positions – can be marked out on the same principle. In the case of the length markings of these chest components, draw a line with a marking knife along the stock of a try-square placed against one face side.

Next, remove the chest pieces from the vice and square the end lines round the four surfaces, again using a try-square and making sure that it is kept firmly pressed against the face side or face edge.

Action hints
* All cutting lines across the grain should be made with a marking knife.
* Cutting lines to be subsequently removed in the cleaning up process (joint marks, for example) should be made with a sharp pencil.
* Never do any marking out except from a face edge or face side.

Planing (or shooting) the ends
It is not always necessary to plane ends square. Give this some thought and you may save yourself a great deal of work. It should only be necessary to plane ends square if their accuracy directly affects subsequent stages.

Cutting to length
Where possible work on duplicated pieces at one time.

Cramp (or clamp)

Face edge marks

Knife lines

The shooting board
Plane the ends of narrow pieces of wood on a shooting board, a jig which guides the plane square to the face edge and prevents splitting of end grain.

A mitre shooting board could also be made to shoot end grain to an angle of 45 degrees. Two squared headpieces are secured at right angles to create two 45 degree angle stops, against which a board is planed.

If, for example, you are cutting a tenon on the end of a rail it will probably not be necessary to plane the end. If it is a stopped tenon joint, the end will need to be square but not planed beautifully. If it is a through tenon joint, the end can be cleaned off after the glue has set.

However, if a narrow piece of wood must be end planed, it is best done using a jack plane and shooting board.

A shooting board consists of two straight-edged boards screwed together to form a rebate (rabbet). Into the top

board is housed a headpiece, against which the timber is held. The jack plane rests on its side on the lower board, thus utilising the top board as a guide.

Shooting boards are not adequate for wide pieces of wood because the force required to hold the work and push the plane is frequently too demanding. Secure wide pieces in a vice. If more than 3mm (1/8in) has to be planed away, first remove some of the waste end grain with a tenon or panel saw.

Action hints
* To prevent the wood splitting at the end of a cut when planing end grain in a vice, cramp on another thinner piece of wood that has been carefully planed to create a good mating surface for the edge of the wide board. The top outside corner of the narrow board should be removed with a chisel. This extra piece of wood reinforces the grain at the end of the plane stroke.
* A marking knife cuts a small 'V' shape line. Stop planing when one part of the 'V' has been removed and the knife line appears as a kind of frame round the end of the board. If you cannot see the effect of the knife line as a shine on the corners of the board end, you have gone too far.

33

Plans introduction

"It is evident that an understanding of the fundamental principles of design and making will enable the amateur to achieve remarkable standards in what he makes. Economy at the expense of quality has too frequently been the maxim of woodwork in general. But the craftsman, whether he be amateur or professional, takes pleasure in producing the best he can. Skill and a growing knowledge of how he can express himself through his work bring freedom to the individual to establish his own identity."
John Makepeace

Plans, the main section of this book, has been organised to provide readers of whatever technical ability with the opportunity to make furniture for their homes. A grading system has been used whereby one star indicates the least demanding objects, and four stars those which require greater practical experience.

Under the direction of John Makepeace, top international craftsmen were commissioned to provide plans for furniture which represent a fairly comprehensive selection of household items, and which have been organised here on a room-by-room basis. All of the designs incorporate some of the special techniques and reflect the characteristic philosophies of these craftsmen.

Construction and design
There are, therefore, very good reasons why each design is as it is. If you turn to one of the most demanding pieces, La Trobe Bateman's kitchen dresser, you will see that certain aspects of it – the tapered legs, for example – would be extremely difficult to reproduce without the aid of power tools. The decision was taken not to provide alternative design suggestions simply because the tapering of the legs is an integral part of the appearance of the whole piece. That is not to say that many aspects of the designs are not open to individual interpretation, indeed it is hoped that the plans will encourage readers to use the craftsmen's ideas, synthesise them, and produce their own designs.

Full and detailed plans, scale drawings, measurements and guidelines for construction were in every case provided by the designers themselves, although some items, notably all the pieces from America, were not made in the designers' workshops. In these cases, individual construction decisions were taken by the builder which might not have been taken by the designer craftsmen had their workshops produced them. As inevitably, readers will make *their* own decisions about construction details.

The main purpose, therefore, of gathering these designs together, besides imparting technical skills useful for tackling virtually every construction problem likely to be experienced by someone wanting to build a table, bed, chair, etc, is to pass on the reasons why each piece has been designed and built the way it has. Understanding "why" will probably influence method and technique.

Tools
In the case where a reader wants to tackle a four-star piece and does not have the necessary tools, much help in the initial stages can be had from saw mills, provided he gives them essential information (possibly even templates) to make the basic cuts. Ashley Cartwright started in business, before he had built up his workshop, by drawing upon this kind of assistance from local saw mills. He expands on this in his introduction to his garden furniture.

Technical skill
All the pieces have been specially made for the book because it was felt that only then could all likely practical difficulties be faced up to and solved before providing readers with step-by-step instructions. The result is a collection of furniture to appeal to a wide range of technical skills.

The carving – hall chest and mirror frame – was achieved by an amateur completely inexperienced in craft, who simply followed Howard Raybould's instructions to the letter. Of course the uncarved chest and frame are simple constructions which some readers might wish to build without attempting to carve them. There are other pieces which can be adapted or "taken so far". Norman Beverton's saw horse has compound angled legs for maximum rigidity, and while it *could* be built as a simpler construction, the reader is given the opportunity to choose to build a stool which will stand him in good stead for years.

Again whether you choose to employ the sophisticated drawer jointing procedure recommended by Wendell Castle for his chest of drawers (the dovetails carry through a theme of the whole bedroom suite) or whether you choose to employ the simpler technique suggested by Sam Maloof in his dining room sideboard drawers is an example of choice theoretically open to the reader.

Of course, joining one piece of wood to another is one of the basic and essential techniques which some amateurs find difficult. In the previous section, space was given to preparing and squaring boards. Again, many woodwork books push traditional jointing methods to the virtual exclusion of more modern, simpler "engineering" techniques. In the plans provided by John Hardy for the sitting room, an emphasis on board preparation and less traditional methods of jointing provides the worker with a thorough grounding in what he regards as the "bricks and mortar of craftsmanship." He has more to say about joints in the tools and techniques reference section at the back of the book. In fact, for the less experienced amateur, this reference section (Part 3 of the book) will be useful when attempting all of the plans.

Scope
It is intended that there be something for everyone in this Plans section. Space age executives, desk-bound astronauts will delight in Fred Baier's study offering. But his designs will be of interest to anyone who likes to work in man-made sheets with simple joints. Wendell Castle's bedroom furniture on the one

hand provides the reader with essential construction details for a side table (which can also be used as a stool), chest of drawers, and dressing table, but more interestingly, gives the reader the option to enhance them through his "stacking" technique. Norman Beverton, in his

"In producing a design for the chair, table and media unit system I have concentrated on what I regard as the bricks and mortar of craftsmanship. It is essential that you understand how to prepare and mark out timber, and the importance of maintaining and using the various hand planes in the successful basic preparation of timber. Without an efficient training in these basic activities, the craftsman is ill-advised to proceed to the making of more exotic joints presented as features in the work of other craftsmen.

"The designs have evolved from this precept and the various wood components have been treated as an engineer might treat steel. Except for him of course the basic preparation has been done _ the engineer starts from a precise base.

"Additionally, the designs have some regard for new technology and materials not necessarily regarded by the traditionalist as falling within his frame of reference.

"We are dealing here with easily manageable short pieces of wood. Providing that simple accuracy in planing, cutting and squaring is maintained there will be a pleasing and satisfying end result."

The workshop by Norman Beverton

Beginnings

"I started working with wood when I came out of the Air Force in 1948. I had done a bit of woodwork at school and again on a course during my time in the Air Force. During the War I planned my future in making furniture. First of all I went to *Guildford Art School* and studied sculpture. I worked in stone and wood at Guildford. Later I rented a small coach house and used it as a workshop. The first machine I invested in was an electrically powered hand plane. Everything else I did by hand. I was making all sorts of things – tables, chairs, wardrobes, cupboards, any kind of furniture. One or two were original designs but mainly I was working to commissions for the family and friends. At that point you have to be prepared to live on bread and water as it were! I hadn't really had any specific technical training other than the Guildford course and I looked upon that time as learning the craft. In fact you don't really ever stop learning.

Materials

"I don't recall seeing anything particularly original around at the time – this was the early '50s, and I tended to look back to the way wood was used in mediaeval times. Wood has a great strength in itself. You can cantilever wood whereas with some materials that isn't possible. Using wood for its constructional quality was the thing as far as I was concerned.

"Even then we used to use materials other than wood. I used lino for its colour, and metal too. I used to make hinges and locks. I would make patterns in wood and have them cast in brass, then file them to shape to fit, say, a knuckle of a hinge – anything to get it just right rather than going out and buying one. You can make lovely locks and keys in this way.

"I worked a lot in plywood as well. The basic difference in using plywood as opposed to solid timber is that you haven't got the weakness of the grain. A piece of solid wood is very strong along the length of its grain. But it's relatively weak across the grain. You just cannot impose much load across a plank of wood, whereas with plywood you can impose loads equally in any direction. Obviously you can use this aesthetically, not simply as a structural bonus. Just a simple example, you could have a boomerang shape as a shelf, or as a table, which is very much something that would use the particular quality that is unique to plywood. I have done a lot in chipboard too. Chipboard has the advantage of being very cheap if you want to cover a big area at minimum cost and, of course, it has this great virtue of always staying flat.

"It's the ideal situation to be coming up with your own designs and the designer/craftsman has to be the best person to do it since he is *close* to the material. A lot of the designers responsible for contemporary mass-produced articles are very often not in touch with the work itself in a practical sense. I have designers come to me with projects, who never work with wood at all, and that very often shows up in the designs.

"We have to assume that anyone about

to embark upon working with hardwoods has a real interest in the material. Either you like to see things made in wood or wooden designs, or you have some special feeling for wood the material. It's a special interest and enthusiasm. After all you are using that most precious thing – leisure time."

Design

"In the early stages my advice is to begin with fairly simple things. Pay them a great deal of attention and give them a lot of time. Don't do anything too ambitious to start with, otherwise you can give yourself so many headaches that it might put you right off. I suggest that newcomers begin with my workbench, which is, after all, a place to work on, and the pleasure that they will derive from that will be enough to take them along the trail. To make something you can *use* is a good thing in itself. Either do that or get hold of a small piece of hardwood and try carving it, a face, anything – just in relief. Don't go into three dimensions straight away. If you carve out something in wood in this way you will begin to experience its qualities and how tools operate. It's a beginning, it's something that you can be pleased with; it's a good first step.

"If you are designing from scratch, from your own idea, then first of all you

must draw a sketch, get it down on paper. If you can't draw, then it's a good idea to make a model. Models can be very useful indeed because you can see how things work. But if you can visualise then you can do it all on paper.

"Say you want to make a circular table and you have the idea to support it on a central pedestal. You'll think first of all about its diameter and you'll have a feeling about how thick you want the edge of the top to be, and already you'll be thinking of what kind of wood you want to build it with. Maybe you are thinking of a fairly good hardwood like mahogany. Then, once you have the circular top fixed in your mind, you'll begin to think about the size and shape of the pedestal. What will it have to be to support that table? Then you begin to sketch things out. If you are thinking of a tripod base, then you think about how long and what shape each arm shall be, bearing in mind that it mustn't fall over and if you put pressure on it at any point it must stay upright. Then you begin to think about the joints and how the top rails will support the top and be joined to the pedestal. You begin to look at all the details – you want it to be as utilitarian as possible. You may begin with a visual image but that can only be realised with functional principles in mind."

The workbench ★★

The bench is designed to be strongly utilitarian and has two special features – first of all the bench top can be changed or turned when it gets damaged, secondly you do have the option to make it a knock-down bench which can be easily stocked out of the way. Beverton's first choice of timber is beech, but if that is too costly or difficult to come by in your area then deal is also a very good timber, but any soft-wood will do. Make sure whichever species you select that your timber is straight and reasonably dry. The overall size of the bench (that is the length and width) can easily be adjusted to suit the space available. We are concerned here simply with the method of construction – the actual measurements are relatively unimportant. The experience gained in making the bench will be a good start to the projects to follow – and without a good workbench you really cannot hope to realise your least ambitious plans.

Cutting list Beech	Length	Width	Thickness
2 Surface rails	2000mm (78¾in)	70mm (2¾in)	95mm (3¾in)
4 Legs	820mm (32¼in)	70mm (2¾in)	95mm (3¾in)
2 Cross-leg rails	750mm (29½in)	170mm (6⅝in)	38mm (1½in)
4 Top rails	750mm (29½in)	100mm (4in)	50mm (2in)
1 Top surface (chipboard)	2000mm (78¾in)	750mm (29½in)	18mm (¾in)

Tools
Cross cut saw
25mm (1in) chisel
20mm (¾in) chisel
Drill and bits
Mallet
Square
Bevel
Small drill with countersink
   bit
Spanner for bolts
Plane
Mortise gauge
Screwdriver

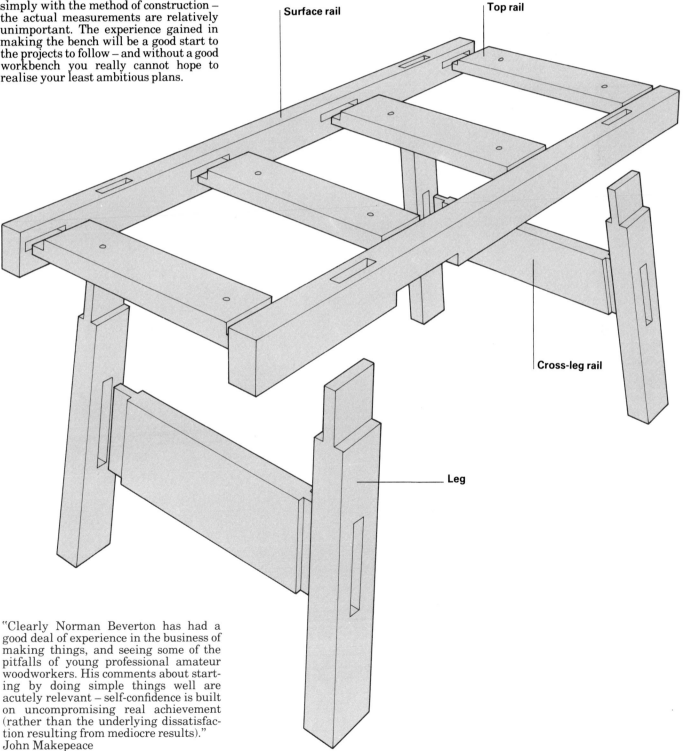

Surface rail

Top rail

Cross-leg rail

Leg

"Clearly Norman Beverton has had a good deal of experience in the business of making things, and seeing some of the pitfalls of young professional amateur woodworkers. His comments about starting by doing simple things well are acutely relevant – self-confidence is built on uncompromising real achievement (rather than the underlying dissatisfaction resulting from mediocre results)."
John Makepeace

The workbench 2

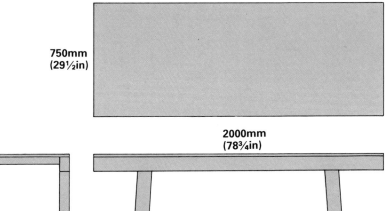

750mm
(29½in)

2000mm
(78¾in)

The legs and rails

1. Make a full-size drawing or model to scale and calculate the angle between the leg and bottom edge of the bench top, which will permit the bottom of the leg to splay 50mm (2in) from a perpendicular erected from the underside of the table top as shown in the illustration. Set your bevel to that angle.

Action hint
* If you find a slight difference in the angle from that given in the accompanying illustration, it doesn't matter provided the same bevel setting is used for each of the four legs.

2. Use the bevel to mark the angle of the tenon shoulders on the leg; use the same bevel setting to mark the angled mortise on the edge of the surface rail.

3. If you plan to build a knock-down workbench the inner side of each mortise should be cut at 90 degrees to the top of the surface rail as shown in the illustration.

4. Draw corresponding mortise guidelines on the inner side of the surface rails, again, using your bevel as a guide. Then, using your square, continue the line across the top and bottom of the surface rail. Use your mortise gauge to set out both tenon and mortise thicknesses precisely. Cutting an angled mortise is perhaps not as straightforward as cutting a right-angled mortise but provided you cut from both top and bottom of the surface rail you will achieve it by trial and error.

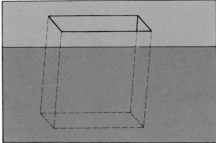

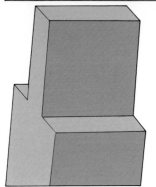

Action hint
* Drill the waste wood out short of the lines and then cut back to them with a chisel.

5. Fit each leg joint individually. Next, with the original bevel setting, mark the slope at the base of each leg. Carry the mark line round each leg and cut and/or plane to it.

Cutting the wedge

The wedge is a tapering piece of wood with an angle at point A equal to the angle that you have set on your bevel. The 90 degree shoulder on the inside of the wedge enables you to knock the wedge out of the construction when you want to dismantle it.

Mark and cut accordingly but ensure that the top of the wedge does not come to a sharp point, as it needs to be lower than the top of the sur-face rail. Finish with your plane.

Action hint
* A dry joint with a wedge will not weaken the structure of the table provided you use a good strong wood for the wedge, such as oak. Again, it might help to make a drawing of this section to enable you to cut the wedge so that the wedge slopes at a corresponding angle to the gap left in the mortise by the leg tenon.

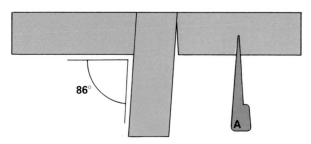

The top rails

Next we move on to the top rails. The object is to cut bare-faced tenons on the top rails because ordinary tenons will be less able to support any weight bearing down on the top surface of the workbench. So, mark and cut the tenons and mortises. Again, fit each joint dry to check that they fit well, and make any adjustments that are necessary. Then dismantle, glue each joint, reassemble and cramp up.

The leg rails

1. Mark and cut the tenons on the leg rails and the mortises in the legs.

2. Fit the whole structure together dry. When you are satisfied that the structure is as you planned it, dismantle, glue the joints, and cramp up.

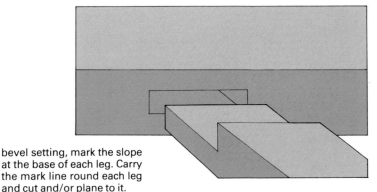

Bench top and vice

1. Cut the workbench top to size from the 18mm chipboard.

2. Bore holes for screws in the top rails (as shown in the illustration) to attach the workbench top.

Action hints
* Calculate the length of the screws you need so that they enter approximately 10mm to 12mm (⅜in to ½in) into the underside of the chipboard top.
* When you have drilled the holes in the top rails, mark point of screw entry into the blockboard with a bradawl.

3. Screw the top to the rails.

Attaching the vice

The last job is to clear the bottom edge of the surface rail to take the vice so that you bring the jaws of the vice up to the level of the top of the bench. Mark the cut. Cut down with the saw and clear it away with a chisel and mallet. Drill holes in the surface rails and packing piece to take the coach screws and affix the vice.

Action hint
* It is essential to fix soft and hardwood jaws to the vice to prevent the metal damaging the work held. If hardwood jaws are used, supplementary softwood jaws can be made for particularly delicate work.

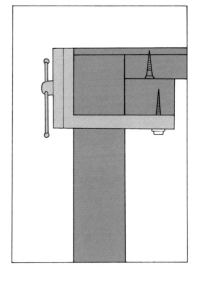

The saw horse ☒

Side and front elevations of saw horse

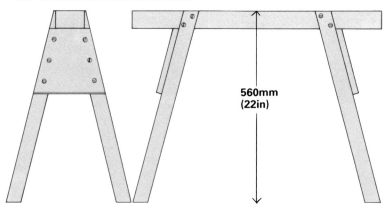

560mm
(22in)

Cutting list Beech or deal	Length	Width	Thickness
1 Trestle	760mm (30in)	90mm (3½in)	50mm (2in)
4 Legs	610mm (24in)	45mm (1¾in)	45mm (1¾in)
2 Webs (plywood)	200mm (8in)	200mm (8in)	20mm (¾in)

The legs

1. The legs are set at equal compound angles of 75 degrees, giving a height of 560mm (22in) from the top of the trestle to the floor.

2. Cut the four legs, allowing for waste.

3. Set your bevel gauge to the splay angle and mark the top of each leg only (see illustration). Once marked, it can be cut and planed to the lines.

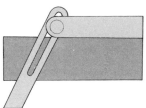

Three-quarter view showing 'bird's mouth' joint and plywood webs

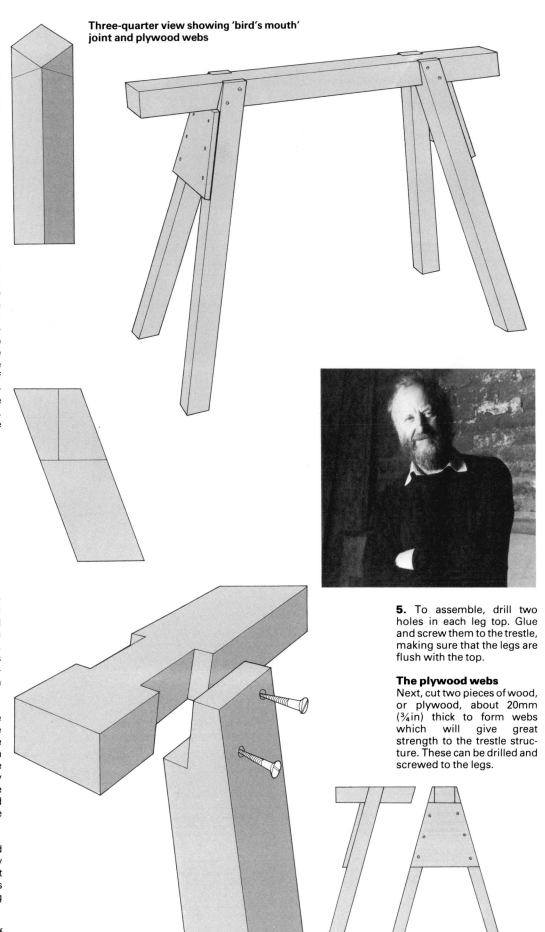

4. Take two legs and lay on a flat surface and, as shown in the illustration, scribe a line to the thickness of the trestle top. This line is the bottom edge of a cut which will produce a 'bird's-mouth' lap joint between legs and trestle top. 10mm (³⁄₈in) from the outside edge at the top of each leg, drop a perpendicular to the mark you have just drawn (see illustration). Cut as indicated. Do the same with the other two legs.

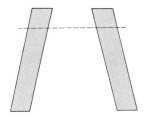

The top surface
1. Cut a length of wood suitable for the trestle top and 152mm (6in) from each end of this piece mark a point on the edge of its top surface. With your bevel (still set to its original angle) mark the position of each leg as shown in the illustration.

2. With a try-square, square lines over the surface of the board and with your gauge mark a cutting line 10mm (³⁄₈in) from the outside edges. You can now cut away between the lines. First use your saw to cut down and then clean away the waste with a chisel.

3. Try the legs in position and if the joints are accurately cut, the legs should be a tight fit into the top. The tightness of the fit ensures a strong trestle.

4. Then dismantle, mark off the lengths of each leg against the bevel and cut.

5. To assemble, drill two holes in each leg top. Glue and screw them to the trestle, making sure that the legs are flush with the top.

The plywood webs
Next, cut two pieces of wood, or plywood, about 20mm (³⁄₄in) thick to form webs which will give great strength to the trestle structure. These can be drilled and screwed to the legs.

The hall by Howard Raybould

"Craft has conventionally been a word used in connection with traditional objects where personality achieves little expression. The basic purpose of my work is that personality should be displayed very strongly. Recently I gave a talk and slide show in Japan at the *Kyoto College of Industrial Design and Textiles*. The reaction to my design philosophy, from those who opened their mouths to speak, was general confusion and bewilderment!"

Aesthetics and function

"We hear that art is art, and furniture is furniture . . . but when I sit in a room and observe objects I cannot accept that they are solely concerned with function. Design is lurking about trying to persuade someone to buy this object as opposed to any other on show. Hi-fi control panels, for example, far from being a random arrangement, are not designed, in structure and appearance, to lure the buyer into making his decision solely on the basis of function – in this case sound reproduction. This is true of virtually all objects from cars to cutlery. I believe that it is true of craft works too."

Looking for ideas

"Now, if you go back far enough to the days when, for various reasons, objects were few and far between, the objects that were around tended to be personalised, imbued with 'magic' (or whatever you like to call it) by the maker and owner. He carved or added something of himself, his culture, his beliefs, and the ornamenta-

tion (so-called) was completely natural. Today this is rarely the case – ornamentation tends to be superficial, trim and divorced from essentials. When I started carving in a traditional workshop, I felt sad that nothing of the collective experience of today, nothing new, nothing characteristic of the times, had been added to the age old traditional approach. Traditional work was in fact an unquestioned motif, recurring themes which were rooted in craft prestige above all else. So, I decided to try and arrange my own reactions, look inside myself for ideas and have a go.

"From the start, it was quite obvious that traditional carving had been well worked out in terms of techniques, if not in terms of application. So, I turned to fair grounds, ships' figureheads, shop signs, old wooden toys, shutters, etc., and I decided to start from the beginning.

"I knew what I liked – I liked colours and crude simplicity. Sometimes I found myself preferring the simpler work in small village churches to more grandiose work displayed in many of our cathedrals. I also found myself enjoying non-intentional irregularities because they seemed to display a directness which exuded the energy of creativity. Had the irregularities been tightened up they would possibly have lost something. In this sense, the amateur contributed considerably to my formation of feelings about carving. I was reacting against accepted principles of design characteristic of mass-production today – the 'perfect flat surface' for example. My feelings

were a product of my own time, but was that something to run away from? After all, in nature, the straight line or flat surface is rarely evident. The straightness and flatness of line seem to me to be a strange and human obsession. I agree it is very economical and practical but it has nothing of the personality of the maker. It also exists alongside some truly abhorrent techniques which are also 'practical'. The high gloss finish of some precious wood table, for example, gives me a feeling of *control at all costs*, I admit such a finish may be able to take bumps, bangs, and spills, but when I make things I try to *encourage* a restrained hand to touch them and use them without fear of denting or damaging the surface. Generally, my pieces will actually improve with handling. Certainly the colours will change as a result, because underneath them, the wood will, in time, darken to warm mellow tones. From a wild and lively youth, a quietening will come with use and age! And this is how I like it."

Materials, tools and finishes

"The wood I buy invariably comes in straight lengths, but the tools I use are anything but tools which produce straight lines and surfaces. Variations of texture in wood are a natural consideration for the 'personalised' carver and one to be exploited.

"Personally, I like the fresh, outdoor appearance of cedar or pine. Some timbers entice the craftsman to work them to perfection and call upon him to enhance

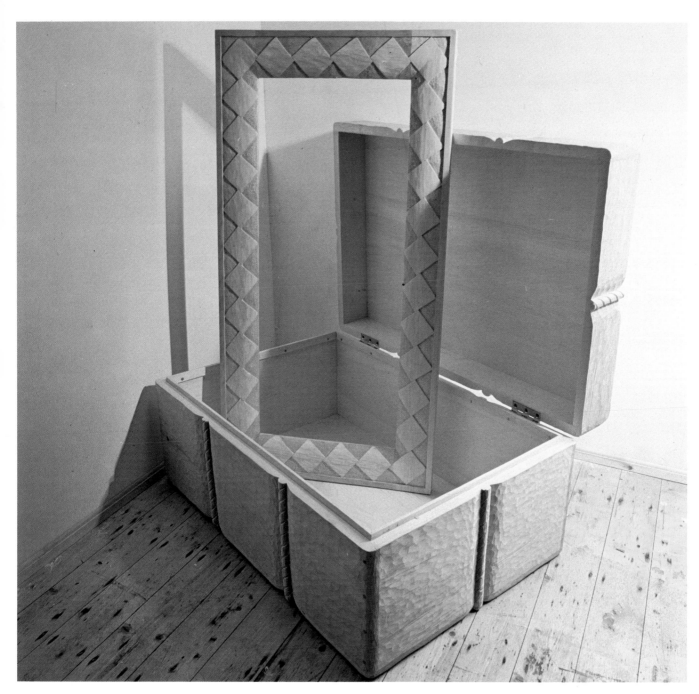

their natural aspects in an individual way. Recently, I have been using Quebec pine – yellow pine, for a lot of my work. It has a quality of being clean to cut, and in terms of movement, it is relatively stable. However, its grain and natural colour need weathering. A freshly carved piece of work doesn't really have much of a woody feel about it. But it is an ideal vehicle for colour experimentation, and this is one of my preoccupations.

"Colour can be applied in various ways. Paint may obliterate grain rather than accentuate it, but I usually apply colour in such a way as to enhance the grain. Rubbing in pigments or making up a water colour . . . applying the colour and then removing any excess . . . I've used colour in these ways either on small details or across the whole job. But at other times I may decide on button polish or some other type of shellac finish."

The process

"There comes a point in a piece of work, whether it's a box, frame, toy or whatever, when it feels complete. For me this is the important thing. Throughout its making, decisions are being made. My chest, for example, starts by looking boxy, and only an image of the idea helps carry me through the early stages. Early on there are a number of alternative possibilities. Later, as it begins to stand more on its own, a less abstract directional course presents itself.

"When carving a figure, the piece goes through a strange period of metamorphosis – frequently it appears as if it was made in the dawn of time . . . weird ghostly shapes which conjure up images of things long past . . . there's a great deal of struggling until it is brought forward to today. And it is always surprising just how much wood has to be removed. Just

when satisfaction seems around the corner, working a final detail brings to light a heaviness somewhere else in the work. It's not as if there is one absolute incredible surface lurking inside the

The chest ★★

wood. It is a matter of feeding the eye with a selection of convincing details which are finally unified into a whole.

"In the end, different life-styles produce different objects. Here in Japan (where I am) craft objects are very humble and quiet – but then they have to fit into humble homes. When I make something I often have an idea of where and in what surroundings it would really look good, but sometimes I make something for a mythical house – maybe the complete object casts a spell of sunshine, sea breezes, sun-lit rooms . . . things which I had imagined as characteristic of this imagined house. It really is a question of stimulating the imagination – looking perhaps for a feeling of relaxation (which would be uncharacteristic of heavy gilt work), of using techniques suitable for the feeling you want the object to exude (using more sombre colours, for example, which might be said to be more typical of the North)."

Ideas for alternative designs

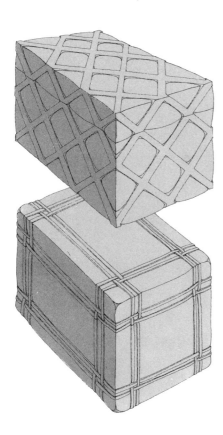

"In his recent book on the history of furniture, Edward Lucie Smith explores people's motives for buying particular objects. He demonstrates that function has only been a minor force and that, perhaps unconsciously, we are all expressing our character in the things we choose to have around us. Howard Raybould's skill, his ability to identify his inner feelings and his good humour all find expression in his work."
John Makepeace

44

Constructional view of chest

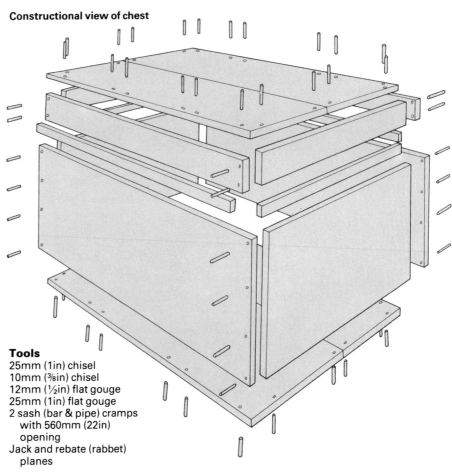

Tools
25mm (1in) chisel
10mm (⅜in) chisel
12mm (½in) flat gouge
25mm (1in) flat gouge
2 sash (bar & pipe) cramps
  with 560mm (22in)
  opening
Jack and rebate (rabbet)
  planes

Cutting list Quebec yellow pine:	Length	Width	Depth
4 Top and bottom surfaces	813mm (32in)	292mm (11½in)	25mm (1in)
2 Front and back sections	813mm (32in)	254mm (10in)	25mm (1in)
2 Side sections	559mm (22in)	254mm (10in)	25mm (1in)
2 Lid sections, front and back	813mm (32in)	89mm (3½in)	25mm (1in)
2 Lid sections, sides	559mm (22in)	89mm (3½in)	25mm (1in)

Building the chest
"I have chosen to build the chest from Quebec yellow pine, but lime is feasible being good to carve though a rather harder wood and a fairly nondescript grain."

1. Edge plane the top and bottom pieces (lid and base), and utilising the rubbed joint technique join appropriately to form the top and bottom surfaces. Make sure of a good fit and plane to size.

2. In building up the front, back and sides, make sure that all opposite sides are aligned – in other words, plane carefully. Glue, cramp up, and leave to dry before drilling for dowels.

3. Cut lid sections to measure, front and back.

4. Refer to exploded diagram for placing of dowels; drill and fix.

5. Once you are sure that top and bottom fit correctly, glue the inner securing battens.

Action hint
* Do not plane outer surfaces, as these will be hand finished with carving tools.

Action hints

* Now that the basic shell is complete, the work of drawing, setting in and carving can begin. But before it does, make sure that the work in hand is secure and well supported. You may well have to use a mallet to set in the outlines, and if your support is unbalanced or inadequate you might find the shell unequal to the strain. Another word of advice – always keep your hand behind the tool; never be in a hurry. It is a slow job which becomes faster not by hurrying but by experience and understanding. Maybe you'll make a few mistakes to begin with, so practise on an off-cut and then begin on the bottom of the chest before you tackle the front, sides and top. Get the feel of what you are doing. The tools are designed to do just this job and there's nothing mysterious about its performance.
* Another thing, parcels are not precise objects. Forget your measuring tape and architect's lines. The box is there; its shape has been formed; it'll be thousands of chips later that you alter that shape. Fix the shape of the rope in your mind's eye, think of it being rounded off, of the 'paper' tucking beneath it. Optical illusion will do the rest!

Carving (1)

1. With a soft pencil mark out the position of the rope and set in its outline with the bevel of a 25mm (1in) chisel facing away from the rope. Work gradually towards a cut 10mm (⅜in) deep. Avoid the temptation to achieve this depth all in one go.

2. Chop out the wood by the side of the rope with a 25mm (1in) gouge. You may find it useful to use the 12mm (½in) gouge in the tighter spots.

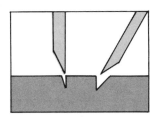

3. The next step is to round off the edges of the chest itself with the 25mm (1in) gouge. Bring the tool's cutting edge in at an angle to the edge, rather than straight on, so that you are performing a slicing action as illustrated right. A surform file might also be useful here, but do be careful of the dowels and remember that the planks are only 25mm (1in) thick. If the corners are rounded too severely they will weaken the strength of the piece.

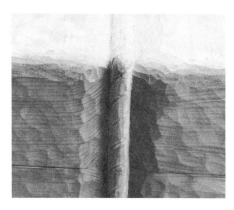

Carving (2)

1. Now the piece is ready for you to shape the rounded contour of the ropes. Where they intersect, have the top rope running with the grain over the bottom rope (which will be running across the grain). With reference to the diagram, turn your 12mm (½in) gouge over and begin the cutting action. If you experience problems in cutting across the grain (which will probably be the case, however sharp your tool) resort to the 25mm (1in) gouge and work with a slicing action.

2. The chest is now looking more like a wrapped parcel. You can maximise this effect by slightly undercutting the ropes.

3. To give the rope its plaited effect, use the 12mm (½in) gouge as follows:

Tackling each length of rope at a time, set in from the side with the 12mm (½in) gouge, and from the other side with the same tool

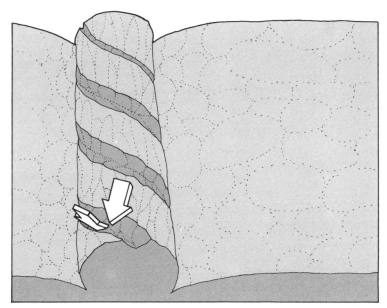

turned over. Beware of crashing straight through the wood on the end grain. Allow 20mm (¾in) between each cut.

Chop out the wood on either side of the cut as shown in the diagram above.

Finishing

"Quite possibly the 'wrapped' surface of the chest will have been damaged (bruised or cut) whilst the work on the rope has been done. You could smooth down the whole surface, but I recommend that you clean up the bruises and cuts with the 25mm (1in) gouge, where necessary balancing the effect by adding further cuts with the gouge.

"Very fine garnet paper can be used sparingly on the 'wrapped' surface and to soften the strands of rope. For final finishing, there are a number of possibilities. Here are some suggestions.

"Polyurethane varnish is hard-wearing and gives a fair amount of protection, but it is a bit 'plastic'. I would use the matt version, smooth it down with fine wire wool, and finish it off with prepared beeswax.

"Prepared beeswax is also a possibility, which will have the effect of emphasising the relief work should it be left in the recesses and polished off on the raised areas.

"I do not recommend linseed oil on Quebec pine. If you do decide to use an oil then cedar oil is better, although personally I do not recommend these products on soft pines."

The mirror frame ★ ★

Cutting list Quebec yellow pine:	Length	Width	Depth
2 Side sections	1016mm (40in)	95mm (3¾in)	25mm (1in)
2 End sections	330mm (13in)	95mm (3¾in)	25mm (1in)

1. Place the pieces of wood on a flat surface and use a rebate (rabbet) plane to cut mirror recesses 6mm (¼in) wide. Note that the two longer strips will form the sides of the mirror so leave 108mm (4¼in) at each end of both strips uncut as these parts will form the corners of the frame.

2. Glue the four strips together so that there is 6mm (¼in) overlap on the side strips at the top and bottom of the frame. This will be planed away later to give a smooth finish. Wipe away any excess glue and secure with sash cramps across the width of the frame at the top and bottom.

3. As additional support for these joints you will need to sink four beech straps at the back of the frame as shown above. First, cut and plane the straps to size from the beech wood. Each strap should be about 64mm (2½in) × 64mm (2½in) × 10mm (⅜in) shaped as in the diagram. Then, cut a shallow recess for the straps to fit and glue them in.

4. When the glue is set, very carefully plane down the straps to the level of the frame, and plane away the 6mm (¼in) overlap on the side strips.

5. The next job is to carve the frame to the cross-section diagram shown here. So, turn the frame over on the flat surface. The uncarved outer edge will be about 12mm (½in) across. Set the bevel of your straight chisel away from the edge and work away from it. Slowly carve out some of the wood by the edge and continue to

Back/front view of frame
The illustration right shows clearly the strapped joints which Raybould suggests, the rebated (rabbetted) mirror recesses, the front edge and surface carving patterns.

set your chisel in until a cut just under 6mm (¼in) has been established. Next, shape the convex contour with the 25mm (1in) flat gouge remembering always to work *with* the direction of the grain.

Cross-section view of frame

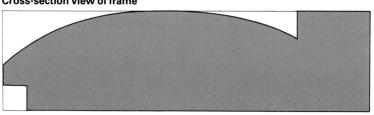

Action hints
* Work slowly and get the feel of how the tool carves the wood. Remember that virtually no wood should be removed from the crest of the contour.
* A good light source is essential for carving. Avoid strip lighting since it minimises shadow.
* When you come to the corners, be aware of the two separate contours meeting. Try and leave a flattish area so that the squares on the design (to be carved later) do not end up looking like creased paper.
* Do not rub down with glass paper. This will only blunt your tools when you start on the next stage. If you *have* to use abrasive paper, a very fine grade should be employed and only when you have finished carving.

46

6. Once you are satisfied, it is time to pick up a soft pencil and draw out the squares. Begin in the corners with squares of about 70mm (2¾in).

Action hints
* Feel free not to be too exact with these squares. If they all look exactly alike, the end result will be mechanical.

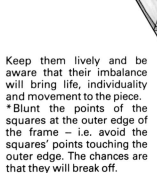

Keep them lively and be aware that their imbalance will bring life, individuality and movement to the piece.
* Blunt the points of the squares at the outer edge of the frame – i.e. avoid the squares' points touching the outer edge. The chances are that they will break off.

7. Beginning very slowly, set in with your chisel along the lines you have drawn. Keep the bevel towards the wood being removed, and the chisel upright. Once again be aware of the stresses being set up in the wood and do not force the body of the tool too deep.

8. Using the 12mm (½in) flat gouge, carve out the area around the squares. Cut down to the line of the chisel and avoid flattening this recessed area. If a chip refuses to be released, set in again with the chisel. Never break the chip off, always cut with your carving tools. Take your time; don't force anything; try to keep the work clean.

9. When the carving is finished it is time to stamp the background. Take a largish nail; cut off its head; and with a triangular file produce four pointed ends as shown in the illustration.

Avoid over-stamping which might break up the fibres of the wood. The idea is only to create an effect to contrast the flat surfaces of the squares. Finally, with a rubber, clean up any remaining pencil markings.

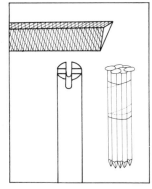

Finishing
Very many different finishes and colours are possible. If you like the look of the wood as it stands, a little beeswax will suffice as a finish. Raybould recommends that you colour the stamped background with button polish, using a 12mm (½in) squared line brush. Then, damp down (not drench) the surface of the squares and apply a *very* thin coat of white emulsion (matt paint) with your brush. Allow to dry and then cut with fine garnet paper or flour paper, so that the natural tool marks show on the surface of the squares through the matt whiteness – the whiteness in the hollows will not be touched.

When choosing colour for the border edge bear in mind where the mirror will be hung – ideally it will blend or deliberately contrast with other furniture in the room. Raybould feels that commercial wood stains look rather aggressive – fine for hardwoods, but on woods like Quebec pine they can look messy. He prefers analin dyes dissolved in polish or bleached shellac thinned down with methylated spirit. An alternative is to damp down the border edge with water, let it dry, then with very fine garnet paper (or flour paper) cut down the raised grain. Then damp again and apply a water based colourant with a brush or cloth (artists' water colours in tubes are ideal). Always start on the light side and build up the colour to the density you require, remembering that it will lighten on drying.

Names of colours often vary according to makes. Raybould recommends a sepia with a touch of burned amber to add warmth. You might like to consider a fluctuation of colour, indeed not all the wood will be the same basic colour and knots can be used to enhance similar visual variations. Further warmth can of course be effected by adding more amber, or burnt sienna, or Vandyke brown.

Action hints
* If the grain becomes fluffy cut it back with abrasive paper.
* Seal the top and bottom ends of the frame (where the end grain shows) before colouring, otherwise it will be degrees darker than the rest of the wood. Use a very small amount of the button polish to about three parts methylated spirits. Do avoid using too much polish or the colour might have difficulty in taking at all.
* When you are satisfied with the colouring, apply prepared beeswax with a brush. Be sparing. Allow to dry for half an hour and then wipe with a cotton cloth, and polish.

The mirror
Measure the mirror dimensions from the internal mirror recesses. A bevelled mirror will add substantially to the cost but the difference will be worth it. Raybould suggests not less than 12mm (½in) bevel and not more than 18mm (¾in). Hardboard is good for the backing plate. It is thin, reasonably damp proof and strong. Take off the edges with a small plane and pin with 12mm (½in) panel pins.

Fixing to the wall

"I recommend using recessed mirror plates which should be fixed into the body of the frame – two plates preferably to prevent the mirror swinging. Alternatively you might prefer using heavy duty picture wire. The process is the same except that you use complementary rings for the wire instead of plates. Hang these nearer the top of the mirror than the middle – it will prevent it swinging out from the wall at the top."

The sitting room by John Hardy

Making woodwork your business

"I started business with a chap called Frank Hills in 1964. Frank had previously taught with me in Hertfordshire and was a sculptor, potter and fine artist by trade. At the time I was working as advisor to the *West Riding Educational Authority* for handicrafts and Frank was teaching at the *Batley School of Art*. We were working weekends and evenings at first but it wasn't working out so I resigned from the West Riding and got a part-time teaching job, at the *Leeds College of Art*.

"Our intention, then, was not to mass-produce but to make one-off pieces. What we did was to make up some coffee tables and try and sell them. One particular table proved to be Heal's best selling coffee table, and they began to place what were for us quite good orders. They put a 70% mark-up on our price to them. Now the London shop is probably a bit more than that, around 75%, which is the recognised mark-up in London.

"Next, these pieces were accepted for the Design Index and we began to get one or two orders through that. The Design Index is run by the *Council of Industrial Design*. You submit to them and your submissions go before a panel. If the panel approves them, they go into a photographic record kept at the *Design Centre*, London. People (interior decorators or private people) looking for furniture go to a cabinet in which there are a wide range of pieces. The essence of the thing is to try and establish a Design Centre stamp of approval.

"Then we started to do some design work for a manufacturing company in Leeds – very cheap upholstered furniture. It was our first incursion into large-scale retail sale. It wasn't successful but it did provide us with a retaining fee which was at least some sort of regular income. Frank had by this time married and started a family. Not being able to devote the necessary time he backed out and I contacted a very good handicraft teacher called Tom Patterson. When he joined me we changed our company name from *Hardy & Hills* to *Design Workshop*. We were still part-time remember. Together, we tried to build on what we had got, which was mainly a reputation with *Heal's* for quality. We made more coffee tables and then came into contact with a man named David Bishop, who was at that time Furniture Buyer at *Woollands* of Knightsbridge.

"David was a bit of a genius, very forward looking, and he asked us to design what he called a day-bed (which was basically a structure to hold a number of cushions into which someone could fall and relax during the day-time). We produced a design and made it in laminated birch plywood. We chose birch ply because the design called for a laminated shape which generally involves quite sophisticated tooling. Normally a laminated shape is made from veneers, not from ply, but we merely bent three thicknesses of ply over a former. It was a very basic thing with cloth cushions. But David put it into a shop he owned in Covent Garden called *Goods and Chattels*. There was a party thrown there to launch his furniture, and our day-bed got quite a lot of publicity.

Sub-contracting to expand

"Next, we organised the manufacture of the bed through another company. We looked after all the liaison work and David sold the beds. That was really the turning point in our business. We had moved from tables, which we made ourselves, to an idea which David had really introduced. We had then sub-contracted the elements of it out and brought all the elements back together again for re-assembly. This really opened up a whole new horizon for us. We realised that it wasn't really necessary, once we had made a prototype, actually to go into the manufacturing business provided (and this was an essential condition) we could find people to do things to a really high standard. *Conran* are of course doing this now on a very big scale, but there are few small people doing it.

"A word of caution, however. The major stumbling block is that in order to approach a factory you have really got to say, "Make fifty," which means you have to have some money. At least we had a cash flow thanks to the day-bed and various other pieces we were making for David. In fact, he was our financier. We never had to build up stocks; we made to order. Then quite tragically David died of a brain haemorrhage and our relationship came to an end. I wrote to his partner, Simon Sainsbury (one of *the* Sainsburys) and paid him for their interest in the development of the day-bed. We had bought back our design.

"Then we changed the day-bed's image. It became a sofa and the corner stone of our business. We re-made it in rosewood and put leather cushions on it and gave it an appeal way up-market. This would be around 1965/6. We were now completely independent. We started selling the sofas and soon realised we had the basis of a much bigger business. As well as the sofa, we could have chairs, tables, etc.

"Our next good stroke of fortune was a personal call I made to *Oscar Woollens* in Swiss Cottage, the best furniture shop in the country. It was run by Kurt Heide and Walter Collins who had built their reputation on Scandinavian furniture – very much in vogue at the time. We had already sold him one or two tables and I called in to show them a chair in rosewood. They fell for it immediately. Fortunately, this was the time of their annual exhibition, a very important event at the top end of the furniture world. They decided to include it in their exhibition and it was the only British furniture they had ever shown. They had a cotton-velvet cloth specially designed in Denmark and we re-made the chair in black lacquer. We got a huge write-up in the *Sunday Times* and that did the trick. Thereafter, we had an urgent letter from France from a company called *Formes Nouvelles* who had a superb shop in Paris and wholesale operations. We signed an agreement and they began to buy. Then we had a letter from Switzerland, sparked by an advertisement taken out by the French shop. Then someone from Belgium did the same. So quite quickly we were selling to the best shops in both countries.

Business realities

"Then it was that we really came up against things. We just didn't have the finance to support the kind of business we were getting. We were showing ten colours in our hides and a hide in those days was costing about £30 and they were an essential element of the design, very soft and very supple and very natural. Then there were the various components – everyone was insisting upon minimum orders. Our clients were first-class people and we began really to let them down. People from whom we were buying laminations were turning out rubbish. We had to re-do them. The whole thing lost its impetus and we couldn't get the stock that we needed to keep the thing going.

"Still we muddled on. The laminations manufacturer went bust, but then a friend of mine who was buying clothes from Denmark found a very small company there and we started to buy laminations from them. They were superb. But still we were under severe financial strain. Luckily the bank was very good to us and gave us a breathing space to get back on our feet. We moved into another building (we had previously been working from an old farmhouse where I lived) and set up a retail shop selling our furniture and other people's. We began to offer an interior design service too. This became very lucrative because by contrast with most other interior designers we had showroom facilities, were agents for all sorts of accessories like carpets and curtains, and, most important, we had workshop back-up. We now offer the design service free provided everything is purchased through us. We are doing a small hotel at the moment, and we have done private houses, offices and pubs . . .

Professional artist craftsmen

"Of course there is a distinction between the professional craftsman involved with the 'realities' of the business and the artist craftsman. The heartening thing now is that there are a number of artist craftsmen who are doing things which aren't looking backwards. When I was at college, people who were trying to do what I set out to do were all producing superbly made copies of Gimson and people like that. They were always backward-looking. Now people are breaking new ground. To some extent they are even using new materials. But it is still a very difficult way to make a living! John Makepeace is the one that everyone thinks of in this country because he has made a success, a financial success and this is, for better or worse, what people are measured by. He's done it because he knows what superb craftsmanship is and because of his personality – he has promoted it."

"Choose a timber that planes sweetly, and one that is close textured to facilitate end grain cutting, e.g. oak, British Columbian or Oregon pine, or teak."
John Hardy

The sitting room

"There is a plethora of bad upholstered furniture on the market — bad construction, bad materials and bad design. Good pieces are difficult to find, and yet relatively easy to make. John Hardy has made a careful study of what is comfortable to sit in, good to look at and durable. In his design he has drawn on his very considerable experience to come up with a handsome and desirable solution."
John Makepeace

designs, recognises some of the traps which inexperienced woodworkers might fall into, and provides an excellent starting point.

Finally, then, the object of the book is to do more than provide plans to copy. The idea is to encourage readers who have not hitherto produced their own designs, to do so in such a way that they reflect sound individual decisions. This section is followed by leading craftsman James Krenov's advice about treating the design and making of a piece of furniture as one process, a welcome and encouraging section for some woodworkers who have shied away from designing their own pieces through a supposed lack of technical "know-how" or drawing skills. *"Today people are turning to the individual craftsman for a new direction."*
Sam Maloof

The chair and coffee table system ★ ★ ★

Tools

Circular saw	12mm (½in) coach bolts
Panel saw	Machine drill with forstener bit (or brace and twist bit)
Hack saw	
Jack plane	Chisel
Plough plane	Metal file
Centre punch	Glass paper
Dormer drill set	Sash (bar or pipe) cramps
	'G' ('C') cramps

Table cutting list

Pitch pine:	Length	Width	Depth
4 Legs	275mm (10⅞in)	125mm (5in)	43mm (1¾in)
2 Holding frame rails	815mm (32⅛in)	98mm (3⅞in)	28mm (1⅛in)
2 Holding frame rails	720mm (28⅜in)	98mm (3⅞in)	28mm (1⅛in)
2 Cladding pieces	775mm (30½in)	130mm (5⅛in)	18mm (¾in)
2 Building board in-fill panels	545mm (21½in)	205mm (8in)	40mm (1⅝in)
40mm (1⅝in) by 32mm (1¼in) solid wood lippings for building board panels			
10 Top slats, ply (+ laminates)	815mm (32⅛in)	77.5mm (3in)	15mm (⅝in)
4 Aluminium 'T' sections for in-fill panels	190mm (7½in)	22mm (⅞in)	3mm (⅛in)

The leg elements

Prepare the leg elements to the finished dimensions given, working very accurately with a sharp plane and making sure that all edges and ends are absolutely square.

"I have emphasised the importance of preparing these elements accurately because we will be using marking jigs, as illustrated, to make positions of the fixing bolts for fastening the leg sections to the main holding frames."

The holding frames

Sizes assume solid wood frames, but could be made from 25mm (1in) birch plywood edged with 9mm (⅜in) lippings along the top edge of each piece (since this is visible when the cushion – in the case of the chair – or the table top elements are removed).

1. Select lippings (edgings) to overlap top edges of frame members. Once the glue is dry, carefully skim the lippings down with a finely set plane to the same level as the plywood.

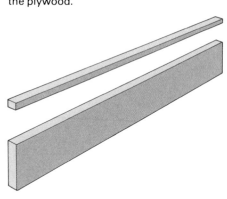

Chair cutting list

Pitch pine:	Length	Width	Depth
2 Legs	600mm (23⅝in)	125mm (4⅞in)	43mm (1⅝in)
2 Legs	275mm (10⅞in)	125mm (4⅞in)	43mm (1⅝in)
2 Holding frame rails	815mm (32⅛in)	98mm (3⅞in)	28mm (1⅛in)
2 Holding frame rails	720mm (28⅜in)	98mm (3⅞in)	28mm (1⅛in)
2 Cladding pieces	775mm (30½in)	115mm (4½in)	18mm (¾in)
1 Inner frame rail (plywood)	775mm (30½in)	88mm (3½in)	25mm (1in)
1 Inner frame rail (plywood)	775mm (30½in)	60mm (2⅜in)	25mm (1in)
2 Inner frame rails (plywood)	573mm (22⅝in)	60mm (2⅜in)	25mm (1in)
1 Building board in-fill panel	545mm (21½in)	530mm (20⅞in)	40mm (1⅝in)
1 Building board in-fill panel	545mm (21½in)	205mm (8in)	40mm (1⅝in)
40mm (1⅝in) by 32mm (1¼in) solid wood lippings for building board panels			
2 Aluminium 'T' sections for in-fill panels	190mm (7½in)	22mm (⅞in)	3mm (⅛in)
2 Aluminium 'T' sections for in-fill panels	515mm (20¼in)	22mm (⅞in)	3mm (⅛in)

2. The plywood should not be finished to its precise size initially. Once you have finished the lippings to the level of the ply treat each part of the holding frame as one piece and finish to the dimensions given and to the same standard of accuracy as with the leg elements.

3. Particular care should be taken with the ends of these

holding frame pieces since they will form the basis of joints for completing seat and table frames.

Marking out the leg fixings

1. Once these frame sections have been accurately prepared, mark out the positions of the holes on both leg and frame sections to house the fixing bolts and dowels (im-

Three views of jig: three-quarter, plan, and face-on

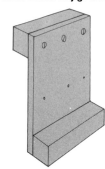

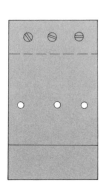

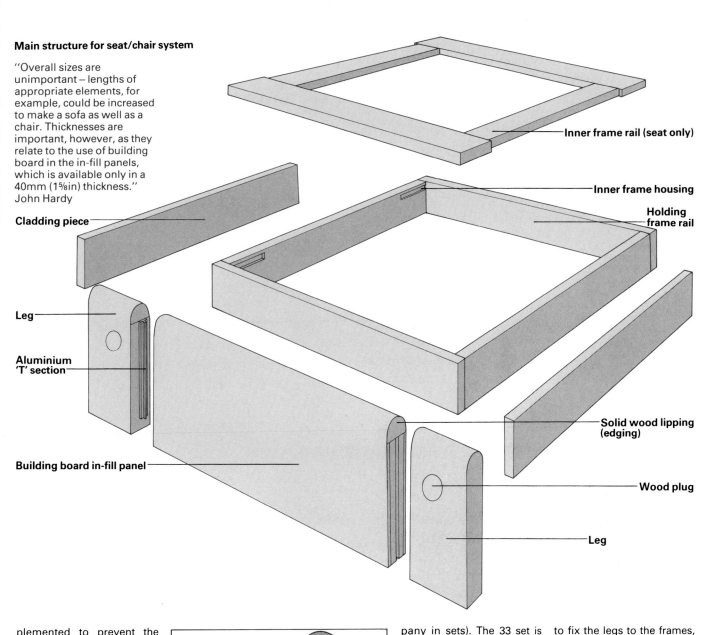

Main structure for seat/chair system

"Overall sizes are unimportant – lengths of appropriate elements, for example, could be increased to make a sofa as well as a chair. Thicknesses are important, however, as they relate to the use of building board in the in-fill panels, which is available only in a 40mm (1⅝in) thickness."
John Hardy

Cladding piece

Leg

Aluminium 'T' section

Building board in-fill panel

Inner frame rail (seat only)

Inner frame housing

Holding frame rail

Solid wood lipping (edging)

Wood plug

Leg

plemented to prevent the legs from twisting). Use a simple marking jig made to the width of the seat frame rail, and reverse the jig for each element in turn.

2. Once marked, holes can be centre punched and drilled with special carbon steel woodworking drills (produced by the Dormer com-

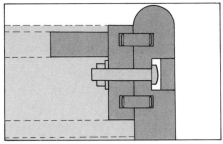

Above: side view leg fixing
Below: plan view frame jointing

Jointing the holding frames
1. Form a firm joint between the four corners of the holding frames.

"A number of joints are suitable for this purpose. Your choice will depend upon your confidence and ability. In the working drawings I have shown a very simple form of fixing – a dowel is inserted through the edge of the frame sections, and ordi-

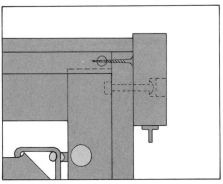

pany in sets). The 33 set is most common and has a range of five drills with 6mm (¼in) shanks. These drills are peculiar in that they have a spur centre ground at the tip which facilitates a very accurate placing of the drill point into the centre-punched spot. Since we are using 12mm (½in) dowels and 12mm (½in) coach bolts

nary wood screws and glue are used to hold them together."

Since end grain has a poor holding effect on wood-screws, it is important to insert dowels in this way and screw into these rather than directly into end grain.

Action hint
* Other joints which might be appropriate include the through dovetail joint and

to fix the legs to the frames, the 12mm (½in) drill is the one to use. A through-hole is drilled for the bolt position; stopped holes are drilled for the dowel positions.

3. Determine the accuracy of your marking and drilling with a dry run of fastening the legs to the frame sections.

the combing (or finger) joint. The combing joint is the same as the dovetail joint but can be pulled apart in any direction when dry, since both male and female members are cut straight.

2. Once these joints have been made, the table frames are complete. They should then be sanded on the inside faces and fastened together, making sure they are absolutely square.

The chair and coffee table system 2

The inner seat frames for the chair

In the case of the chairs further work must be done to house the supporting elements for the Pirelli rubber seating platforms.

1. The inner seat frames are again prepared from 25mm (1in) plywood, veneered on the top face with a veneer of the same wood you have chosen for the rest of the system. Use a balancing veneer on the reverse face.

Action hints

* Use three sash (bar or pipe) cramps and two substantial pieces of wood as cramping bars (cauls) to effect the veneering. Apply the glue to the various pieces concerned and then cramp together between the cramping bars in the sash cramps.
* Once dry, remove from the cramps and dimension accurately to given sizes.

2. Bore the holes for the special attachments to hold the rubber diaphragms. These 22mm (⅞in) diameter special attachments, shown in the illustration, have been especially designed by the Design Workshop and are available for purchase. Pirelli do provide a full instruction booklet with the Pirelli diaphragms together with their own attachment, the Pirelli screw. The holes should be drilled with a machine forstener bit in a machine drill. If this is not available, a simple drilling jig should be made in order to drill an accurate hole using a brace and twist bit.

3. Cut four small slots positioned at each end of the side members of the inner frame to take the back and front rails containing the special attachments.

4. Clean up the various pieces of the inner frame and slightly arris exposed sharp edges. Taking care that the final inner frame is exactly square, glue the four pieces together. A good method to ensure that the frame is square is to measure its diagonals and adjust the cramping until these are exactly equal. Then glue the inner frame into position. The structure can be further strengthened by fixing two screws into each of the side members of the inner frame from the outside of the outer frame, and one screw into the centre of each back and

Veneering the inner seat frames

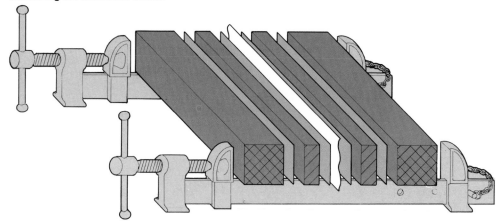

Illustration above shows two boards, four veneer sheets separated by Kraft paper to prevent glue spoiling surfaces. Cramps exert consistent pressure via the cauls.

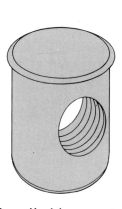

Above, Hardy's own seat attachment.

front member in the same way. See illustration right.

5. Once both seat and table frames are complete, clean up with a sharp plane and glass paper to give a fine sanded finish all over.

Final preparation of leg elements

1. Counter-bore the leg elements as previously illustrated to take the bolt heads and decorative plugs turned from the end grain of the same wood as the rest of the chair construction. These holes are bored with machine forstener bits.

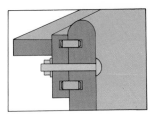

Action hint
*You could leave the bolt head showing on the face of the leg. If you do this, you will obviously need to use a longer bolt than is shown in the drawing.

2. Following this, radius the ends of the legs using a plywood or formica template to mark the curvature prior to planing as closely as possible with a hand plane. Finish with glass paper for a perfect curve.

3. When these operations are complete, clean up the leg pieces with a very finely set plane and glass paper to a high standard finish.

Attaching the aluminium extrusions

1. The aluminium extrusion pieces are used to support the front and back panels of the table or chair. They are made from a standard extrusion readily available (22mm (⅞in) × 22mm (⅞in)). The various lengths are cut with a hack saw and are filed and papered at the end to give a clean finish.

2. Bore the screw holes in appropriate places along the aluminium extrusions. The screw heads must lie flush with the aluminium.

Action hint
*Because of the 'T' shape of these aluminium extrusions it is not easy to countersink the screw holes. John Hardy suggests counter-boring them with a slightly larger drill sufficient to accept the screw head.

3. Attach these extrusions with fine screws so that they run exactly in the centre of the inside edges of each leg.

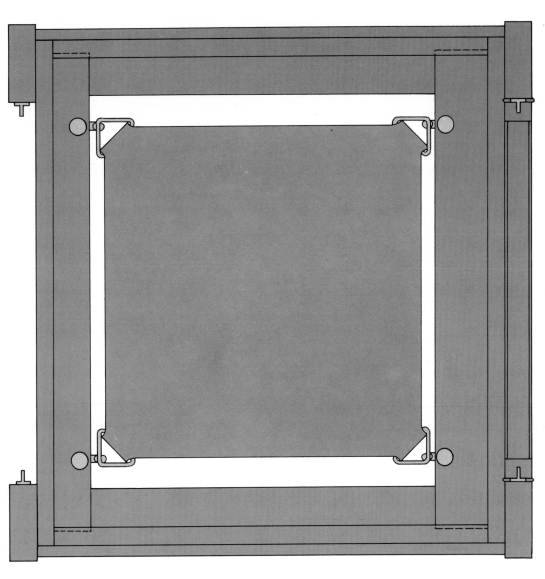

Fastening the legs to the holding frames

The coach bolts may now be pulled into the leg counter-bores by fastening a nut on the outside of each leg and pulling each bolt into the leg tightly. Thereafter, the accurately turned wood plug should be inserted into the

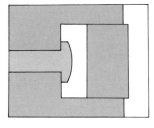

Top: plan view seat support elements.
Below: cross-section chair elements.

leg and glued to hold the bolt in position as shown here.

Action hint
*Leave the plug slightly protruding so that when the glue is dry it may be carefully planed down to the level of the leg and glass papered to a fine finish.

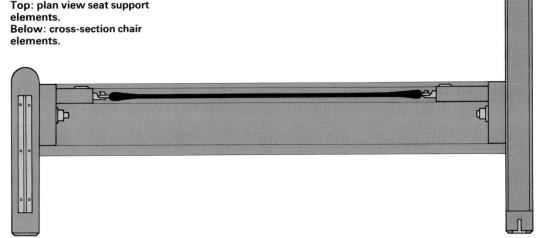

The chair and coffee table system 3

Preparing the in-fill panels

1. Now that the legs are fastened onto the frames, check that the original measurements and the actual dimensions of your pieces coincide. If they do not, make appropriate adjustments to the size of the in-fill panels. It is vital that these panels fit perfectly between the faces of the extruded elements that are fastened to the inside edges of the legs.

2. The in-fill panels are made from 40mm (1⅝in) thick building board. This is a very lightweight, polystyrene cored material which when edged with solid wood lippings provides a reasonably strong panel.

Action hint
*Since you cannot plane building board edges, cut accurately to size with a circular saw. If this is not available, most suppliers will provide a cut-to-size surface for a small extra charge.

3. Then lip the boards all round with a softwood lipping. Apply them in the following order:

Glue the two side lippings, exerting light pressure from sash cramps. When dry, finish down with a hand plane to the level of the building board surface. A 3mm (⅛in) groove, 22mm (⅞in) deep is then cut into the edges of the lippings exactly down the centre using either a hand grooving plane or a circular saw. (See also the plywood sandwich as an alternative method under instructions regarding the media unit rail sections.)

Next, apply the top and bottom lippings in the same way, cutting a further groove in the bottom edge of the panel.

4. Finally these panels are radiused along the top edge so that when placed in position between the legs they line up exactly with the radiused leg tops.

Lipping the building board in-fill panels

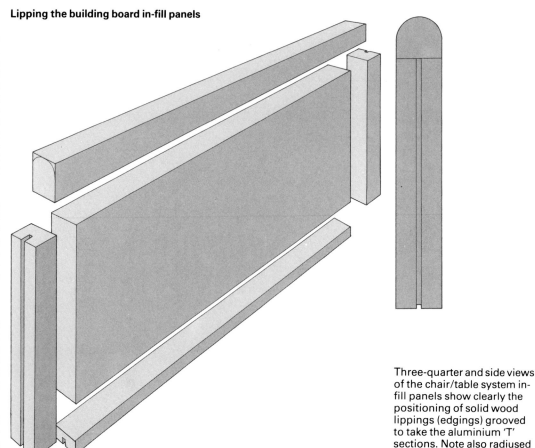

Three-quarter and side views of the chair/table system in-fill panels show clearly the positioning of solid wood lippings (edgings) grooved to take the aluminium 'T' sections. Note also radiused top edge.

Preparing and fixing the cladding pieces

Before the upholstery stage, solid timber cladding pieces made out of the same timber as the rest of the construction should be prepared and fixed to the outer edges of the seat or table side frames for decorative effect.

The cladding pieces are prepared from 18mm (¾in) solid timber to the dimensions shown. They should be planed to size, glass papered to a high standard of finish, then fixed to the edges of the frame by means of screws from the inside face of the outer frame. This permits you to remove them at any time in the future as necessary. Ensure a good fit between back and front legs.

Constructing the table tops

1. Construct these from 18mm (¾in) plywood faced on one side with formica and on the other with wood veneer to match the solid timber used in the main body of the units. The idea behind this is to permit you to reverse the various tops to give either a formica or wood-grained table top surface.

Action hint
*Do not try to dimension the tops to fit exactly into the recess created by the table legs, cladding pieces, and front and back in-fill panels, until *after* the veneering process has been completed.

2. Using a plane cut a small 'V' break between each table top piece to add a decorative effect to the surface. The table top pieces are *contained* by the table but left loose.

The upholstering of front and back in-fill panels

"I suggest that the design has a mixture of linen (to cover the in-fill panels) and linen and leather (for the seat cushions) but this is up to you. They could as well be entirely leather or entirely heavy laid linen or canvas."

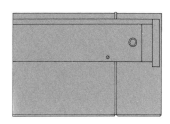

Top left shows cross-section of table top elements and illustrates the planed 'V' grooves. Illustration right is a cross-sectional view along the same pieces.

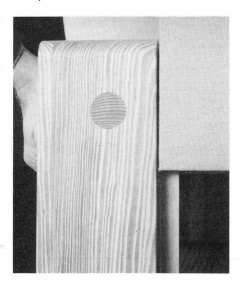

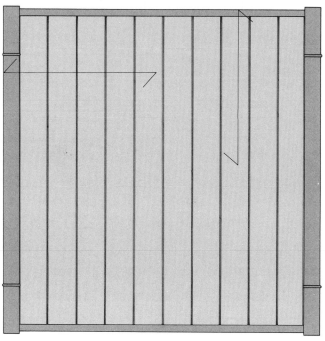

1. Cut the canvas or linen over-size and apply to the in-fill panels with Copydex as directed by the manufacturers. Glue the material over onto the side edges of the panels which will fit against the aluminium extrusions.

2. Copydex is a very strong agent but has the advantage of allowing you to peel the whole lot off if you make a mistake.

Action hints

* You could tack the material to the side edges of the panels to ensure that it stays fast to the surface.
* Remember in fastening the material round the panel edges they should not intrude into the grooved areas, since this would impede the assembly of the panels onto the extrusion pieces.
* Aluminium extrusions were also attached to the bottom edges of the in-fill panels simply to allow the chair and table to be moved easily over a carpet.

Final assembly

Assemble the in-fill panels. Fix the Pirelli rubber platforms. These platforms or diaphragms are manufactured by the Pirelli Tyre Company in various sizes. (John Hardy has ascertained that Pirelli will supply single items to the public.) He recommends these platforms more than the popular Pirelli webbing, since they present a large flat surface which does not in any way mark the underside of the cushion material. However, a tool is necessary to fit these onto the chair, since considerable tension is needed to stretch them between suspension points indicated on the drawing. As we have said, Pirelli provide their own method of anchoring these platforms to the frames and provide a detailed instruction booklet to facilitate the process. Design Workshop's own patented aluminium bush slips easily into the holes bored earlier and John Hardy points out that they have the advantage of providing a nice detail on the front and back rails of the inner frame.

Finishing the wooden parts of the units

"In the prototypes I have made, a teak oil made in Denmark was used. It is a very fine oil which gives a natural appearance to the wood. Which finish you use does depend on which wood you have chosen for the designs. Some woods, such as oak, contain tannic acid and dirty easily. Such woods require a more substantial sealing finish."

The chair and coffee table system 4

Chair cushions

The seat and back cushions used here are filled with a mixture of Chinese duck feather and curled chicken feather. This is simply more economic than the best filling – 100% Chinese duck feather – which has in fact become so expensive that the feather company actually recommends a mixture of the two types of feather as being a suitable alternative. *The important factor as far as the design is concerned is that the cushions should not resemble slabs of concrete.* They should not be filled, therefore, with lumps of polyester or rubber. The advantage of feathers is that the cushions will mould themselves into the support of the chair. Their disadvantage is that they will need to be plumped up occasionally after use. *They are, nevertheless, an integral part of the overall design concept.*

An alternative filling:

100% curled chicken feather, which is cheaper but does tend to matt down when the artificial curl produced in the manufacturing process collapses.

This filling will also provide the essential quality demanded by the design – that they should bed down into the shape of the seat.

The construction of the cushion unit: the cotton case containing the feathers is compartmentalised during the sewing process. These compartments prevent the feathers congregating at one end or corner of the cushion by retaining them in smaller

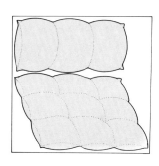

localised areas. The cases for feather fillers will of course be sewn by the supplier of the cushion themselves.

Preparing the cushion cases

1. Make nine compartments in the *seat* cushion (i.e. 3×3). Three compartments in the *back* cushion, running verti-

cally, would be sufficient.

Action hints
* Remember to leave sections of the case unstitched through which to insert the fillings.
* The cushion cases are shown here as having a centre panel of linen or canvas relating directly to the front and back in-fill panels of the chair. The outer edges of the cushion are made of leather and this relates

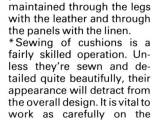

directly to the legs of the chair. When the cushion is placed on the chair a line is maintained through the legs with the leather and through the panels with the linen.
* Sewing of cushions is a fairly skilled operation. Unless they're sewn and detailed quite beautifully, their appearance will detract from the overall design. It is vital to work as carefully on the leather or canvas as one would work with a piece of wood. If you are not an expert sewer it may be worth finding someone to sew them for you.

2. Make cardboard or even hardboard patterns for the pieces comprising the seat and back cushions. Lay these patterns on the rolled out material and cut around them with a sharp knife. Allow 12mm (½in) for seams on either side of each sheet of material. On the prototype, the cushion has been sewn by normal methods and thereafter stitched with two rows of stitching as decoration detail around the edges of both cushions.

3. The back cushions are zipped on the bottom edge; the seat cushions are zipped along the back edge.

The media unit ★★★

The media unit
Designed to match and relate directly to the seat and table units, the media unit is very similar in terms of its manufacture, especially in the case of its legs. Once again the dimensions of the unit are infinitely variable both in length and depth.

Media unit cutting list Pitch pine:	Length	Width	Depth
4 Legs	600mm (23⅝in)	125mm (4⅞in)	43mm (1⅝in)
4 Rails	745mm (29⅜in)	80mm (3⅛in)	43mm (1⅝in)
4 Rails	405mm (16in)	80mm (3⅛in)	43mm (1⅝in)
22 Top slats, ply + laminates	410mm (16⅛in)	77.5mm (3in)	15mm (⅝in)
4 Fillets	850mm (33½in)	15mm (⅝in)	15mm (⅝in)
8 Aluminium 'T' sections	575mm (22⅝in)	22mm (⅞in)	3mm (⅛in)

The legs
These are carbon copies of the chair back legs. The dimensions are the same and all processes of building are the same up to the stage where holes were bored into the chair legs.

Attaching the aluminium extrusions
Having produced the legs, the aluminium extrusions may be fastened to them in the same way as before, except that this time the positions of the fastening screws is determined by the position of the media unit rails which should hide the screw heads when the unit is assembled.

The media unit 2

Action hint
*Since the aluminium extrusions are visible, it is a good idea to anodise them after drilling for the fixing screws. Anodising is an electro-chemical process which changes the surface of aluminium to aluminium oxide. A satin-silver finish is recommended, similar to that seen on aluminium curtain tracks, aluminium parts of cameras, etc. There are many anodisers about who will do this work inexpensively for you.

The rail sections

1. The rail sections, which join the legs together, can be made either from solid wood or plywood (which would then be lipped and veneered in the same way as the chair frames). Which you decide to use will probably hinge on

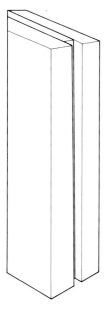

the availability of a circular saw (which you will need in order to cut locating grooves into the solid timber rails). It would be difficult to hand saw and chisel these grooves because a tight fit is essential.

If you do not have a circular saw, make the rail sections out of two pieces of 19mm (¾in) plywood between which is sandwiched a piece of 3mm (⅛in) plywood left short at either end to equal the depth of the extrusions. You have thus created the required groove at either end of each rail section.

When the sandwich is made, it is then lipped on its top and bottom edges with 3mm (⅛in) lipping and veneered on its two faces with the appropriate timber veneer.

"That you elect to manufacture this section from plywood rather than solid wood is not in my view detrimental to the function or appearance of the final design."

2. Once the legs have been accurately dimensioned, end-squared and radiused on their tops in the same way

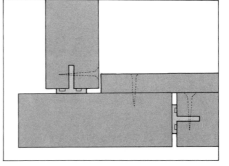

as was done for the chair and table legs, use a marking or drilling jig to drill through the rails and the extruded pieces to let in screws to fasten the rails to the legs.

Action hint
*"On the drawing I have shown two wood screws inserted from the inside face of

the rails through the extrusions and into the rails again. But since the drawings were done I have considered using socket head screws (Allen screws) from the outside of the rails and secured with nuts on their inside face. This may prove to be even more secure and provide an interesting detail on the outside face of the rails." See right.

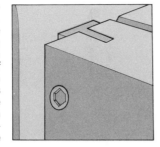

Final assembly
1. Once you have drilled the fixing holes, the unit frames may be screwed together, ensuring that they are square before fastening.

Action hint
*It is a good idea to hold the frame in cramps whilst screwing to ensure that the rails are fixed tightly to the faces of the extruded pieces attached to the legs. See right.

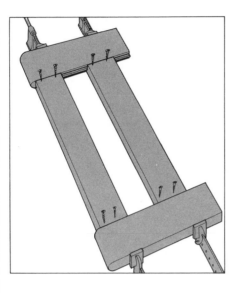

2. Once assembled, the wood fillets (pieces of solid wood) may be drilled and screwed onto the inside faces of the rails to support the top elements. These simple solid wood fillets are planed accurately to the dimensions shown, drilled and counter-bored to accept screw cups and then screwed to the rear side of the rails as indicated.

The top elements
Finally, make the top elements or shelves in exactly the same way as the table tops for the table unit. Use 18mm (¾in) plywood, faced on one side with formica and on the other with the appropriate wood veneer. Remember, once again, not to dimension these accurately until after they have been veneered. Finish as the table tops were finished in the previous designs.

The kitchen by Richard La Trobe Bateman

*"I want to make furniture that cries out to be used –
furniture which can be knocked about, and even 'used up'.
Its design exploits that particular relationship we have
with something we use every day. It does so first by
employing coarser timbers – oak, ash, elm, for example.
Furniture made with these timbers seems to improve with
use."*
Richard La Trobe Bateman

Richard La Trobe Bateman

"I started as an apprentice draughtsman for a Tyneside shipyard with a view to becoming a naval architect. But it wasn't something I wanted for myself, and in the late '50s I dropped out and became a prototype hippie – doing time as a pavement artist, that sort of thing. Then I went to *St. Martin's School of Art* in London and discovered a natural aptitude for 3-dimensional work. I ended up in the sculpture school there under Anthony Caro. In retrospect I realise that this was *the* time and place for learning.

"Later I went to America with the idea of designing cars. I went to see the big white chief at General Motors in Detroit and was interviewed on and off for two days. At the end of the time they said, 'There's one thing you've overlooked – we're here to make money!'

"From Detroit I came back to Coventry and worked for a time for Rootes. Then, because a friend of mine had done it, I applied and was accepted at the *Royal College of Art*. While I was there I made some way-out furniture which was not very good. But I came very much under the influence of Professor David Pye. Also, I did see how easy it all was – you make a hole in one piece of wood and stick another piece into it! And I began to understand how nice wood is to work with. The point is that it is nice *all the way through*. The Victorians never understood this and that is why their very highly finished Victorian cabinets are so repulsive – there's just no homogeneity. As far as I'm concerned it is vital that as little is done to the surface of the object which makes it different from the wood below the surface. It is stuff – you can carve it, bend it, it can be very fine, it can be clumsy, you can see it growing, and no trees are the same even within the same botanical species.

"After the RCA I got a teaching job. I lived in a basement flat in Earls Court and organised my first workshop there. Still, my future wasn't premeditated. Nothing I was doing was deliberate in that sense. Friends gave me some commissions, and later I went to the British Craft Centre and was accepted on the Index of Craftsmen. Later still I was invited onto the Committee that chooses craftsmen for the Index, and then I discovered that there was a thing called the Crafts Movement. I no longer felt alone.

Practical ability and vision

"So I was learning all the time, but I am a very slow learner – lacking in gumption. Gumption is a terribly important thing in running a workshop – I make up for gumption in other respects, but the guy who mends the roof, does the plumbing, the guy who can cope with the world, the handyman – he's important. But what he very often lacks is a creative ability. He has all the gumption but none of the vision! And in the end vision has got to be *the* most important thing. That's why this book is essentially different from the other do-it-yourself books which set out to allow people who are good at doing things in a relatively mindless way to make sensible things without too much trouble. In the end vision is a very personal thing, even if readers follow all the instructions to the letter the end result should be different for different people, and *intentionally* so. Each person may think he is making the same piece of furniture as everybody else that reads the book, but if you were to put the whole lot together, you would be amazed how

Above, the illustration shows the high-back chair which became a starting point for his own exploration of craft.

different the pieces are. And that's because a lot of themselves will get into the pieces whether they like it or not.

Sculptural and mechanical structure

"The way that I got going was by coming up with a very striking high back chair. I don't think that it's so striking now but it remains interesting and it got me some sort of name. If I hadn't made that chair I don't think I would have got any attention at all. I then made different variants of it. I now had the basic structure for this chair and I tried (and am still trying I suppose) to get the best chair I can out of that basic arrangement of parts. You see how the process takes over? I didn't start out to be interested in the structure, but now that's what interests me. You see there are two elements in structure which are quite clear. One is sculptural and the other is mechanical. Furniture is a very good way of pulling these two aspects of structure together – of pitting them against each other in a very positive way. Many abstract sculptors have explored structure. But because the viewer does not sense the need of a physical (utilitarian) requirement in these sculptural pieces, he doesn't experience the tension between its sculptural and mechanical aspects. Sculpture can be anything – it can lie on the ground in a heap of rubble, it can be a tower 100ft tall, it can be anything the artist likes. In sculpture there are no rules, but once it's a *table* one has certain predetermined conceptual rules. With furniture you can play the game of exploring the tension between mechanical and sculptural structure.

"Next year I might be making what others would categorise as sculpture. Alternatively, some manufacturer might come to me and ask me to design some furniture for him – then I am in another ball game. Both things could excite me. Categories are other people's pegs of convenience. I am not being pushed.

Wet wood

"Currently, my main interest is in working with wet wood. I was given a book on woodland crafts, and looking through it I came to realise that the wooden objects that had always excited me most were timber building structures, farm gates, fences, hurdles and so on. It was not their rustic quality that excited me (although I am not averse to that) but their *directness*. It is the difference between what David Pye calls *free* workmanship and a *highly regulated* workmanship. From time to time I do like the discipline of somebody forcing me to do a bit of cabinet making, highly regulated work. But for me what is called free workmanship is what gives me a buzz. So in wet wood working I am in a sense coming into my own. Normally, you force the shape on wood that you want. But when cleaving wood, how the thing splits is how *it* splits. Form is decided by the material."

"Although Richard is increasingly interested in working with newly felled timber, his plans really call for rather well-seasoned material. Early "stick" furniture – chairs and stools where the sections are small – moves relatively little, and the shrinkage can be turned to advantage. The warping of wide boards is more difficult to handle – or to accept in practice.

The designs Richard has proposed are rather demanding – particularly the dresser – but it is such a desirable and useful idea.

Richard is a good example of a person achieving success through enthusiasm, a constant search for integrity as a designer and sheer determination."
John Makepeace

"These pieces are all part of a continuous series of works exploring one or two themes. I have tried in my designs to demonstrate the beauty of ordinary objects in a simple, workmanlike way out of common materials. And within the constraints of this brief I have tried to develop new and interesting structures."

Richard La Trobe Bateman

The bench ★★

Cutting List Elm:	Length	Width	Thickness
2 Seat boards	1600mm (63in)	140mm (5½in)	35mm (1⅜in)
4 Legs	475mm (18⅝in)	50mm (2in)	50mm (2in)
2 Seat bearers	300mm (11¾)	75mm (3in)	30mm (1⅛in)
2 Cross rails	225mm (8⅞in)	75mm (3in)	30mm (1⅛in)
1 Stretcher rail	1300mm (51⅛in)	50mm (2in)	40mm (1⅝in)
1 Diagonal rail	1240mm (48¾in)	45mm (1¾in)	40mm (1⅝in)
4 Buttons	75mm (3in)	40mm (1⅝in)	25mm (1in)

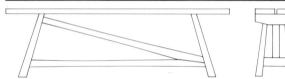

The leg frames

Establish all cutting angles by setting out full-size front and side elevations of one leg frame on white painted hardboard (see Leg Frame instructions for the table).

1. Begin by making the two leg frames each comprising a seat bearer, two legs, and a cross rail. Either bridle joints (as specified for the table) or stub mortise and tenons can be used between legs and seat bearers. Cut two further slots into each seat bearer to accept wooden buttons, designed to permit any future movement across the top.

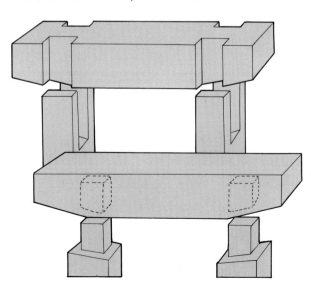

2. The cross rails are stub tenoned into the legs and although the angles achieved may vary slightly from those indicated on the drawing, it is more important that the two frames are identical.

3. Small pilot holes should be drilled approximately 30mm (1⅛in) from the ends of each seat bearer to assist the accurate position and pitch of holes for the seat-fixing dowels. If it is decided to carry dowels through to the bench surface, simply bore dowel holes at leg splay angle through the seat top boards.

Stretcher and diagonal rails

1. Glue and cramp the two leg frame assemblies together and stand them aside while the stretcher and diagonal are prepared. These should be spliced and screwed together dry to assist accurate marking of angled cuts for shoulders on tenons. At one end the tenon may be shared between diagonal and stretcher. Alternatively, only the stretcher could carry the tenon whilst diagonal simply rests upon it short of the tenon and screw-fixed to it. Any tapering towards centre on all sides of the stretcher and diagonal is optional (as is the degree to which it is done) and should begin beyond the spliced section, and be done with a compass plane before the members are finally jointed.

2. Mark out and cut the leg frame mortises to take the diagonal and stretcher rail tenons (i.e. in one seat bearer and both cross rails).

Assembly

1. If both stretcher and diagonal rail tenons fit tightly (which of course will depend on the accuracy of your full-size drawings, angle measurements, and cutting of mortises and tenons) then glue up the assembly.

2. Alternatively, dowel and button-fix the leg frame which has a mortise only in its cross rail to the two top boards which should be laid face down on a flat surface

and so spaced that their outer edges are flush with the ends of the seat bearer. Assuming that the frames will be joined to the top boards by secret dowels, continue the pre-drilled pilot hole from the underside of the seat bearer into the top boards and then counter-bore to receive the dowel. Finally, offer up the other leg frame to the inverted top boards, first assembling and gluing the diagonal rail and then the stretcher.

Finishing

The bench was finished in teak (tung) oil.

The table ★ ★ ★

An advantage of these designs is the degree of freedom they allow the builder to deviate from specifications without impairing the finished result. In the case of the table, for example, the top may be made from one, two or more boards, and there is no need for the legs and stretchers to taper towards centre.

The unusual overhang of the table top increases comfort when seated at its head and jolts one's notional sense of balance. It does not, however, detract from the stability of the construction. Rather, it may recommend itself to many as a refreshingly different structural nuance from the other elements which bring to mind the more vulgar (i.e. commonplace) appearance of the traditional structure of a refectory table.

Cutting list Elm:	Length	Width	Thickness
2 Top	2000mm (78¾in)	460mm (18⅛in)	40mm (1½in)
4 Legs	695mm (27⅜in)	75mm (3in)	75mm (3in)
2 Top support bearers	910mm (35¾in)	100mm (4in)	50mm (2in)
2 End frame cross rails	550mm (21⅝in)	105mm (4⅛in)	50mm (2in)
2 Stretchers	1200mm (47¼in)	60mm (2⅜in)	45mm (1¾in)
1 Diagonal	1360mm (53½in)	60mm (2⅜in)	45mm (1¾in)
4 Buttons	75mm (3in)	40mm (1⅝in)	25mm (1in)

Tools
Band saw
Circular saw
Cross cut saw
Jack plane
Compass plane
Plough plane
Bevel
Square
Mortise gauge
Chisel
Gouge
Mallet
Drill and countersink
Screwdriver
Cramps
Router (optional)

Constructional illustration of the kitchen table
The angled mortise and tenon is a feature of Bateman's series. See top page 68 for Action hint.

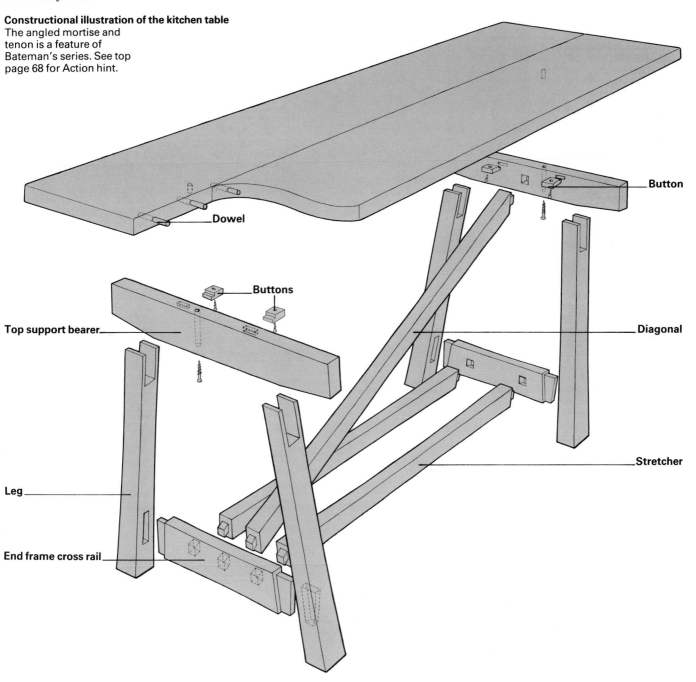

Button

Dowel

Buttons

Top support bearer

Diagonal

Leg

Stretcher

End frame cross rail

The table 2

Action hint
*Angled mortise and tenon joints

There are a number of angled mortise and tenon joints in La Trobe Bateman's furniture. The illustrations show the mortise and tenon joints at either end of the table's diagonal rail. With reference to them, Bateman suggests cutting an ordinary right-angled mortise in both cases,

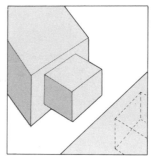

The top

1. If the top is constructed from more than one board, plane up their surfaces and edges so that adjoining boards fit flush.

2. With the boards face side flush together, mark off positions for locating dowels at approximately 150mm (6in) centres and their depth positions with a marking gauge set to half the thickness of one board (see top right illustration). Be sure to work from the face side (top surface) of each board.

3. Drive a bradawl into the spot exactly where the lines intersect – this will act as a lead hole to guide the drill bit when boring for dowels.

Size of dowels should be 15mm (⅝in) diameter or nearest size available commercially, and 75mm (3in) long penetrating half-way 38mm (1½in) into adjoining boards. Ends of dowels should be chamfered and inserted dry (not glued) since they simply act as locating pins. Pre-drill holes for wood screws at 305mm (12in) intervals along centre line of

and preparing the tenon in the following way:

1. With a bevel mark the position of the tenon shoulder and a line parallel to it which will become the end of the tenon itself.

2. Mark the edge lines of the tenon at right angles to the shoulder line. Cut and plane as page 179.

one board and centred in every other gap between locating dowels. Turn board over and carve grooves as shown in photo bottom left. The grooves should be deep and long enough to accept 75mm (3in) screws.

4. With boards together locate positions for pilot holes in adjoining board then drill and tap with wood screw. After assembly turn the top over and give the surface a final planing. Finishing ends and edges is best left to final assembly.

The leg frames
Action hints

*Whenever a design entails cutting compound angles which need to match, as is the case here, accurate results are more easily achieved by first setting out full-size drawings then transferring the angles, by means of an adjustable bevel or even hardboard templates, to the wood. With more than one angle to consider, and to avoid possible error through having continually to alter your bevel, you might consider fashioning a second bevel from two pieces of plywood pivoting on a small nut and bolt.

*The smooth side of hardboard coated with matt white paint is an ideal surface on which to draw full-size plans.

Leg frame joint showing buttons

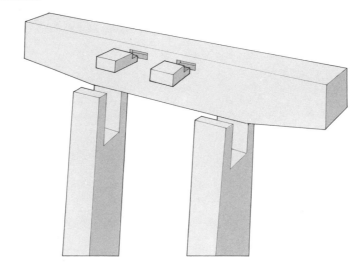

1. Cut the table top support bearers. Ensure that these fall short of the table edges by at least 5mm (³⁄₁₆in) to allow for possible top shrinkage.

2. When making the bridle joints which will hold the legs to the bearers, the legs should be cut and finished before the rail housing slots are marked and cut out of the bearers to form a snug fit with the legs.

3. Bore a hole off-centre in the underside of each support bearer (so that the screw eventually misses the table top joint); then counter-bore to take a fixing screw into the table top. See drawing and photograph left.

4. The table top will be further secured by buttons which turn and plug into mortises cut into the ends of the support bearers. Cut these mortises and fashion the four buttons.

5. Fit the top joints dry and measure and cut the lower cross rails allowing for tenons to fit into blind mortises cut into the inner sides of each leg.

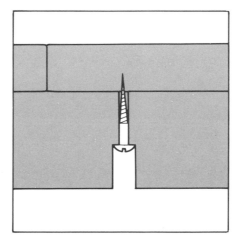

The horizontal stretchers

1. Cut the diagonal and two horizontal stretchers, then mortise into cross rails as shown in the illustration. These should be left in square section until the table is assembled dry when the degree of tapering (i.e. thinning to centres) can be gauged by trial and error until the desired effect is achieved. (See also notes on the stretcher and diagonal rails of the bench.)

2. At this point, when the structure is assembled dry, the chamfer on edges can also be applied. This is a feature of all the edges of Bateman's table (which he built for us), but is intentionally absent on the rest of his kitchen equipment as built by Norman Beverton.

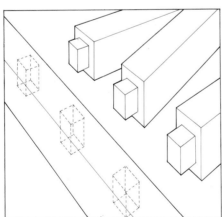

Assembly

Having glued and cramped both leg frames as sub-assemblies, turn the table top face down and screw fix in these frames. Then offer up the stretchers and diagonal.

Finishing

Action hints

* If it is intended to seal all the timber with, say, a matt polyurethane, it is easier to do so before final assembly, taking care not to allow the sealing to affect what will be glue-jointed surfaces.

* "I used matt polyurethane for the table top, cut half-in-half with white spirit. I just painted it straight on and left it — not coat after coat, wire woolling in between. It would be too smooth that way." Richard La Trobe Bateman.

* If the construction is in elm, do not sand with a finer paper than 100 grit (perhaps 120 for end grain) along the grain. Being a soft timber, scratch marks can show, but Bateman's is an aesthetic decision. Elm does not in his opinion lend itself to heavy sanding.

The cook's counter ★ ★ ★ ★

Cutting list Elm:	Length	Width	Thickness
4 Legs	760mm (30in)	60mm (2⅜in)	50mm (2in)
2 Top support rails	1400mm (55⅛in)	80mm (3⅛in)	40mm (1⅝in)
2 Top cross rails	375mm (14¾in)	80mm (3⅛in)	25mm (1in)
2 Lower cross rails	475mm (18¾in)	80mm (3⅛in)	25mm (1in)
1 Lower back rail	920mm (36¼in)	80mm (3⅛in)	25mm (1in)
1 Lower shelf support bearer	890mm (35in)	80mm (3⅛in)	25mm (1in)
2 Centre shelf support bearers	420mm (16½in)	50mm (2in)	25mm (1in)

	Length	Width	Thickness
2 Centre shelf support bearers	965mm (38in)	50mm (2in)	25mm (1in)
1 Diagonal brace	1075mm (42¼in)	45mm (1¾in)	20mm (¾in)
6 Timber buttons	75mm (3in)	50mm (2in)	25mm (1in)
Beech:			
1 top	900mm (35⅜in)	600mm (23⅝in)	50mm (2in)
Local stone (slate, marble, whatever is available):			
1 Top	500mm (19¾in)	600mm (23⅝in)	50mm (2in)

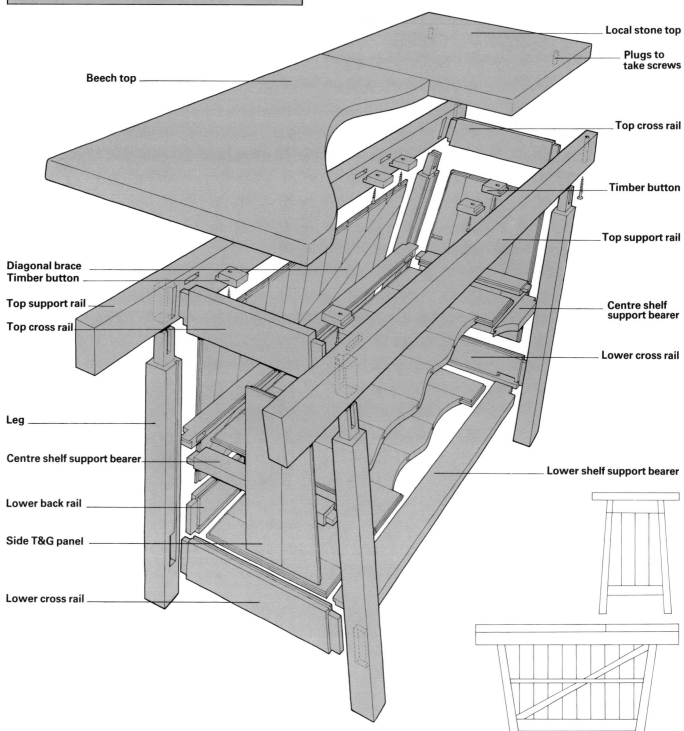

Local stone top

Plugs to take screws

Beech top

Top cross rail

Timber button

Top support rail

Diagonal brace
Timber button
Top support rail
Top cross rail

Centre shelf support bearer

Lower cross rail

Leg

Centre shelf support bearer

Lower back rail

Side T&G panel

Lower cross rail

Lower shelf support bearer

The cook's counter 2

The sub-frame construction
Study the cutting list and set out front and end elevations full-size in order to strike off the various angles involved.

The legs
1. Each of the legs tapers in length from 60 to 50mm (2⅜in to 2in) in its wider

plane and from 50 to 40mm (2in to 1⅝in) in its narrower plane. Mark out and cut the four legs from one board as suggested in the illustration.

2. Carefully select the most suitable leg for each corner of the sub-frame and true up their inner faces. This is crucial as angles and gauge lines to be marked later on cross members and tongue and grooving will be set from these faces.

3. Mark the legs for length, top tenons and lower mortises to house the lower rails. Then mark the groove positions which will house the back and end tongued and grooved panels.

4. Cut the tenons in the leg tops first (note from the illustration that these are slotted to accept haunched tenons from top cross rails).

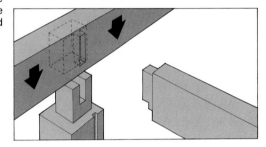

The top support rails
Mark out and chop stub mortises into the underside edges of the two top support rails. Also cut notches to accept the tongues of the fixing buttons, and counterbore for fixing screws to attach local stone to front and back top support rails.

Dry Assembly
Assemble the structure dry and check that you have two identical (front and rear) leg frames.

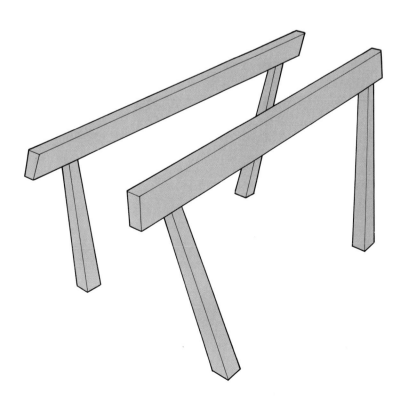

The cook's counter 2

Top cross rails, lower back rail, lower cross rails

1. Mark out and cut the four haunched tenons in the two top cross rails. Chop out their mortises, which continue into the slots already cut in the leg-top tenons.

2. Mark out and cut the lower rails (which continue round three sides of the sub-frame) and then the tenons which will enter the mortises already cut into the legs.

3. Additionally, cut mortises into the inner faces of the

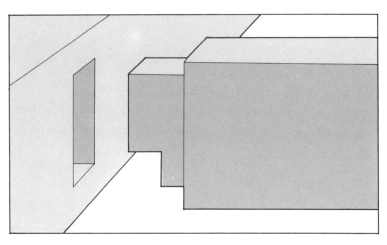

lower cross rails to carry the bare-faced tenons of the lower shelf front bearer. These are positioned 6mm (¼in) before the lower cross rail tenons enter the front legs.

The lower shelf front bearer

Cut the lower shelf front bearer to length and mark and cut bare-faced tenons to fit into the lower cross rails.

Dry assembly

Assemble the whole sub-frame dry, and check that it is square (in plan) and rigid.

The tongue and grooving

1. The next step is to determine the width and depth of grooves in legs and rails to accept the T&G cladding panels. If the T&G has been bought prepared, end grain tongues should be cut to the same dimensions as already exist down its long edges.

2. Cut T&G boards to length to clad both side panels, back panel and lower shelf. It is possible now to assess the number of T&G boards needed for these panels and their length. Determine the position of the vertical tongues on the side boards which joint into the legs by

working out from the centre of each panel so that the end boards in each panel are equal in area. The angle of the tongues will naturally correspond with the angle of the inner faces of the legs.

3. Knock the sub-frame apart and gauge-mark positions for all grooves by working from inside faces. Do not at this stage cut the centre shelf support bearers for the centre shelf T&G boards as these will be stub-tenoned into the end panel T&G.

4. Cut all grooves either with a circular saw, plough plane, spindle cutter, or router.

Back T&G panel and diagonal brace

1. Assemble the back panel dry on a flat surface. Cut the diagonal brace to length and width (it tapers from 50 to 40mm (2in to 1⅝in) along its length). Lay this in position diagonally across the assembled panel and using a knife, scribe the T&G so as to mark shoulders for end grain tongues which will fit into the diagonal brace.

2. Remove the diagonal, and with the boards still in place scribe two further lines parallel to and 5mm (³⁄₁₆in) inside the first two slightly converging lines. The whole panel is to be cut right through along the second pair of lines, but *when* this is done depends on how you intend cutting the rebates (rabbets) for the tongues.

3. Cramp the boards away from the legs and cut the tongues either with a router, depth-adjusted circular saw or grooving plane. If you elect to use a rebate (rabbet) plane (or prefer to cut the tongues on the boards individually) you will need to cut the boards along the inner marking lines to separate the T&G sections.

4. The diagonal member has grooves cut to a depth and width of 5mm (³⁄₁₆in) from its

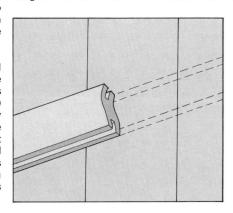

face edges so that in position its face side and those of the surrounding T&G boards are flush on the inside of the unit.

5. Where they reach the 'pointed' ends of the diagonal, the grooves turn into tongues cut to fit the appropriate leg and rail grooves.

End T&G panels

These are cut and assembled in a similar way to the back panel without the complication of the diagonal brace. However, each of the end panel leg adjoining T&G boards should be blind mortised to receive stub tenons cut in the two long centre shelf support bearers. The rear centre shelf support bearer is also cut to fit round the inner corner of each rear leg. Prepare centre shelf T&G boards and shorter bearers.

The centre shelf is set 440mm (17¼in) above ground level.

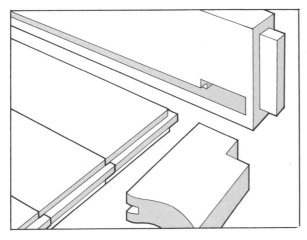

Assembly

1. The entire back panel can be assembled by laying it flat and working from the lower rail upward. First apply the legs, then build up the lower half of T&G panel by starting with the longest board. When complete, insert diagonal brace and assemble the top half in the same sequence.

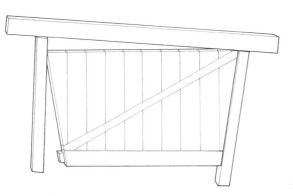

2. Owing to the angle at which the leg top tenons splay, it may not be easy to apply the top rail, in which case disengage one of the legs and swing it away sufficiently for top tenons to be inserted into rail mortises.

This operation may entail a slight 'easing' of joints. The front top rail and legs are similarly assembled and need no further explanation here.

3. End frames, having an opposing angle, are assembled from top to bottom and since this operation must include all the legs it is best done by re-assembling the whole unit upside down. With its top rail on the floor, lean the back panel against a wall at an angle exactly opposite to that which it will finally splay. Insert the top cross rails (flush on the floor) and each of the T&G boards. At the same time insert the wider cross rails and the five shelf bearers.

4. The front legs, already assembled with their top rail, can now be offered to the protruding tenons and tongues.

5. Dismantle and reassemble in the same order, but glue and cramp all joints except the tongues and grooves which should all remain dry.

6. Lay the beech top face down on the floor, then manoeuvre the inverted leg assembly into position and fasten down into the top with four brass screws passing through the timber buttons. Stand the unit right way up.

7. The local stone, which should first have been cut to size, is marked through the two buttons and counter-bored pilot holes in the top rails. In these positions bore holes sufficiently large to take plugs – either plastic, fibre, or wood – into which the four brass fixing screws

will pass. Take great care with this operation since a too tight fit might expand the plugs to cause the stone to crack at the corners (this will also depend upon the strength of the stone).

8. Fit the centre and lower shelf to complete the counter.

Finishing

The beech top, as a butcher's block, should remain untreated (as of course should the stone). The remainder of the counter was finished in teak (tung) oil.

The breakfast stool ★★★

Cutting list Elm:	Length	Width	Thickness
2 'Z' frame seat supports	160mm (6¼in)	80mm (3⅛in)	25mm (1in)
2 'Z' frame front legs	640mm (25⅛in)	60mm (2⅜in)	25mm (1in)
2 'Z' frame base rails	430mm (16⅜in)	60mm (3in)	25mm (1in)
1 Foot rest	290mm (11⅜in)	75mm (3in)	25mm (1in)
1 Leg support rail (rear)	206mm (8⅛in)	60mm (2⅜in)	25mm (1in)
2 Rear legs	916mm (36in)	40mm (1½in)	25mm (1in)
1 Back rest	360mm (14⅛in)	80mm (3⅛in)	50mm (2in)
1 Seat	360mm (14⅛in)	300mm (11¾in)	30mm (1⅛in)

The stool is made up of triangular structures so placed as to ensure great rigidity.

First set out full size on white paper or white-painted hardboard plan, front and side elevations. The drawings will not show the true size and angles of much of the construction since the angles are compound and the actual pieces are not parallel to the drawn elevations. But provided that the stool is made up in the order below, the woodworker will be able to make good use of them.

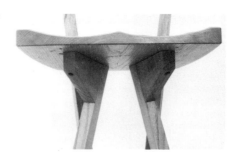

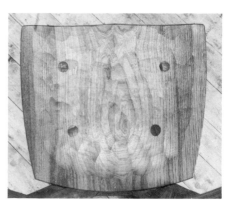

The seat bearers
1. Mark out and cut the two seat bearers, front legs and base rails which assembled make two 'Z' frames. Each frame will be jointed with five 60mm (2⅜in) long dowels that have been chamfered and grooved for gluing. Leave frame tops and bottoms square.

Front and side elevation of stool

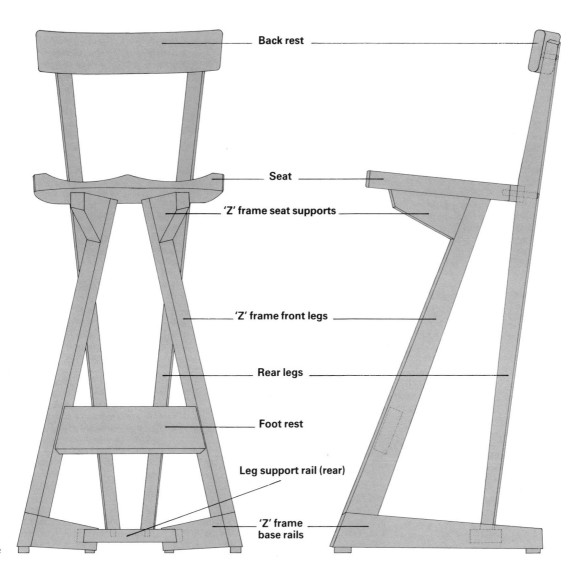

Back rest

Seat

'Z' frame seat supports

'Z' frame front legs

Rear legs

Foot rest

Leg support rail (rear)

'Z' frame base rails

2. Cut and fit the foot rest. Dry cramp to the 'Z' frame. Then, calculate, mark and cut exact dimensions and angles for the rear leg support rail. Finally, dry cramp all the frame components together and scribe angles for its top and bottom surfaces; dismantle, cut and plane.

3. Now finish all parts of the 'Z' frame and glue up. The mortises in the rear leg support rail to accept the two rear legs can be cut later.

The seat
1. Cut the seat blank to shape.

2. Carefully mark around 'Z' frame tops on seat underside and determine positions for 3mm (1/8in) pilot holes for dowels parallel to seat supports in an orderly pattern, since the dowel tops will eventually be visible

'Z' frame side elevation

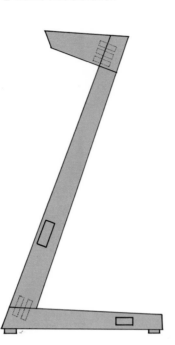

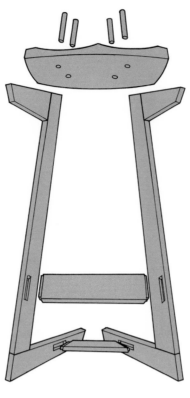

from above in the seat depression.

3. Carve out the seat. Bateman used a 50mm (2in) No. 4 gouge. Finish completely without boring back edge dowel holes.

4. Butt glue seat to 'Z' frame. When dry, use a brace and bit to bore holes along pilot holes to accept 15mm (5/8in) dowels.

5. Glue pins into position (the dowel tops were cut and beech wedges were glued and inserted into the top). Saw about three-quarters of the depth of each pin through its diameter. Glue and drive in the dowel making sure that the saw kerf is at right-angles to the grain of the seat surface (otherwise the surface may split). Drive in the beech wedge as far as possible and carve flush.

Back legs and rest
1. Offer up the back legs to the seat and rear leg support rail, scribing the tenon shoulders from the latter. Cut the mortises in the leg support rail parallel to front edges of rear legs.

2. Dry cramp rear legs into position, mark and bore holes for dowels. Glue up base and seat joints, wedging dowel ends.

3. Carve the back rest out of a solid piece, or band saw thinner boards and stack.

4. Fit back rest into position and scribe round legs. Let the inner edges of the legs into it.

5. Dry cramp and bore dowel holes, using packing pieces to prevent splitting out should you wish to expose the dowels in front. Glue on, wedging dowels as before.

The dresser ★ ★ ★ ★

Kitchen dresser front elevation

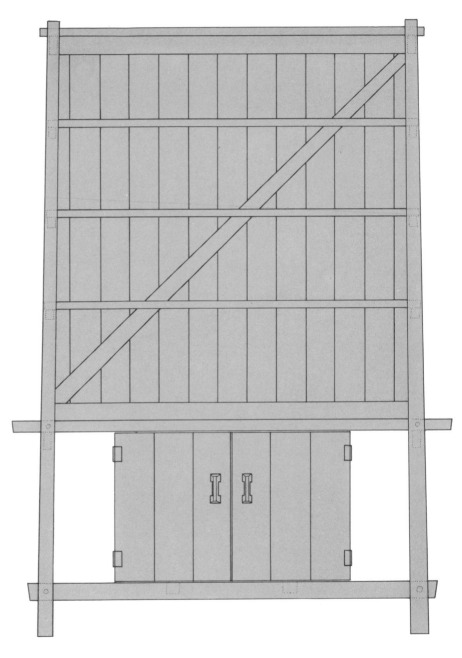

With any design that involves many angles, it is a good idea to make the working drawings full-size, if errors of measurement are to be avoided. It is strongly recommended that the front and one end elevation be scaled up and drawn full size on a dimensionally stable surface such as the smooth sides of hardboard panels painted white.

With the aid of an adjustable bevel, all cutting angles can be transferred from drawing to work. Having achieved a good fit with the angles, the rest of the design admits a fair degree of tolerance without impairing the finished result.

The legs, shelf support bearers and top and lower rails

1. Begin by cutting the four long leg uprights, each of which tapers from 60 (2⅜) to 40mm (1½in) in one plane and from 40 (1½) to 30mm (1⅛in) in the other. True up the inner faces of each leg, for it is from each leg's inner corner that all gauge lines and bevel angles will be taken. Cut the base line leg angles.

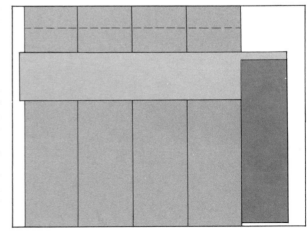

Kitchen dresser side elevation

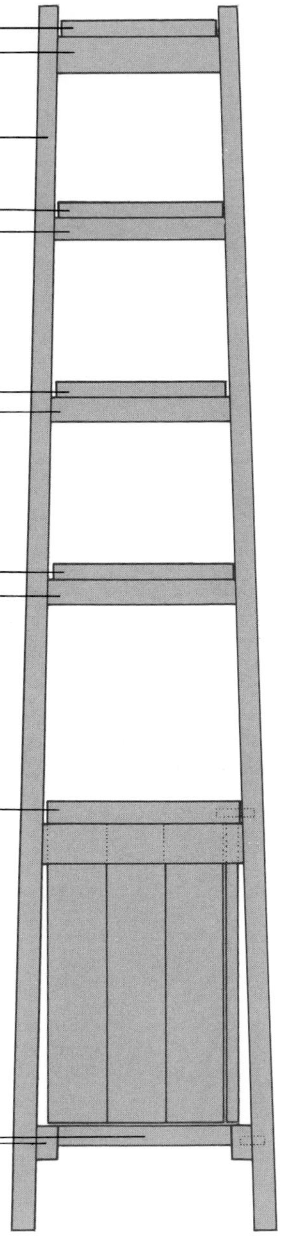

2. Mark out the ten (five-a-side) shelf bearers, then carefully cut tenons at each end. The shoulders of these tenons will reflect the vertical angle of convergence between uprights, viewing the dresser end on. See page 68 Action hint.

3. With the four legs clamped together mark across their inner faces the positions of all shelf bearers (left), then gauge, being careful to work from legs' inner corners, for mortise cuts and panel grooving. Chop out mortises, trial fit, then dismantle.

4. In the same way mark out and cut the back panel top and lower rails. Cut mortises in the legs for the top rail tenons but do not, at this stage, cut mortises for the lower rail.

Tongue and groove cladding and diagonal brace

1. On a wide flat surface assemble the back panel T&G cladding and mark out for cutting, ensuring that both end T&G boards are of equal proportion.

2. Cut bare-faced tongues on ends of all T&G boards and along tapering edges of leg-adjoining boards. Cramp entire panel.

3. Cut diagonal brace to exact length and width (which tapers from 50 (2) to 40mm (1½in) along its length) and lay it in position diagonally across the assembled panel.

4. Using a marking knife scribe along both edges of the diagonal marking the T&G boards (these two lines will cut to form the shoulders of bare-faced tongues). Remove the diagonal brace and scribe two further lines parallel to and 5mm (¼in) inside the first two converging lines.

Action hints

*The whole panel of boards will be cut through along the second pair of lines but before this is done decide how you intend cutting the shoulder for bare-faced tongues. If they are to be cut with a router, depth adjusted circular saw, or grooving plane, cut the shoulder first with boards in place. Alternatively, with second line cut through make the tongues with a rebate plane.

5. The diagonal brace is grooved along its edges to a depth and width of 5mm (¼in) gauged 5mm (¼in) from its face side so that in position it forms a flush surface with surrounding T&G boards.

6. At its 'pointed' top and bottom ends these grooves reverse to tongues sharing grooves in legs and rails.

7. Gauge and cut panel grooving 5mm by 5mm in top and lower rails, then trial fit the panel with its rails. Now the positions of lower rail mortises can be marked and cut in rear legs so also the grooves in legs to accept panel tongues.

Dresser

Cutting list

Elm:	**Length**	**Width**	**Thickness**
4 Legs	2025mm (79¾in)	60mm (2⅜in)	40mm (1½in)
5 Shelves, top	1200mm (47¼in)	290mm (11⅜in)	25mm (1in)
second	1175mm (46¼in)	305mm (12in)	25mm (1in)
third	1205mm (47 7/16in)	320mm (12⅝in)	25mm (1in)
fourth	1235mm (48⅝in)	330mm (13in)	25mm (1in)
main	1520mm (59⅞in)	345mm (13⅝in)	35mm (1⅜in)
5 Bearers, top	340mm (13⅜in)	60mm (2⅜in)	25mm (1in)
second	355mm (14in)	40mm (1½in)	25mm (1in)
third	370mm (14½in)	40mm (1½in)	25mm (1in)
fourth	385mm (15⅛in)	40mm (1½in)	25mm (1in)
main	410mm (16⅛in)	65mm (2½in)	25mm (1in)
1 Back panel top rail	1140mm (44⅞in)	85mm (3⅜in)	20mm (¾in)
1 Back panel lower rail	1260mm (49⅝in)	90mm (3½in)	20mm (¾in)
1 Diagonal brace	1640mm (64½in)	50mm (2in)	20mm (¾in)
12 *Cladding back panel	1165mm (45⅞in)	105mm (4⅛in)	10mm (⅜in)
2 Cupboard underframe bearers	1400mm (55⅛in)	60mm (2⅜in)	30mm (1⅛in)
2 Cupboard underframe bearers	350mm (13¾in)	40mm (1½in)	20mm (¾in)
Cupboard			
4 Longitudinal members	770mm (30¼in)	45mm (1¾in)	20mm (¾in)
4 Corner uprights	485mm (19⅛in)	30mm (1⅛in)	20mm (¾in)
4 Cross rails	320mm (12⅝in)	45mm (1¾in)	20mm (¾in)
2 Centre shelf supports	300mm (11¾in)	30mm (1⅛in)	20mm (¾in)
24 *Cladding (incl. doors)	483mm (19in)	105mm (4¼in)	10mm (¾in)
4 Door battens	375mm (14¾in)	50mm (2in)	20mm (¾in)
2 Door braces	425mm (16¾in)	35mm (1⅜in)	20mm (¾in)
2 Door handles	100mm (4in)	30mm (1⅛in)	30mm (1⅛in)

*Cladding quoted for T&G board widths of 105mm (including tongues). If narrower, increase number of boards. Note appearance is improved by wider boards.

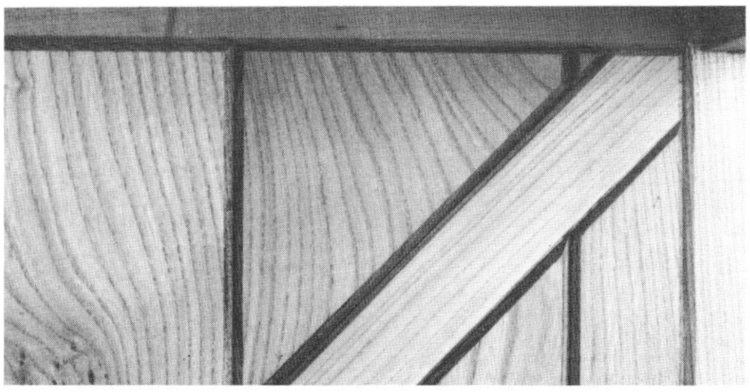

The dresser 2

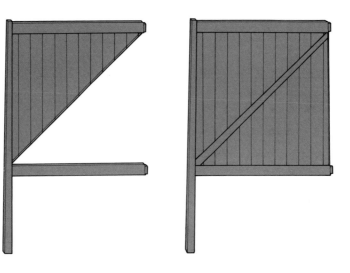
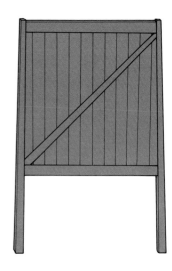

Assembly
Assemble the back panel from left to right or vice versa.

1. Begin by inserting top and lower rail tenons into one leg mortise. Start with the longest board and progressively build up one half of the panel, insert diagonal brace and complete the other half. All this should be done dry.

2. Apply the opposite leg but this time glue the mortise and tenons only. Go back and disengage the first leg. Apply glue to both mortise and tenons, then reassemble and cramp the whole structure until glue has set.

3. Cut the main shelf (the one directly above cupboard) to length, then glue and insert its two front locating dowels. Mark and bore the backs of front legs to accept these dowels dry.

4. With the structure still lying on its back, assemble both end 'ladders' by first gluing shelf bearers into rear legs. Lay main shelf in position on its rear edge and resting on its bearers with the two locating dowels upwards.

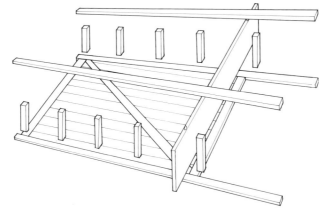

5. Glue all tenons and mortises in front legs, then lower the legs into position. The two locating dowels of the main shelf will help position the 'ladder' sides at 90 degrees to the back and either the top shelf or a piece of waste board G-cramped across top bearers will assist accurate positioning whilst glue sets.

Cupboard
This can be constructed as a separate unit, then suspended under the main shelf and supported in position by the underframe.

Basically, the cupboard consists of two end frames clad on their outsides with T&G panels. The frames are connnected by four stretchers which are grooved to carry the back and floor panel T&G.

The doors, which are of batten and brace design, simply hinge onto end frame uprights, and the centre shelf is supported on two rails (shelf bearers) that form part of each end frame.

1. Begin by making the two end frames consisting of four corner uprights and four cross rails with mortise and tenon joints. The two rear corner uprights are grooved to accept back panel T&G. Both shelf bearers are mortised and tenoned into corner uprights and their position laterally should be determined by storage requirements. Each of the two top cross rails must be slotted for buttons and drilled for screw fixing to main shelf.

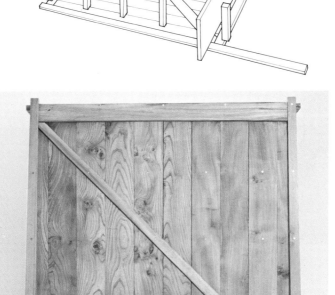

Constructional illustrations of dresser cupboard

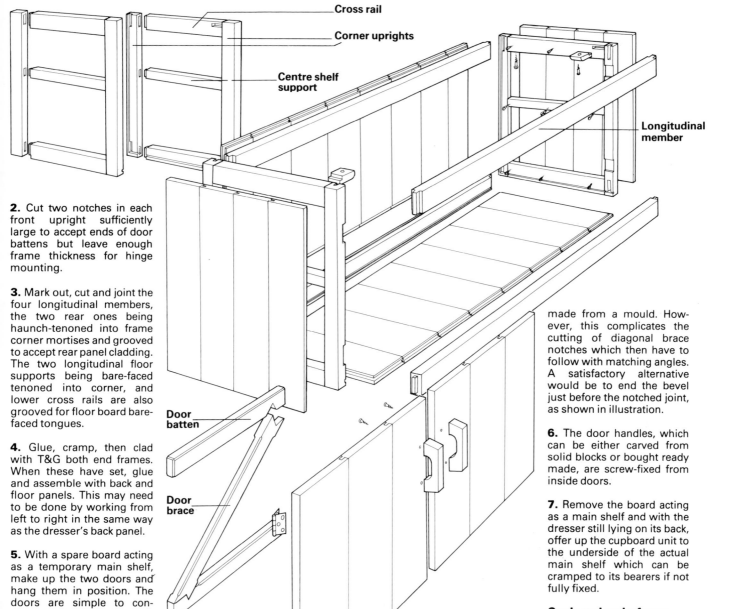

Cross rail

Corner uprights

Centre shelf support

Longitudinal member

Door batten

Door brace

2. Cut two notches in each front upright sufficiently large to accept ends of door battens but leave enough frame thickness for hinge mounting.

3. Mark out, cut and joint the four longitudinal members, the two rear ones being haunch-tenoned into frame corner mortises and grooved to accept rear panel cladding. The two longitudinal floor supports being bare-faced tenoned into corner, and lower cross rails are also grooved for floor board bare-faced tongues.

4. Glue, cramp, then clad with T&G both end frames. When these have set, glue and assemble with back and floor panels. This may need to be done by working from left to right in the same way as the dresser's back panel.

5. With a spare board acting as a temporary main shelf, make up the two doors and hang them in position. The doors are simple to construct, each having two horizontal battens and a diagonal brace notched into battens top and bottom. In the open position, the battens on doors look more attractive if bevelled as if they were

made from a mould. However, this complicates the cutting of diagonal brace notches which then have to follow with matching angles. A satisfactory alternative would be to end the bevel just before the notched joint, as shown in illustration.

6. The door handles, which can be either carved from solid blocks or bought ready made, are screw-fixed from inside doors.

7. Remove the board acting as a main shelf and with the dresser still lying on its back, offer up the cupboard unit to the underside of the actual main shelf which can be cramped to its bearers if not fully fixed.

Cupboard underframe
Mark the position of cupboard underframe and the length of its two cross rails, which are also drilled for dowel jointing into all four leg uprights.

Final assembly
1. Dismantle up to the main shelf, then stand the remainder of the dresser upright. Screw fix the main shelf from behind the back panel lower rail.

2. Fasten the underframe to the cupboard by screwing through the two cross bearers. Then take the whole unit, which will resemble a sedan chair, and offer it to the underside of the main shelf.

3. Glue and insert the four

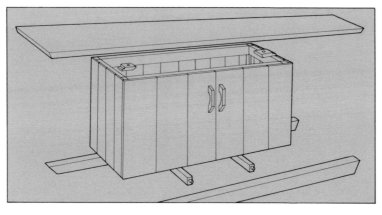

leg dowels to hold it in position whilst cupboard and frame are screw-fixed to underside of main shelf, including the two button fixings which are to allow for differential movement.

Lastly, cut to length and fit the remaining shelves, each of which should be set in to clear all four legs by approximately 2mm.

Finishing
The dresser was finished in teak (tung) oil.

The dining room by Sam Maloof

A first generation American, Sam Maloof was born in Chino, California in 1916. Before serving in the United States Army between 1941 and 1945, he worked as a graphic artist, architectural draftsman, and industrial designer. Following his discharge from the Army he began to work with wood with the dream of having his own workshop where he could design and make objects which reflected his own ideas. Despite his background as a graphic artist, his designs are achieved in the process of making a piece and not on the drawing board.

"When the designer is also the woodworker, he can feel the character of the piece as it is being made, make changes as he wants. How different this is from being subservient to a drawing."

Since the late '50s, he has won many awards, exhibited in numerous galleries and museums, lectured and taken workshops, and appeared in various books, magazines, and two films.

"Perhaps most famous for his chairs, his design approach is one which may well be followed by readers. It is similar to the way country chairmakers have worked for years in that it enables the maker to respond to a particular timber and to experiment with the way a piece is constructed – learning as the piece evolves."
John Makepeace

Design

"Most of my pieces are made from a storehouse of ideas that I have tucked away in my mind. I design as the pieces are made. Design and craftsmanship go hand-in-hand; one cannot be separated from the other. I also feel very strongly that any piece should serve a purpose. Too often, beautifully crafted chairs seem to dare one to sit on them. I want my pieces to be not only appealing to the eye and to the touch, but to be used.

"I had no formal training, and what I did in the early days was by trial and error. Even today my approach to work is perhaps contrary to what school-trained craftsmen do, and I find it rewarding that some of my concepts of joinery have proved that one does not have to adhere to the past. I did not know about other craftsmen, and was not influenced by what others were doing, or by trends. To this day I have not let what others are doing change my way of working. I respect how other woodworkers work, and hope that they respect my approach.

"In designing, one of the difficulties is to make a piece so simple that its very simplicity makes it a beautiful, functional object. A simple object is the most difficult to achieve.

"Originality, only to be different, has no value. An object that is derived to make an impression only survives that first impact.

"The most important thing is to live, work and think as an individual. Many young people today are seeking a way to identify themselves – to break away from the established precedence that for too long has been a pattern and a way of life."

Tools and materials

"Being self-taught, and in the early days not having any power tools, I had a golden opportunity really to learn how to use hand tools. Even now that my shop is well-equipped, approximately ninety per cent of the finish work is done by hand.

"As for materials, I mostly use American black walnut; though I do use Brazilian rosewood, Indian rosewood, teak, cherry and English brown oak.

"Every woodworker has his own way, his own method and own deep feeling about wood. I am partial to walnut, but do not ignore the other woods I mention. I do take care to choose the right grain of wood for chair legs, for example, and if when going through my wood pile I find a piece that is interesting but incompatible with previously selected pieces, I will set it aside until I find a use for it.

"So often people have asked me why I work in wood rather than other materials, such as plastics. My answer has always been that anyone who has worked in wood knows how intimate it is, how beautiful it works, how beautiful it is to the touch and to the eye."

Chair construction

Sam Maloof's dining room furniture was not made by him for the book. The following guidelines for his method of chair construction are, therefore, particularly interesting in the ways they differ from the subsequent instructions.

"In constructing my chairs, I follow a procedure which you might find useful:
1. I start with the seat, doing whatever joinery work is necessary.
2. Back and front legs are then attached.
3. Before anything else, I do the sculptural work on the construction so far.
4. I then attach the arms, and sculpture them into the back and front legs.
5. The next step is to put the spindles in, and fit the upper back of the chair, sculpturing it into the back legs.
6. Finally, I use a scraper and a 400 grit sandpaper, finishing with steel wool."

Finishing

"There are, of course, many finishing processes. The one I use is a formula of one half linseed oil and one half turpentine. I apply one coat, let it set for a bit and then wipe it off completely. This procedure is followed for several days. I then apply a generous mixture of boiled linseed oil and beeswax with a pad of steel wool. This too is left to set for a while and wiped off, the procedure being repeated for several days."

n does not keep pace
, companions, perhaps it is because
s a different drummer.
step to the music which he hears,
r measured or far away.

Henry David Thoreau

The dining room

The chair ★ ★ ★

Sizes are sawn and not finished. Walnut:	Length	Width	Thickness
2 Back legs	864mm (34in)	*	38mm (1½in)
2 Front legs	559mm (22in)	64mm (2½in)	38mm (1½in)
2 Arms	520mm (20½in)	51mm (2in)	38mm (1½in)
†2 Side rails	508mm (20in)	70mm (2¾in)	38mm (1½in)
2 Side stretchers	508mm (20in)	38mm (1½in)	38mm (1½in)

	Length	Width	Thickness
1 Front rail and 1 Back rail	508mm (20in)	102mm (4in)	38mm (1½in)
1 Cross stretcher	508mm (20in)	38mm (1½in)	38mm (1½in)
6 Back pieces	457mm (18in)	*	38mm (1½in)

* These pieces can be cut after overlapping with a template when marking out.
†From offcuts you will also need four seat bearer strips and, two curved seat rails.

	Length	Width	Thickness
† Seat (plywood)	457mm (18in)	457mm (18in)	4mm (⅛in)

1. Make a full-size drawing of the side elevation of the chair so that joints with angled shoulders can be accurately marked out and a template made for the back leg.

Action hint
*If possible, try and choose pieces for the back legs that enable the grain to follow the shape. Time spent in selection at the timber yard could pay dividends. If the tree from which you are choosing your boards was cut close to the ground, a flaring out at the base of the tree to the roots will yield boards with a curve that will accommodate the legs. Similarly, if the top cut has been made near a branch. If this choice is not available, cut the back legs so that the short grain forms the upper part of the leg.

Preparation
Prepare the timber and mark out and cut the joints. For all the angled shoulders to any tenons, a sliding bevel can be set to the full-size drawing. The arms can be made wider than shown and finally shaped to your own requirements.

Constructional illustration of chair

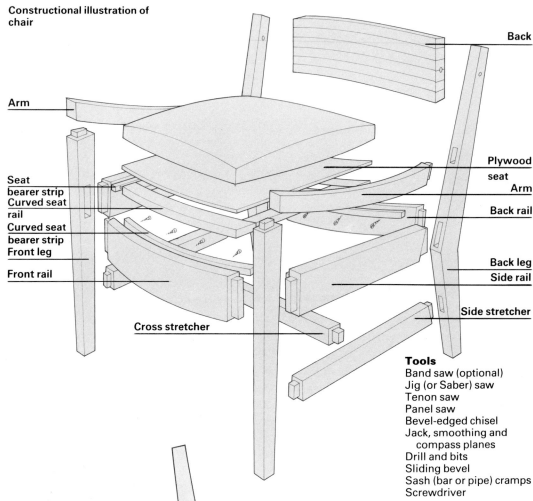

Arm

Seat bearer strip
Curved seat rail
Curved seat bearer strip
Front leg
Front rail

Cross stretcher

Back

Plywood seat
Arm
Back rail

Back leg
Side rail

Side stretcher

Tools
Band saw (optional)
Jig (or Saber) saw
Tenon saw
Panel saw
Bevel-edged chisel
Jack, smoothing and compass planes
Drill and bits
Sliding bevel
Sash (bar or pipe) cramps
Screwdriver

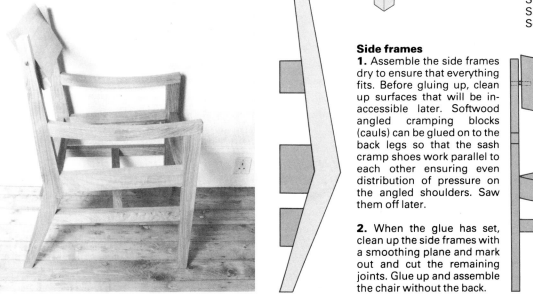

Side frames
1. Assemble the side frames dry to ensure that everything fits. Before gluing up, clean up surfaces that will be inaccessible later. Softwood angled cramping blocks (cauls) can be glued on to the back legs so that the sash cramp shoes work parallel to each other ensuring even distribution of pressure on the angled shoulders. Saw them off later.

2. When the glue has set, clean up the side frames with a smoothing plane and mark out and cut the remaining joints. Glue up and assemble the chair without the back.

The swivel back

1. This is stack laminated out of six horizontal strips. Make a template out of the first strip and use it to mark out the other five. Saw these, and the first strip with a band saw, jig saw (Saber saw) or coping saw. Glue and cramp together and clean up with a spokeshave or compass plane. Finally saw to length and clean up the ends with a smoothing plane.

2. Mark out centres on the ends and drill to take the 'T' nuts. Use hexagonal socket machine screws as these have a better appearance than the usual slotted

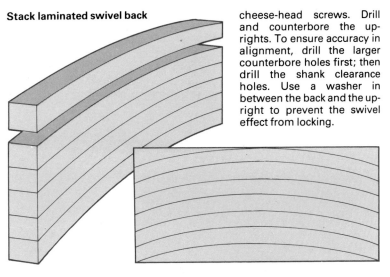

Stack laminated swivel back

cheese-head screws. Drill and counterbore the uprights. To ensure accuracy in alignment, drill the larger counterbore holes first; then drill the shank clearance holes. Use a washer in between the back and the upright to prevent the swivel effect from locking.

The seat

1. Seat bearer strips need to be screwed and glued to the insides of the side rails.

2. Glue and cramp the curved front and back rails to the plywood of the seat. These can be made from offcuts. The surface plys should run from front to back as this is the best direction in which to bend the ply. When the glue is dry, glue on the side rails. The plywood seat should fit in to place making allowance for the leather or fabric cover. Drill holes through the plywood to

allow air to escape when the cushion is compressed.

3. Glue the foam to the plywood using an impact adhesive and allowing a generous overlap. This excess can be cut away with a household electric meat knife or with a tenon saw held almost flat, cutting on the back stroke, only. Leave an even overlap of 10mm (³⁄₈in). The leather can next be stapled to the frame forming a tidy envelope effect at the corners. Finish the underside with a black cotton cloth stapled neatly into position.

The table ★★

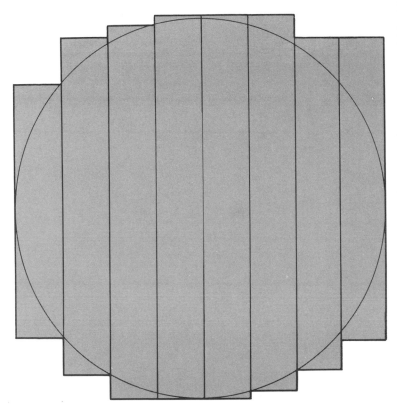

Sizes are sawn and not finished, except column length.			
Walnut:	**Length**	**Width**	**Thickness**
1 Column out of 3 pieces	736mm (29in)	115mm (4½in)	38mm (1½in)
2 Legs	1092mm (43in)	102mm (4in)	51mm (2in)
2 Top rails	1092mm (43in)	76mm (3in)	51mm (2in)
*1 Top out of 4 pieces	1245mm (49in)	159mm (6¼in)	25mm (1in)
2 pieces	1016mm (40in)	159mm (6¼in)	25mm (1in)
2 pieces	838mm (33in)	159mm (6¼in)	25mm (1in)
8 Buttons cut from pieces	48mm (1⁷⁄₈in)	48mm (1⁷⁄₈in)	48mm (1⁷⁄₈in)

*Your decision about constructing the top may be influenced by the materials available.

The top
Action hint

*Making the wide surface from narrower pieces has always presented its own problems, the main one being to produce a board wide enough and yet stable. It is not true that a few wide boards (with fewer edge joints) will produce a more stable top than a number of narrower boards with more edge joints. Here, use boards no wider than 203mm (8in), and 152mm (6in) is advised.

1. For the sake of economy, first draw a circle on white painted hardboard and divide it (as shown in the illustration) into your chosen board widths. Measure the lengths to which the table top boards must be sawn.

The table 2

2. If you have access to a thickness planer all to the good. Plane the boards about 1mm (¹⁄₁₆in) over-thickness. A local joinery firm might undertake this for you, and of course it can be done by hand. Planing will make the grain clearly visible and help you arrange the boards to interesting effect. But bear in mind that alternating annual rings aids stability (see page 176).

3. Next shoot the edges carefully to form good butt joints. 6mm (¼in) thick loose tongues or 10mm (³⁄₈in) diameter dowels will improve location and make gluing up easier.

4. Glue and cramp up the boards.

Action hint
* To facilitate gluing boards to form any large surface, do it in stages. First glue and cramp up the four centre boards, then when dry, the outer boards. Eventually, the surfaces should be flat enough to be skimmed clean with a smoothing plane.

5. Draw out the shape of the table top with an improvised beam compass, made by driving two nails through a strip of waste wood – the distance apart being equal to the radius of the circle. Mark this out on the underside of the top. A power jig saw (saber saw) is perhaps the best tool for cutting so wide a circle, but a coping saw or bow saw could be employed provided some of the waste is first removed with a panel saw. Clean up the sawn edge with a spokeshave or compass plane.

Constructional illustration of table

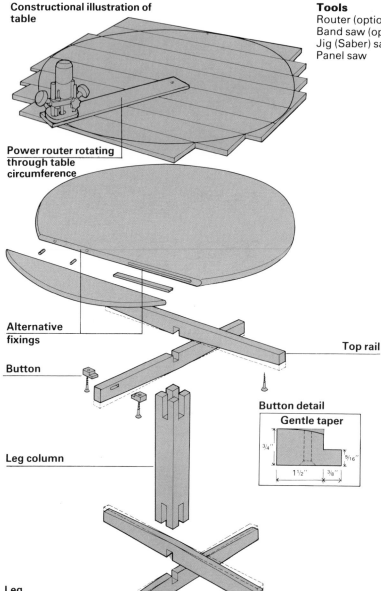

Power router rotating through table circumference

Alternative fixings

Button

Leg column

Leg

Top rail

Button detail
Gentle taper

3/4''
5/16''
1 1/2''   3/8''

Tools
Router (optional)
Band saw (optional)
Jig (Saber) saw
Panel saw

Jack, smoothing, compa: and plough planes
Mortise and bevel-edgec chisels
Sash (bar or pipe) cramp

Alternatively, use a router. Fix a power router to one end of a strip of plywood by removing its baseplate and fixing the tool to the plywood with the baseplate screws. Drive a pivot through the other end of the plywood into the centre of the underside of the table, so that the distance between pivot and router bit is equal to the desired radius of the table. Using a 6mm (¼in) diameter parallel cutter, increase the depth of the cut by 3mm (⅛in) with each rotation until the circle has been cut and a clean edge achieved.

The base
1. Build the central column out of three pieces of wood glued together to form a 102mm (4in) square section, but cut the centre piece shortest to form the notched joint that will take the cruciform legs and top rails.

2. Prepare the timber and cut the cross halving joints for the cruciform legs and rails. Remember to make an allowance when cutting these joints for cleaning up the surfaces with a smoothing plane. Otherwise slack joints will result.

Fixing the top
The top is best secured to the top rails by buttons let in to shallow mortises cut in the sides of the top rails. This will allow the top to move without straining the structure.

The sideboard ★★★★

Sizes are sawn and not finished.			
Walnut:	**Length**	**Width**	**Thickness**
1 Top	1181mm (46½in)	515mm (20¼in)	25mm (1in)
2 Sides	864mm (34in)	464mm (18¼in)	25mm (1in)
1 Centre partition	711mm (28in)	464mm (18¼in)	25mm (1in)
1 Bottom	915mm (36in)	464mm (18¼in)	25mm (1in)
2 Drawer rails	915mm (36in)	57mm (2¼in)	25mm (1in)
2 Doors	572mm (22½in)	457mm (18in)	25mm (1in)
1 Back (plywood)	915mm (36in)	686mm (27in)	6mm (¼in)
2 Drawer fronts	457mm (18in)	108mm (4¼in)	25mm (1in)
4 Drawer sides	432mm (17in)	108mm (4¼in)	12mm (½in)
2 Drawer backs	457mm (18in)	108mm (4¼in)	12mm (½in)
2 Drawer bottoms (plywood)	457mm (18in)	432mm (17in)	4mm (³⁄₁₆in)
4 Shelves	457mm (18in)	407mm (16in)	20mm (¾in)

The sideboard 2

The carcase

Action hint

* The centre partition could well be made from a less expensive hardwood, with a 50mm (2in) lipping or "facing" of the show wood butt-jointed to its front edge. In fact it is solid wood.

1. As with all carcase work, this sideboard demands care in butt-jointing narrow boards to make wider surfaces. First, plane the timber to 1 to 2mm (say 1/16in) over-thickness. This may involve the services of a local joinery firm.

2. After the butt-jointed boards have been planed to finished thickness, the ends can be planed square. This is a simple matter with the top. The sides and centre partition should be marked out together to ensure continuity of measurements, as should the dimensions of the bottom, and front and back drawer rails.

3. Next, cut all the carcase joints. The sides are housed and stub tenoned into the top. An intermediate stub tenon is necessary half way along the housing for extra strength. Cut similar joints to fix the bottom to the sides, and the partition to the bottom. The drawer frame is stub tenoned into the side panels and fits round the centre partition panel as shown in the exploded diagram. The four shelves will be fixed to the side panels by means of stopped housings (dadoes).

Constructional illustration of sideboard

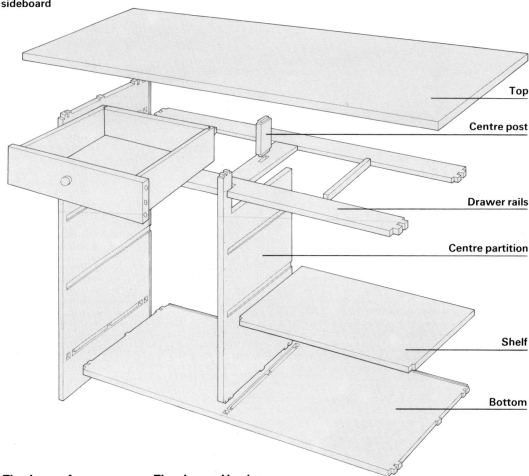

Top

Centre post

Drawer rails

Centre partition

Shelf

Bottom

The drawer frame

The front and back drawer rails are assembled as part of a frame (see illustration). A post is tenoned into the rails above the centre partition and into the underside of the top to prevent the top sagging and jamming the drawers. This may be made from an off-cut.

The plywood back

When all the carcase joints have been cut, the grooves to take the plywood back can be cut; this is best done with a router. Then, having cut the shelves, dry assemble the carcase. When you are satisfied that everything fits, all the internal surfaces can be cleaned up with a smoothing plane and sanded. You may consider pre-finishing these surfaces before gluing up. Take care to keep the finish away from the joints and try to glue up the carcase as soon as possible, so that the exterior can also be finished. This will stabilise the timber and prevent it from moving.

Assembly

Glue up in stages. First assemble the drawer rail frame taking great care to keep it absolutely flat. Next, assemble the main carcase without the top. Make sure the back grooves line up at the corners. Slightly curved cramping blocks (cauls) are necessary to ensure even pressure on housing joints in wide boards.

When dry the back can be slid into position and the top glued into place.

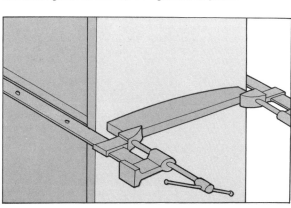

Drawers

Carefully fit the drawer fronts to the drawer openings. Aim for a tight fit; this can be adjusted later. Then fit the drawer sides; these should slide easily. The drawer joints can now be cut. The drawer sides can be housed

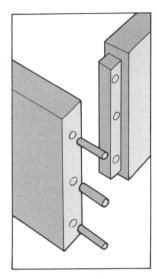

into the drawer front and pegged with dowels after gluing up. The housing joint should penetrate two thirds of the thickness of the front. The back can be housed into the drawer sides. Grooved drawer runners are then tenoned into drawer fronts and backs. The runners are grooved to fit the drawer rails.

They should slide easily at this stage. Grooves are then cut to accept the drawer bottoms. A dry assembly before gluing up is advisable.

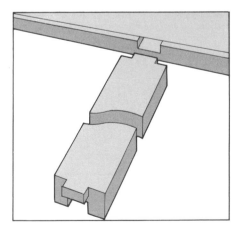

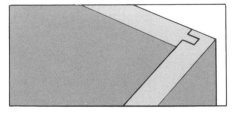

Doors

1. Exercise a great deal of care when assembling the doors. Stability can be aided by using carefully selected narrow strips when butt jointing the boards for the doors; each strip should certainly be no wider than 152mm (6in). Make the doors to give a clearance of 1mm (1/16in) all the way round.

2. Mark out and drill the holes for the pin hinges. These are not manufactured items. 'T' nuts can be purchased over the counter as can the 6mm (1/4in) machine screws. The brass rod and tube will have to be bought and then cut to length. To enable the door to open, the pivoted edge has to be rounded. This is best done with a jack plane after marking out the curve, and finally sanded off.

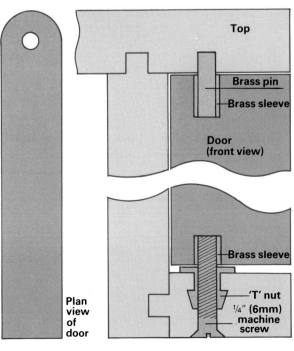

Plan view of door

Top

Brass pin

Brass sleeve

Door (front view)

Brass sleeve

'T' nut

1/4" (6mm) machine screw

The study by Fred Baier

"My grandfather, an engineer, did woodwork in his spare time. I never knew him but we had some of the things he made, like cabinets, boxes and violins. The tools were just lying about so I began to use them. It wasn't the wood so much as the things that I could make out of them for myself – cross-bows and other things! Then at school I studied mathematics, physics and chemistry to 'A' level until I realized I wasn't very good at the physics and chemistry so I dropped them for art and woodwork.

"Then I went to Birmingham Art College where I worked a lot with plastics and metal as well as wood. In a way, Birmingham had an influence on me as a designer because I got very keen on pattern making and the whole industrial scene. During one holiday I made the wooden patterns for metal casting of components for engines and the like. When the firm that I was working for closed down they said that if we wanted any of these patterns we could have them, so we moved literally tons of the stuff out and painted them. We made sculptures out of them and playthings for kids, and the shapes started me thinking about making similar shapes as furniture.

"I work mostly with wood because I am proficient in it – I have got the tools and I know how to use them. I am not interested in the purist's approach; I enjoy making visual puns. For example, there is something nice about some of my pieces looking like metal objects, yet obviously they are made out of wood. It's really the resulting objects – the shapes – that interest me and people's reactions to them, rather than the material of which they are made. This is nothing new. In the

Brighton Pavilion, for example, we have *painted* wood grain. You may have seen something similar in pubs, but this is really good. I took an American professor of woodwork around the Brighton Pavilion and he never noticed! You will begin to see the scope of visual puns – things which look as if they are done one way and in fact are something altogether different. I admit that those sorts of joke do fall short of some people.

"I tend to choose wood for its grain and lightness of natural colour – I use sycamore a lot. Colour is an important element in my work and I've spent time researching different wood colouring techniques. Unfortunately, they don't sell ready-mixed colours any more. You go to a decent supplier of finishes and he will only sell powdered pigment. There is one sort you mix with mineral spirit base and another you mix with water. But remember that if you use water, always wet the surface of the wood first to raise the grain. Then sand it smooth again before applying the stain. It is very difficult to get an even tone with spirit on a large area or complicated shape because it dries too quickly. In the main I use a water mix.

"On top of the colours I like all those modern finishes, especially acid catalysed lacquer – melamine, like liquid formica! I tend to steer clear of polyurethane and P.V.A. except for jigs.

"I am not concerned to provide a service. It's a very selfish attitude. It is important for me not to make my living by making furniture. Mine is more of a fine art approach. What I am doing is exploring possible forms within certain limitations in order to expand people's

ideas both of what is possible structurally and what is nice to look at. If I am commissioned, then ideally the client will employ me because he has confidence in my judgement – he will make that decision after looking at my previous work. I will then work on the idea in principle for him and submit it to him. If approved, then I will work it out.

"When I was commissioned to make the Conference Table (see below) the stipulations were that it had to seat sixteen people and fit into one particular room, access to which was up a 3ft spiral staircase. They provided a set of plans for the room and I was invited up to look at it. I noticed that all the wood details were made from plywood. And outside there was a natural view – trees and spires – interrupted by a great row of electric pylons (which I particularly enjoyed). I sat in the room and drew it. And then I did what I nearly always do; I went to the Science Museum and wandered around looking at things. I got rather excited about aeroplane parts – wings, propellers, turbo engines and things. I made some drawings of what I saw and went home to develop an idea through exploring the relationship between the various components I had drawn, and my drawings from the building. The result was a picture of a wheel type structure with fins fanning out. Put a cone in the middle and it's just like the impeller in a turbo engine. When I took the idea back, the cone was criticized, with some validity. It had to go, but something had to replace it to maintain the structural quality of the piece. So I used a system of tensioning wires, similar to the structure used in the wings of a bi-plane.

The desk ★★

Why furniture?

"The reason I design furniture is something to do with pushing boundaries forward. But in the end the things that I make have got to work out to a satisfactory and stable conclusion. If you play about with structures and forms, you discover new weaknesses and new strengths – you open up the field a bit. If you look at the history of furniture you get to the point at the turn of the century when for the first time for ages embellishment is reduced to a minimum. It all becomes to do with structure, woodwork, simple things. Then there is a little bit of the Art Nouveau thing, and after that, right the way through, it's all to do with geometry. I have been concerned with shapes and figurative things based on a 20th Century technological theme. But now it's going to change. All my pieces, up till now, have been objects – objective studies of other things (it's a refined pop-arty thing really). But what I want to do now concerns 'process'. In a way the desk led me to it. It's got the feeling of something coming up and breaking through a surface. Can you see the main stay breaking through the surface and the top piece? It's dynamic rather than static. Also, it seems to defy gravity – there is only one leg and everything seems to hang off it. In a sense it is a transition. I was beginning to waver between figurative work and something that is really *happening* in the piece.

"Everything, in the end, is a result of refined thinking. Someone comes up with an idea and then it is gradually refined by further thoughts. The trouble is that there are not nearly enough people to inject new thoughts or new forms. Too many people base their ideas on previous people's work. I am trying to take things a step further in my own way."

"Fred Baier has never thought of himself as an expert woodworker; he is an ideas man with a keen wit. So often, the best artefacts around us demonstrate that precious quality – not jokiness, but the understatement that is more profound. His work may look dramatic, but that is the natural result of assessing the need without being over burdened with tradition. Fred really enjoys old furniture too, largely because it reflects the best of *its* time."
John Makepeace

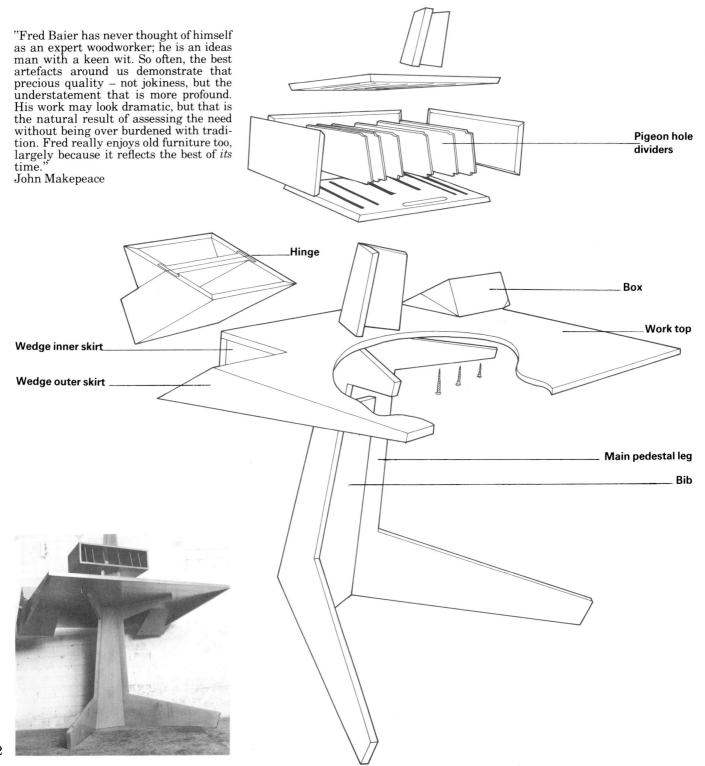

Pigeon hole dividers

Hinge

Box

Work top

Wedge inner skirt

Wedge outer skirt

Main pedestal leg

Bib

Cutting list

Plywood:	Height/ Length	Width/ Depth	Thickness
2 Main pedestal legs	1226mm (48¼in)	870mm (34¼in)	20mm (¾in)
1 Work top	1016mm (40in)	762mm (30in)	20mm (¾in)
2 Wedge skirts, outer	725mm (28½in)	108mm (4¼in)	20mm (¾in)
2 Wedge skirts, inner	203mm (8in)	108mm (4¼in)	20mm (¾in)
1 Back skirt	610mm (24in)	108mm (4¼in)	20mm (¾in)
1 Bib	757mm (29¾in)	235mm (9¼in)	20mm (¾in)

Pigeon hole			
2 Top and bottom	457mm (18in)	241mm (9½in)	12mm (½in)
2 Sides	241mm (9½in)	127mm (5in)	12mm (½in)
1 Back	445mm (17½in)	115mm (4½in)	12mm (½in)
4 Dividers (beech)	203mm (8in)	115mm (4½in)	6mm (¼in)
2 Dividers (beech)	165mm (6½in)	115mm (4½in)	6mm (¼in)
Boxes			
4 Tops and bottoms	330mm (13in)	228mm (9in)	12mm (½in)
4 Sides	228mm (9in)	102mm (4in)	12mm (½in)
4 Fronts and backs	228mm (9in)	102mm (4in)	12mm (½in)

Tools
Circular saw
Cross-cut saw
Tenon saw
Chisels
Mallet
Jack plane
Plough plane
Drill and countersink
Screwdriver
Bevel
Square
Paint brush
Cramps
Picture frame cramp
Band saw (optional)

Front view of desk

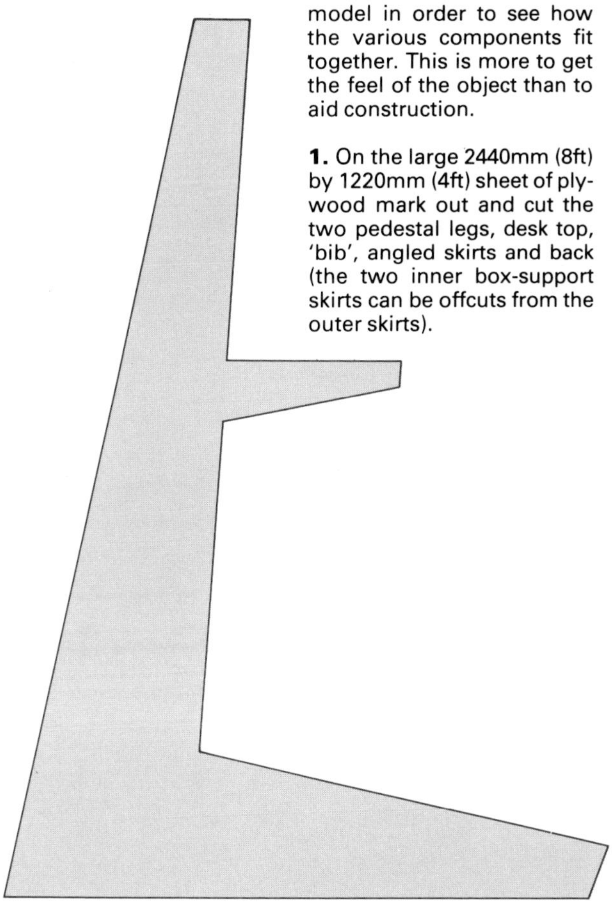

The study desk
Furniture constructed from man-made boards is often quicker and simpler to construct than designs incorporating frames and sub-assemblies. Another advantage is that absolutely flat surfaces featured in many modern designs come ready made and stable. However, in the absence of framework etc., the constructional strength depends on good jointing if additional and unsightly corner blocks are to be avoided.

Anyone unfamiliar with this type of construction might find it useful to construct a scale cardboard model in order to see how the various components fit together. This is more to get the feel of the object than to aid construction.

1. On the large 2440mm (8ft) by 1220mm (4ft) sheet of plywood mark out and cut the two pedestal legs, desk top, 'bib', angled skirts and back (the two inner box-support skirts can be offcuts from the outer skirts).

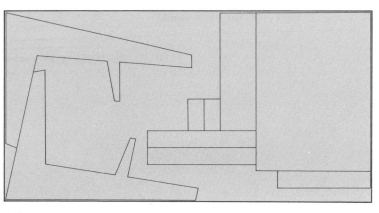

Artist's impression of desk elements cutting plan from an 8ft by 4ft ply sheet.

Main pedestal leg to scale

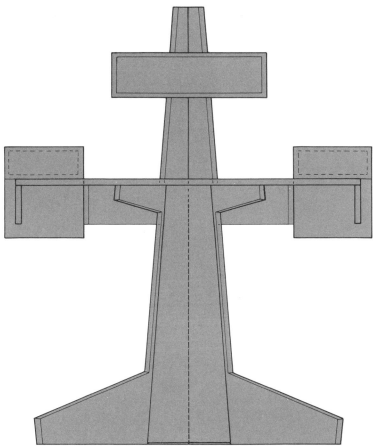

The desk 2

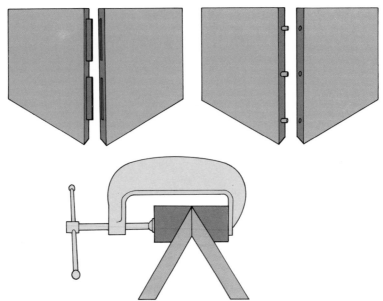

2. Plane the inside back edges of the two pedestal legs each to an angle of 31 degrees so that they meet to form an angle of 62 degrees. Do not plane to a knife edge but leave blunt for shoulder of plough plane to be used in grooving for loose tongues.

3. The two angled edges must be glued to form a strong joint and therefore not allowed to 'slip' during the gluing and cramping operation. To prevent this, a method of locating one surface with the other is necessary. On the example shown loose plywood tongues were inserted into a series of slots cut into opposite angled edges. These slots are 76mm (3in) long by 6mm (¼in) wide and cut 10mm (⅜in) deep

gauged 25mm (1in) from the 'pointed' edges, and were cut first with a plough plane (you could use a router) then squared out with a 6mm (¼in) mortise chisel. They are staged at approximately 127mm (5in) intervals along the edges leaving 64mm (2½in) at both top and bottom. If the desk is to be painted, the same job can be done with short dowels or screws with their heads countersunk and filled.

The glued joint requires cramping across the angle which can be done with the aid of blocks each cut to 31 degrees. To make them easier to remove later, insert and glue a single sheet of brown 'kraft' paper (not newspaper) between blocks and legs.

Cutting the bib and column

1. To strengthen the central column just below desk top a 'bib' is inserted 40mm (1½in) from the column's leading edge stopping 3mm (⅛in) from the floor. This can be marked out for vertical angles by holding it in position then planing the edges to 31 degrees so that it can form a rub glued joint with pedestal.

2. At this stage, bore and counterbore the pedestal arms for top fixing screws.

3. A section of the pedestal column must now be removed to accommodate the pigeon holes. The cuts for this must be made at 90 degrees to perpendicular and the waste portion of the column retained to be used as a template for marking out and cutting the angle of the desk-top slot through which a lower section of the pedestal column will pass.

The desk top

1. On the desk's top surface mark the spot at which the apex of the pedestal column will break through, then, using the waste portion as a template, scribe the angles at which the whole 'V' section will follow through. The actual length of each arm of the 'V' can be assessed by measurement along the pedestal column 20mm (¾in) (the ply thickness) above the desk top arms.

To mark the underside of the top, the same 'V', but with fractionally longer arms, must be reproduced farther

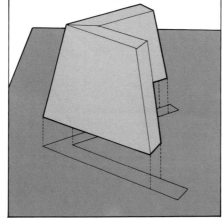

to the rear. Again the waste piece of pedestal can be used as a guide to set the angle for drilling a pilot hole at the apex. Using the point at which the drill breaks out underneath, repeat the 'V' profile. The waste portion can be of further use as a guide for the chisel angle when paring the slot.

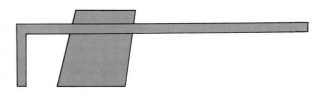

2. Depending on your attitude to waste, both inner skirts which house the 'drawer' boxes and flank the rear desk top can be cut either before or after the rear and outer side skirts have been fitted.

The outer skirts, which diminish from 110mm (4½in) to zero over a distance of 780mm (30in), are cut to support the boxes at an angle of 30 degrees from horizontal. Use the waste portion of both to form the inner skirts which should be drilled for box fixing before assembly.

3. Glue and screw all four angled skirts to the underside of the top. With the top inverted on the bench, make

The boxes
These resemble large flip-top cigarette packets with lids hanging on their fronts instead of backs.

1. Construction can be according to preference, type of finish, or tools available. On the example shown, front and rear corners were mitred and glued with loose-tongue locators in the same way as pedestal column. The sides were pushed and glued into rebates cut into the inner surfaces all round. Cramping of mitres was achieved with picture frame cramps.

Alternatively, the boxes can be constructed with rebated (rabbeted) joints all round, then glued and pinned. If this method is adopted, decide where you would prefer the edges of plywood to appear. The amount of edge can be reduced by cutting rebates to three-quarters the plywood thickness. Another method is to edge veneer the appropriate pieces but this must be done before box assembly.

The pigeon holes
1. This can be constructed in the same way as the boxes either with tongued mitres or rebated joints. If the latter are used it is suggested the forward-facing edges are strip veneered with knife mitres at the corners. The back panel can be rebated (rabbeted) within the box.

2. Before assembly, both top and bottom must be grooved on their inner surfaces to hold the six dividers. These grooves, which should stop 6mm (¼in) before dividers, can be cut to a stop with a tenon saw, then the waste removed with a chisel. The two pencil depressions can be cut with a small gouge.

Since the interior of the pigeon hole will be visible to anyone sitting at the desk, painting or wood finishing should be completed before assembly.

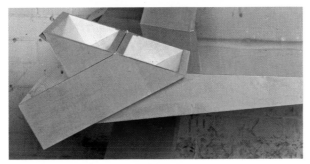

3. The pigeon hole is fixed within the cut-out portion of the pedestal column by 6mm (¼in) dowels into both panels and pedestal. Exact location for dowels can be achieved by knocking panel pins (finishing nails) part way into ends of pedestal, snipping off heads to leave a point, then pressing pigeon hole in position to mark for dowel hole centres.

a rub-glued joint between rear skirt and top. Further fix by screwing into both inner skirts.

4. The desk top is glue-fixed to its support arms and further secured by 40mm (1½in) dome-head screws (with washers) passing through the three pre-drilled vertical holes in each support arm.

2. Take the two completely encased boxes and cut off their top corners to an angle of 45 degrees, then clean up the cut edges. Replace the corners to form lids by hinging with strap hinges as shown.

3. Both boxes are held in place by two screws passing from inner skirts to box and two screws from lower front lip in to chamfered edge of desk top. Be careful to select suitably short screws.

Finishing
Naked edges of plywood panels on pedestal, desk top etc, can be edged with iron-on veneer which can be applied during any stage of production.

The completed desk can be painted, stained, and polished as desired or to blend with other decor.

The chair ★

Cutting list Plywood:	Height	Width	Thickness
Pedestal legs	610mm (24in)	515mm (20¼in)	20mm (¾in)
Back	381mm (15in)	279mm (11in)	20mm (¾in)
Seat	381mm (15in)	457mm (18in)	20mm (¾in)

Main pedestal leg to scale

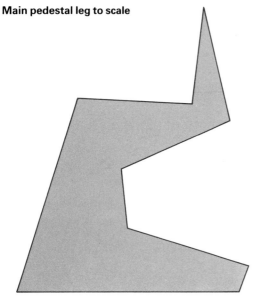

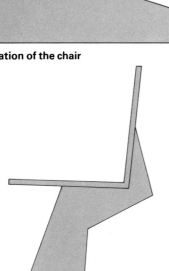

Side elevation of the chair

Front/back view of the chair

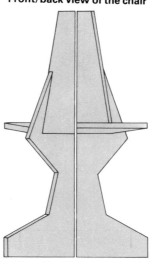

Building the chair

1. Mark out and cut the two leg frames, seat panel and back rest.

2. Plane the inside fore edges of the leg frames to 31 degrees so that they meet to form an angle of 62 degrees. Do not plane to a sharp edge but leave blunt for shoulder of plough plane.

3. Both edges are located for gluing by the insertion of plywood tongues in exactly the same way as described for the desk's pedestal column except that the tongues are staged at 50mm (2in) intervals along its edges.

4. If the chair pedestal is to be painted, locate with 25mm (1in) screws which would dispense with the need for cramping. The screw heads should be countersunk and holes plugged flush with the surrounding surface. Before assembly apply edge veneer to all panels.

5. Both seat and back rest are glued and dowelled to the pedestal. Dowels, which are 25mm (1in) long, do not pass right through but stop 6mm (¼in) short of surfaces. Dowel hole centres can be located by pressing the panels onto partly driven headless pins.

6. Glue and dowel the back rest first, followed by the seat, which should be slightly bevelled along its rear edge to abutt and be glued to the back rest.

7. Stain, lacquer, or paint the chair accordingly. Soft upholstery could be tied, stretch-fitted or attached by surface-mounted press studs.

Action hint

*If intending to use stain, be particularly careful to remove any stray glue from any surface with one damp cloth, then with another. Finally give it a fair sanding.

The shelving unit ★

Cutting list Plywood:			
2 Verticals	**Length**	**Width**	**Thickness**
	330mm	216mm	20mm
2 Shelves (top and bottom)	(13in)	(8½in)	(¾in)
	965mm	178mm	20mm
2 Shelves (centre)	(38in)	(7in)	(¾in)
	508mm	305mm	20mm
2 Centre box pieces	(20in)	(12in)	(¾in)
	305mm	305mm	20mm
2 Centre box pieces	(12in)	(12in)	(¾in)
	305mm	343mm	20mm
1 Centre box back	(12in)	(13½in)	(¾in)
	324mm	324mm	20mm
4 Fillets	(12¾in)	(12¾in)	(¾in)
	305mm	20mm	20mm
8 Fins	(12in)	(¾in)	(¾in)
	228mm	12mm	20mm
	(9in)	(4in)	(¾in)

Plan view and, below, side elevation

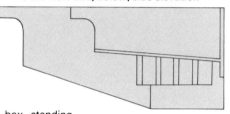

Construct the unit in either plywood, blockboard, veneered or laminated chipboard according to preference or availability.

1, Mark out the four shelves, two verticals, four box sides, back panel and eight 'fins'.

2. Begin by making the central box. Rebate (rabbet) all four of its rear edges to receive the back panel. Take two adjoining sides and bore each with a series of twelve holes, in four rows of three, pitched at an angle of 110 degrees. These are to receive 40mm (1½in) screws, countersunk on the inside of the panels.

3. Glue and cramp the four simple butt joints to form a box, insert but do not, at this stage, glue the back panel. Plane off the outer four corners at 45 degrees to form a bevel exactly equal to the thickness of the shelf material.

4. Gently dry cramp the four internal corner fillets in position and drill pilot holes through the corners and fillets, four into both horizontal shelf fixings and three into the vertical. Take out the corner fillets and counter-

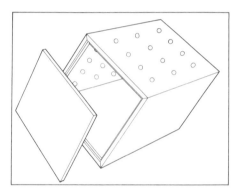

bore to receive the shanks of 45mm (1¾in) screws. Also countersink on insides for screw heads. Glue corner fillets in position.

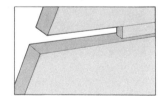

5. Shape all shelves, then make joints between verticals and top and bottom shelves. These are cut as halving (cross lap) joints which continue as housing (dado) joints along both sides of each board (the housing joints will counteract any tendency to warping). Edge and counter-bore shelves for wall screws.

6. Cut the eight 'fins' to length, then bevel their long edges to 110 degrees. Should edge-veneer be used, it is easier to apply before final assembly with the box sides.

7. With the box standing upright on a flat surface, arrange the 'fins' along two sides to centre over predrilled screw holes. Then glue, butt and screw from inside the box.

8. Offer up the two vertical panels and horizontal shelves, then glue and screw from inside the box. When the glue has set, turn the whole unit over and insert the back panel into rebates (rabbets) already cut into the rear edges of the box.

9. Apply the glue and slide in both top and bottom shelves. If the unit is finished after wall mounting, the screw holes can be plugged with suitable lengths of dowel or covered with small plastic buttons available from hardware merchants.

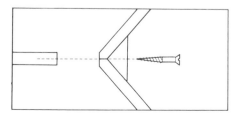

The child's bed ★ ★ ★

Cutting list Plywood:	Length	Width	Thickness
1 Headboard	915mm (36in)	476mm (18¾in)	20mm (¾in)
1 Baseboard	1524mm (60in)	915mm (36in)	20mm (¾in)
1 Tailboard	915mm (36in)	274mm (10¾in)	20mm (¾in)
3 Long chassis members	1695mm (66¾in)	610mm (24in)	20mm (¾in)
5 Chassis cross members	813mm (32in)	152mm (6in)	20mm (¾in)
Head bogie (one drawer)			
2 Shaped sub-frames	864mm (34in)	355mm (14in)	20mm (¾in)
2 Drawer box top and bottom	915mm (36in)	419mm (16½in)	20mm (¾in)
2 Drawer box sides	915mm (36in)	216mm (8½in)	20mm (¾in)
2 Drawer front and back	368mm (14½in)	178mm (7in)	12mm (½in)
2 Drawer sides	1219mm (48in)	178mm (7in)	12mm (½in)
1 Drawer bottom	902mm (35½in)	368mm (14½in)	6mm (¼in)
Alternative (two drawers)			
4 Drawer fronts and backs	368mm (14½in)	178mm (7in)	12mm (½in)

	Length	Width	Thickness
4 Drawer sides	585mm (23in)	178mm (7in)	12mm (½in)
2 Drawer bottoms	406mm (16in)	368mm (14½in)	6mm (¼in)
Tail bogie			
2 Shaped sub-frames	368mm (14½in)	355mm (14in)	20mm (¾in)
1 Pr. feet	813mm (32in)	159mm (6¼in)	20mm (¾in)
2 Drawer box top and bottom	483mm (19in)	419mm (16½in)	20mm (¾in)
2 Drawer box sides	483mm (19in)	254mm (10in)	20mm (¾in)
1 Drawer box back	381mm (15in)	216mm (8½in)	20mm (¾in)
2 Drawer front and back	368mm (14½in)	216mm (8½in)	12mm (½in)
2 Drawer sides	590mm (23¼in)	216mm (8½in)	12mm (½in)
1 Drawer bottom	445mm (17¼in)	368mm (14½in)	6mm (¼in)

Also required: 50mm (2in) diameter beech dowel (for 'climb aboard' drawer pulls) 1676mm (66in) if single head bogie drawer, 1880mm (74in) for double.

4 Runners (Ramin)	432mm (17in)	12mm (½in)	6mm (¼in)

Action hint
*The design is suitable for adaptation to individual needs and can be made more manoeuvrable by fitting ball castors, four under the head bogie and two under the tail. Also by using nuts, bolts, washers or screws for connecting bogies to chassis members, the bed can be made to dismantle for storage or transportation itself.

The main frame
1. Start by cutting out the head, base, and tail boards, both long chassis members, and the five cross members. Cut long and cross members with halving (cross-lap) joints, then slot together to form an 'egg box' chassis.

2. Drill the mattress baseboard with 10mm (⅜in) diameter holes on a 100mm (4in) grid but vary this to avoid the cross members. If the head, tail, and baseboard are to be edged, apply at this stage before assembly.

3. The headboard is glued and screw-fixed to the two chassis uprights, then the baseboard abutted to it. If the owner's name is to be saw-pierced out of the tailboard, it should be cut before assembly with the chassis.

The 'egg-box' chassis

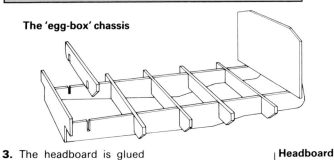

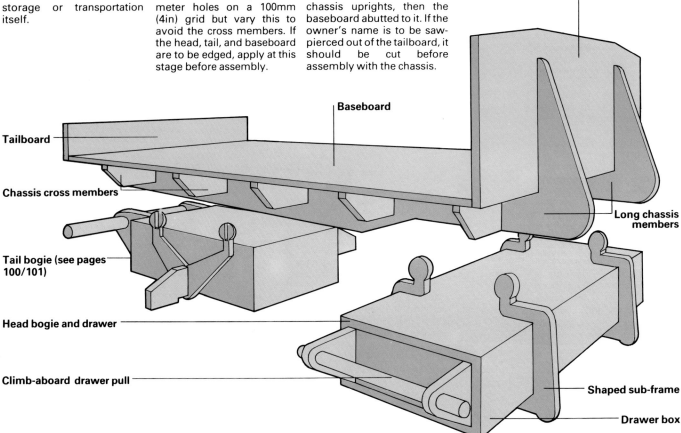

Tailboard

Chassis cross members

Tail bogie (see pages 100/101)

Head bogie and drawer

Climb-aboard drawer pull

Baseboard

Headboard

Long chassis members

Shaped sub-frame

Drawer box

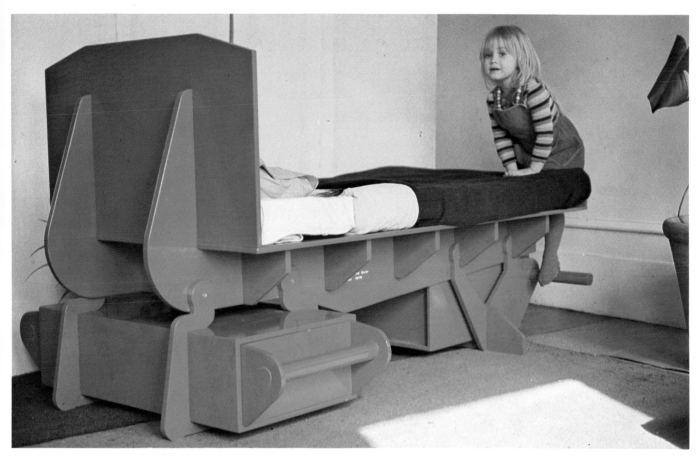

The head bogie

The head bogie

This comprises a long, open-ended box held in place by two shaped sub-frames. The box may contain either one long or two short drawers, depending on room space.

1. Mark and cut the head box members. The joints could be lap joints, or glued and nailed in dovetail fashion for improved grip.

2. Use a cardboard template to mark out the two shaped sub-frames which hold the drawer unit (reversing it as appropriate), then cut them out. These are fastened to the drawer unit by two blocks centred underneath, and to the long chassis members above. Fastening to the chassis members can be by glue and screw from the inside between the chassis

members, or with nuts, bolts and washers only if the facility to dismantle is preferred.

3. If one drawer is to be incorporated it should be capable of passing through the box unimpeded ('like a train through a tunnel'). The 'climb aboard' drawer pulls must in that case end flush with the drawer sides. The

pulls can if necessary be firmly fixed with a gap-filling glue, such as Cascamite, following drawer construction.

4. Should the drawer be mounted on ramin runners (glued and pinned on the inner sides of the box, 50mm (2in) below the top and running almost its full length), then cut matching grooves along both outer drawer side faces. If runners are fitted (you may decide that because they are visible at both shaped ends they spoil the unit's appearance), they should of course be mounted prior to drawer construction. If you dispense with them, make the drawer slightly undersize and simply allow it to run on the bottom edges of its sides. Wear due to friction can be reduced by letting it run on two strips of thin gauge plastic 'rails' or the occasional application of candle wax.

5. If the bogie features two drawers, they can either run up to a common stop in the centre of the box, or their fronts can be extended down to stop against the box's lower front edge. The two drawers could share the same runners.

The child's bed 2

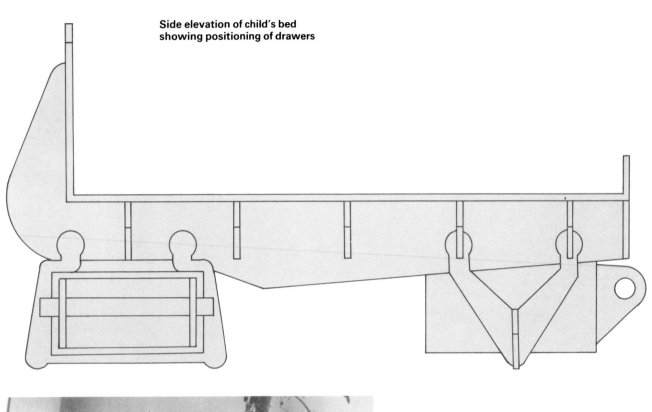

Side elevation of child's bed
showing positioning of drawers

Drawer construction
1. Cut out the front, back, sides and bottom drawer members, possibly using a cardboard template to assist the marking of the sides. In all cases use simple housing (dado) joints to bring these members together.

2. As can be seen from the illustration, the 6mm (¼in) plywood bottom panel slides into matching grooves cut 5mm (³⁄₁₆in) deep, gauged 6mm (¼in) from drawer side and front bottom edges. In the case of two drawers, drawer backs are not grooved but cut short so that they rest upon the bottom panels. In the case of one drawer, the bottom panel must rest upon an extra 6mm (¼in) bead attached to one drawer front.

Tail bogie

1. This is similar in all respects to the head bogie except that the drawer box has a rear panel which should fit within the box sides. Again, the drawer itself would run smoother if mounted on runners.

2. The framed sub-assembly forms a cradle which holds the drawer box up against the two cross members nearest the tail. The feet, shaped at their ends like an inverted chassis member, are cut to pass under the drawer and act as its support. The whole 'bogie' assembly is glued and screwed to chassis but if the facility to dismantle is required then the four rounded frame arms should be dry-slotted with ends of cross members and the drawer box screw fixed from inside its top panel into the lower edges of cross members.

Feet/head elevations of child's bed

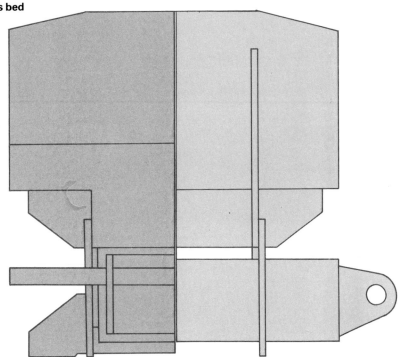

Constructional illustration of tail bogie

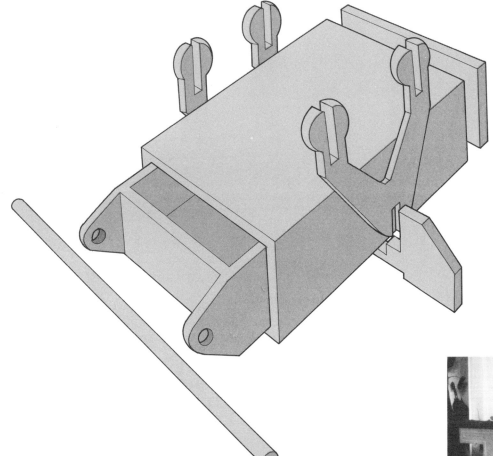

Finishing
Truck beds benefit from being painted in bright colours either to match surrounding decor or contrast each other. There are no hard and fast rules except that the baseboard top in contact with mattress should be left untreated.

Paint can be applied during or after assembly. The example shown was painted blue with 'coach lines' applied in metallic silver with the aid of masking tape.

101

The bedroom by Wendell Castle

Wendell Castle

Born in 1932 in Emporia, Kansas, Wendell Castle's workshop produces around 140 major pieces of furniture a year. He is President of Wendell Castle Inc., Scottsville, New York, and Director of *The Wendell Castle School of Woodworking*, also in Scotsville.

He looks to natural forms – plant-like, animal-like, shell-like shapes, etc. – as the fount of his design inspiration, and employs the laminating or stacking technique to achieve a synthesis or metamorphosis of these forms as furniture.

This type of furniture-making permits an unlimited volume of unbroken wood surface, and provides the woodworker with the opportunity of moulding any number of different shapes. "In developing ideas which will eventually become items of furniture, the woodworker who avails himself of the technique will not be bound by the geometric demands associated with traditional furniture design. As a result, the free sketch tends to replace more traditional draughtsmanship. The designer approaches his task more like a painter – who begins with charcoal sketches – than the architect – whose initial considerations involve engineering factors."

Ideas for the laminating technique

"The most practical consequence for the woodworker is that he can look almost everywhere and anywhere for his ideas, except the existing field of furniture. Since almost all possible design ideas have long ago been exhausted, he may already feel that new approaches to furniture which depend upon techniques employed in contemporary and period furniture are doomed to failure. Further exploration in that area will very likely lead to witting or unwitting plagiarism. Somewhere, sometime, a similar piece will have been created.

"The lamination technique opens doors for the furniture designer. If he employs it, he will be limited only by the horizons of his artistic fantasies and ingenuity.

"First, he can choose from a wide variety of sources for his ideas. My personal preference is for organic forms. These offer an enormous range of design possibilities; but there are innumerable other sources, for example mechanical objects – gears, hardware, machinery – architectural forms, crystals, minerals, which can be transformed by a fertile imagination into exquisite furniture forms. It is up to the individual; the only condition is that the object of his muse is sufficiently powerful to sustain the design process.

"I would like to point out that I have long held a fascination for fabric folds. Interesting forms produced by fabric folds have been used over and over again in my designs."

The design process

"Initially, the chosen form should be explored thoroughly with the eye, so that its uniqueness and beauty are fully comprehended. This involves a suspension of all pre-conceived notions, so that it appears in a totally new manner.

"At this point, begin to make idea sketches. These sketches are the means to alter the chosen form as much as is necessary to create a functional piece of furniture. What is important is that a wide range of possibilities be explored quickly and fearlessly. Don't be afraid of the bad or the grotesque, or be content with two or three solutions. The widest array of possibilities should be investigated at the preliminary stage. Sometimes seemingly bad ideas have a way of leading to good ones, so keep your sketches however unsatisfactory they appear at the time. Soon, a few good ideas begin to emerge and these are then carried forward to the next stage.

"Once the basic sketches have been done, begin to refine them to reflect detail and scale. In the end, you will need a perspective drawing, or final set of sketches prior to a full-scale working drawing.

"In this perspective drawing stage, practical demands of construction join aesthetic considerations. The sketching of flowing form can lead you to gloss over construction problems which you will be unable to solve later. There are numerous considerations – problems relating to balance, weight and the like, the placement of drawers for a bureau, the correct hinging of a mirror for a dressing table, etc. In all these the successful designer will fall back on draughtsmanship skills and shop experience.

"This stage of the process ends with a set of scale drawings representing the object from its most characteristic views.

"It is important to point out here the necessity to think cross-sectionally when employing the technique. This will help you understand how the construction can

be clamped together when building it, but most important, it will enable you to achieve walls which are as thin as possible without compromising the piece's design or inherent strength.

"Many people are under the illusion that forms carved from wood laminations begin as one chunk of wood grooved together, leading to a process of construction similar to sculpture – chiselling away unwanted parts to achieve the final form. Such is not the case at all. Laminated forms give the impression of weight and mass, but most are hollow. This is not simply for reasons of weight and materials costs – the critical factor has to do with conventional stability. Given sufficient bulk, the most expertly laminated wood can simply crack because of internal stress brought about by ordinary changes in humidity. Hollow forms beat this in two ways. Thin structures are more flexible and stresses, resulting from changes due to fluctuating atmospheric humidity, are more readily set off. Secondly, hollow forms nearly double the wood surface exposed to the outer air, thus permitting a more rapid and uniform rate of expansion and contraction throughout.

"Like most of the contributors to this book, Wendell comes to Parnham to lecture in the *John Makepeace School for Craftsmen in Wood*.

Wendell Castle's work has been enormously influential in North America. Design students, craftsmen and furniture makers are widely caught up in the idea of organic forms."
John Makepeace

The night stand ★ ★ ★

Laminating technique
Action hints
*Because it has an even, straight grain, Wendell Castle specified Honduras mahogany as the most suitable timber in which to construct the entire suite. Brazilian mahogany was used to build the example illustrated because of its similarity to Honduras mahogany and the fact that it is easier to obtain in Great Britain.

However, any straight-grained wood can be used provided that laminations of it blend together making joints almost invisible. Cascamite powdered resin glue was used on all joints.

*Start by scaling up the two "drape" profiles to full size and produce patterns for carving the bases of all laminated panels. A standard full-size pattern for cutting all dovetail joints would also help produce a uniform appearance throughout the range.

*All drape panels taper from thin at the top to thick at the base so if laminations are cut from opposite ends of the same board they should be arranged so that grain directions help disguise joints.

Cutting list

Mahogany:	Length	Width	Thickness
1 Top	410mm (16⅛in)	410mm (16⅛in)	38mm (1½in)
22 Sides	508mm (20in)	variously tapering	38mm (1½in)

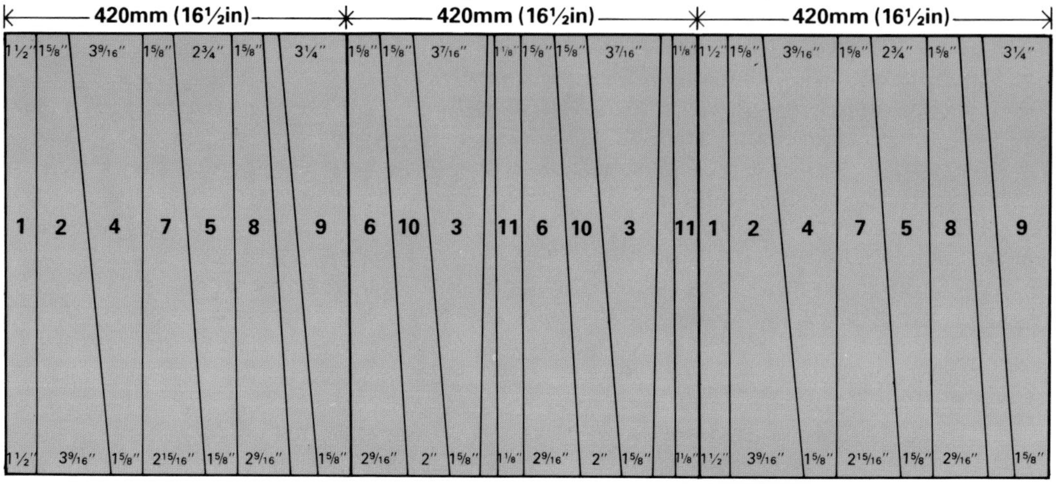

The night table
This design doubles as a seat for the dressing table and can be cut from a single board 1943 mm (6ft 4½in) by 420mm (16½in). Remember to allow for planing and saw-dust waste.

1. First cut three 508mm (20in) lengths from the board then, with reference to the cutting diagram, cut all twenty-two variously tapered pieces which will form the laminated "drape" sides.
2. Arrange pieces according to the profile pattern so that one side forms a "mirror" image of the other.
3. Take a piece of waste wood and cut it into a stepped pattern so that when it is laid under the base ends they are "jacked up" into their glue positions. Glue and cramp each side and, if necessary, cramp between laminations 2 and 9. When the glue has set, trim each side 457mm (18in) deep.

Lamination cutting plan
Below is a plan which was drawn for the piece photographed above, and is useful mainly as a principle of economy in cutting laminations. To preserve a uniform finished edge of each table element (and because it made economic sense to cut the available boards in this way) 1 and 11 do not taper. Finally, 11 was turned on edge in the profile pattern. You might consider using hardboard templates.

Profile pattern

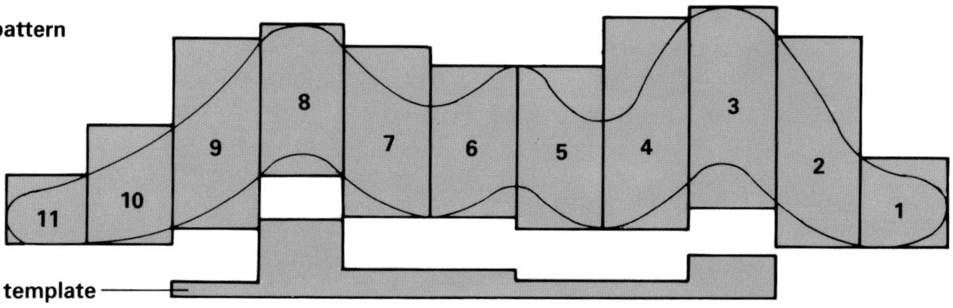

Jacking template

Carving the "drapes"
Mark out the base "drape" profile across the laminations and carve the inside (not the outside) of both panels. Carving can be done with whatever tools you prefer for this operation, but care must be exercised not to carve in the area for dovetail joints. See illustration.

"I would carve the drapery folds with a gouge, then true up with round bottom moulding planes. Sanding can be done with sanding drums mounted on a grinder or small power drill." Wendell Castle

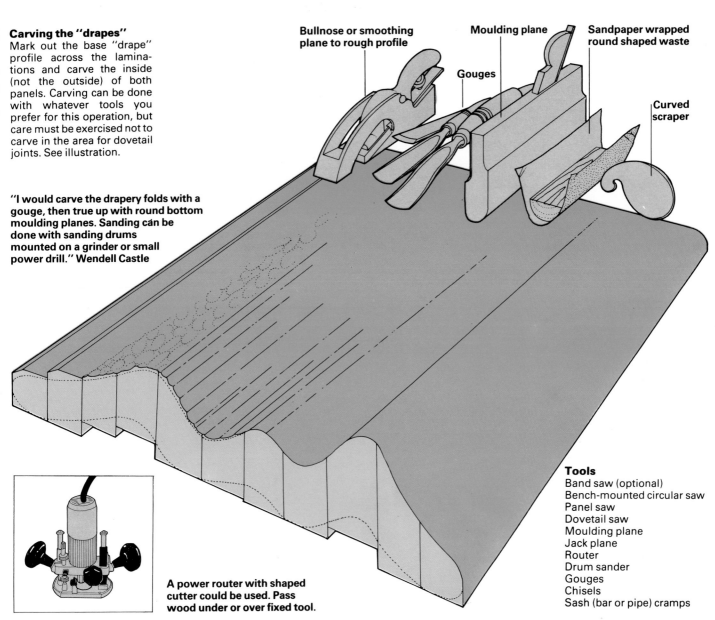

Bullnose or smoothing plane to rough profile

Moulding plane

Sandpaper wrapped round shaped waste

Gouges

Curved scraper

A power router with shaped cutter could be used. Pass wood under or over fixed tool.

Tools
Band saw (optional)
Bench-mounted circular saw
Panel saw
Dovetail saw
Moulding plane
Jack plane
Router
Drum sander
Gouges
Chisels
Sash (bar or pipe) cramps

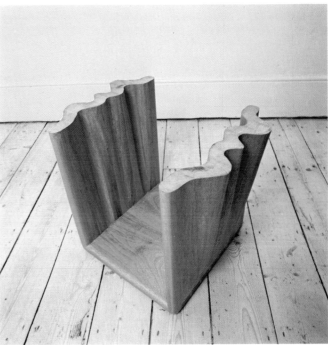

The night stand 2

Cutting the joints

1. The top can either be cut from one piece of timber or made up of glued laminations. Cut it to size then lay out and, with a sharp knife, mark out dovetails in each end.

2. The actual dovetails are cut to the very shallow angle of only 3 degrees, and since they are exposed as a feature of the design any variation will affect the finished appearance.

3. Having removed all waste from between tail members, use them as templates for marking out their mating pins to be cut into the tops of

Suggested dovetail lay-out

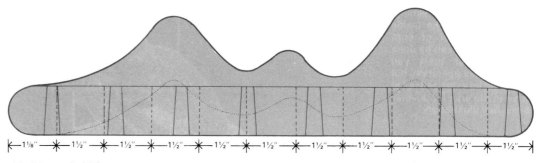

side "drapes". All four corner dovetails must be cut to a mitre with their mating side panels.

4. Now carve the outer surfaces of both sides to a rough

profile then glue to the top.

5. When the glue has set, continue carving the outside "drapes" into the area near the joints.

Radius all edges until they

are almost semi-circular, which can be achieved with a router fitted with an appropriate profile cutter for following into and around corners. Alternatively, use a moulding plane.

The dressing table ★★★★

Cutting list Mahogany:	Length	Width	Thickness
1 Top (later to be cut in three)	1067mm (42in)	410mm (16⅛in)	25mm (1in)
22 Sides	762mm (30in)	407mm (16in) variously tapering in width	38mm (1½in)
1 Through shelf	1054mm (41½in)	362mm (14¼in)	25mm (1in)
1 Rear panel	1054mm (41½in)	152mm (6in)	25mm (1in)
2 Well sides	362mm (14¼in)	140mm (5½in)	25mm (1in)
*1 Flap drop	356mm (14in)	134mm (5¼in)	20mm (¾in)

Drawers			
*2 Fronts	330mm (13in)	127mm (5in)	20mm (¾in)
2 Backs	298mm (11¾in)	89mm (3½in)	12mm (½in)
2 Sides	350mm (13¾in)	102mm (4in)	12mm (½in)
2 Bases (plywood)	343mm (13½in)	289mm (11⅜in)	4mm (³⁄₁₆in)
3 Handle blocks (optional)	118mm (4⅝in)	55mm (2⅛in)	20mm (¾in)

* Double thickness measurement to follow Wendell Castle's instructions to carve eye-lid drawer pulls from drawer front panels and flap drop.

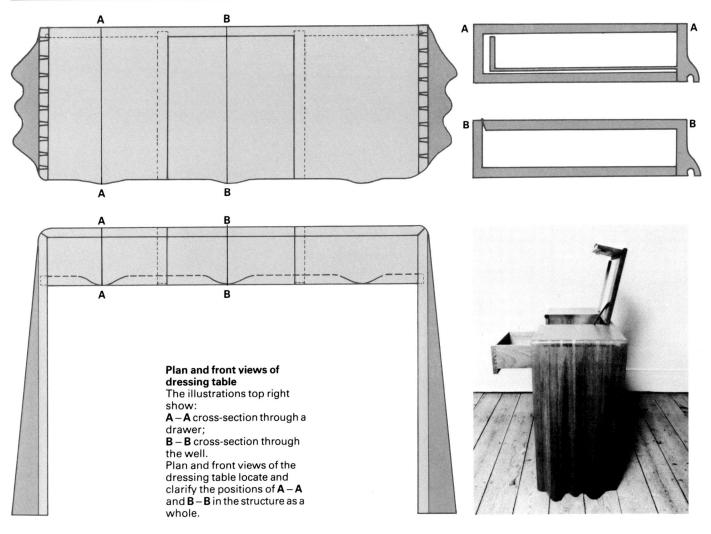

Plan and front views of dressing table

The illustrations top right show:
A – A cross-section through a drawer;
B – B cross-section through the well.
Plan and front views of the dressing table locate and clarify the positions of A – A and B – B in the structure as a whole.

The dressing table Action hints

* The outer frame of the dressing table is really a tall, long version of the night table and is similarly constructed from 38mm (1½in) mahogany. Exactly the same patterns can be used for carving the "drape" profiles and joints.
* To maintain an even grain pattern it is recommended that the three table top panels be cut from a single plank, similarly the drawer fronts and flap drop.

Jacking template and glued laminations

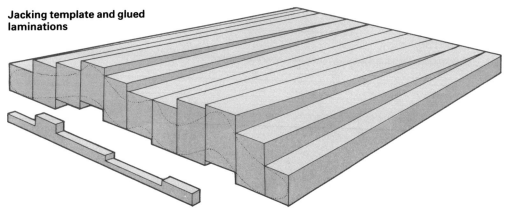

The dressing table 2

1. Make up the two side panels and top exactly as previously described for the night table but only radius the front edges leaving their back edges square. Cut to size the through shelf panel which runs the length of the unit, and also the back panel.

2. Rebate (rabbet) both ends of the shelf panel 3mm (⅛in) deep by 20mm (¾in) and cut stabilising stopped tenons 12mm (½in) from both front and rear edges. Next, cut bare-faced tongues into both ends of the rear panel.

3. Take both laminated side panels then slot and groove their inside faces to accept the stopped tenons on the through shelf, and tongues on the rear panel.

4. Dry assemble top, sides, and shelf, then mark out and cut top into its three sections.

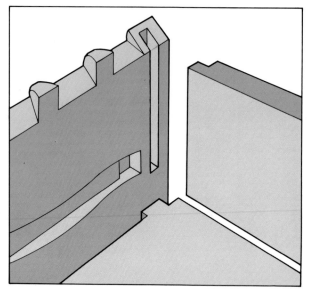

You may need to adjust the length of both the through shelf and rear panel so that the lift-up lid will fit snugly.

Rear panel

5. Recess both ends of the rear panel upon which will rest the rear edges of the flanking worktops.

To obtain a clean appearance to the centre well section of the dressing table, its side panels have mitred secret dovetail joints cut into the inner edges of both worktops. The dovetails are cut into the tops with their pins in the side panels. The well side panels' rear and bottom edges have a 3mm (⅛) rebate and are stop-tenoned 12mm (½in) into both the through shelf and rear panel. In the event, the well side panels were housed into the flanking worktops. But mitred secret dovetails are thematically consistent and preferable visually.

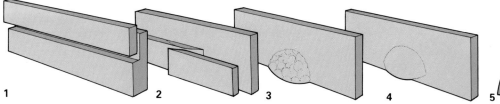

Carving drawer pulls from solid fronts, Wendell Castle's way:
1. Saw away waste from upper section of drawer front.
2. Band saw to curved drawer pull profile.
3. Hand carve to final form.
4. and 5. show bottom edge of finished pull just above bottom edge of drawer.

Drawers

1. Both drawers are of conventional design and simply rest on the through shelf. Their outer sides are flush and were built with lapped dovetails into the outer end of each front piece. The inner sides have vertical tongue and groove dovetails to facilitate front overlap. The rear panels of both drawers are lap-dovetailed into the sides – thus producing a clean appearance to the outside of drawers. See Sam Maloof's furniture for an alternative and simpler drawer construction.

Constructional illustration of drawer

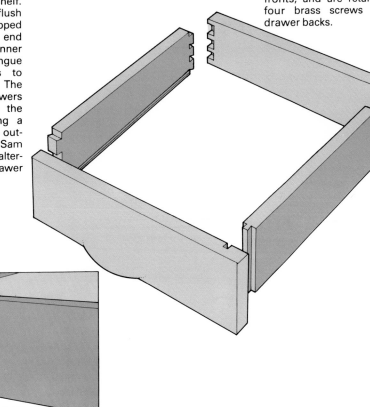

Corner detail

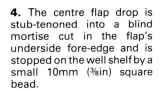

2. The plywood drawer base panels simply slide into grooves in drawer sides and fronts, and are retained by four brass screws to the drawer backs.

3. Handle pulls for drawer and flap drop were shaped from blocks which had first been roughed out, then glued in position and finally blended into the panels to appear as if they had been carved from the drawer fronts. This method is less attractive than Wendell Castle's method illustrated on the previous page which preserves a consistent grain pattern across drawer faces.

4. The centre flap drop is stub-tenoned into a blind mortise cut in the flap's underside fore-edge and is stopped on the well shelf by a small 10mm (3/8in) square bead.

5. Two battens with stopped recesses were mounted on the underside of the centre flap and hold a 305mm (12in) square mirror tile to act as a looking glass.

6. The flap itself is mounted on two 50mm (2in) recessed brass hinges. A single brass folding stay is mounted in the right-hand side of the well to hold the flap in an inclined back position when open.

The chest of drawers ★ ★ ★ ★

Cutting list Mahogany:	Length	Width	Thickness
1 Top	1308mm (51½in)	508mm (20in)	32mm (1¼in)
28 Sides	915mm (36in)	variously tapering	38mm (1½in)
2 Back panels (plywood)	686mm (27in)	635mm (25in)	6mm (¼in)
1 Back rail (rear)	1283mm (50½in)	76mm (3in)	32mm (1¼in)
Drawer frames			
8 Long members	1283mm (50½in)	76mm (3in)	25mm (1in)
12 Cross members	356mm (14in)	76mm (3in)	25mm (1in)
2 Centre dividers	750mm (29½in)	95mm (3¾in)	25mm (1in)
4 Drawer dividers	260mm (10¼in)	38mm (1½in)	25mm (1in)
8 Drawer runners	407mm (16in)	38mm (1½in)	25mm (1in)

Drawers			
*2 Fronts	610mm (24in)	121mm (4¾in)	20mm (¾in)
*6 Fronts	610mm (24in)	203mm (8in)	20mm (¾in)
2 Backs	604mm (23¾in)	80mm (3⅛in)	12mm (½in)
6 Backs	604mm (23¾in)	162mm (6⅜in)	12mm (½in)
4 Sides	458mm (18in)	95mm (3¾in)	12mm (½in)
12 Sides	457mm (18in)	178mm (7in)	12mm (½in)
8 Bottoms (plywood)	445mm (17½in)	597mm (23½in)	6mm (¼in)
8 Handle blocks (optional)	118mm (4⅝in)	55mm (2⅛in)	20mm (¾in)

*Double thickness measurement to follow Wendell Castle's instructions to carve eye-lid drawer pulls from drawer front panels.

Chest of drawer carcase showing top and bottom drawer frames only

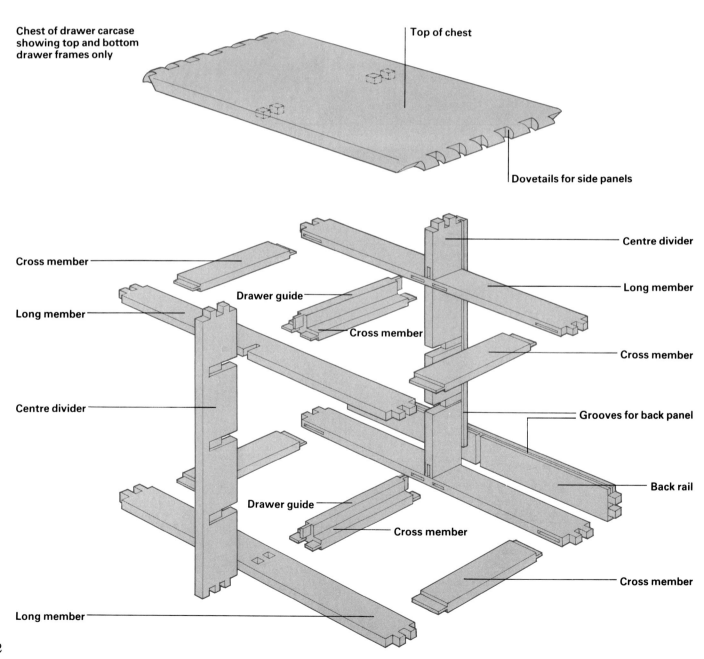

Top of chest

Dovetails for side panels

Cross member

Long member

Drawer guide

Cross member

Centre divider

Centre divider

Long member

Long member

Drawer guide

Cross member

Cross member

Long member

Cross member

Grooves for back panel

Back rail

Cross member

The carcase

The carcase consists of four horizontal frames which carry eight drawers, a central division, back rail, top, sides and back panels.

Using the same principle as before to cut the laminations, make up the two shaped side panels exactly as previously described. Take care not only to avoid carving in the area for top dovetails, but also to remove a minimum of wood in the area for jointing framework. In fact only the side panel bases need good profiles on their inner faces.

Do not cut the top corner dovetails until a good square fit with horizontal frames has first been achieved.

1. Mark both side panels for cutting to length then square across their inner faces for stub-tenon mortises and recesses for drawer runners. Cut out the recesses for drawer runners but do not chop out the mortises until after the frames have been made.

Lamination position for chest of drawers

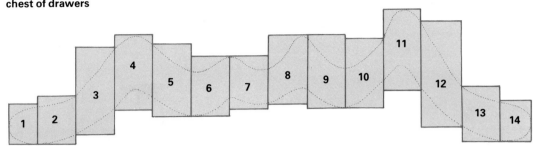

Profile pattern – depth and width measurements

*1. 1″ × 1½″
2. 1½″ × 1¾″
3. 1½″ × 3″
4. 1½″ × 2½″
5. 1½″ × 2⅞″
6. 1½″ × 2⅜″
7. 1½″ × 1⅞″
8. 1½″ × 2¼″
9. 1½″ × 3″
10. 1½″ × 2⅜″
11. 1½″ × 3″
12. 1½″ × 3¾″
13. 1½″ × 1⅞″
*14. 1″ × 1½″

*Boards 1 and 14 were turned on edge when constructing the profile.

Jacking template

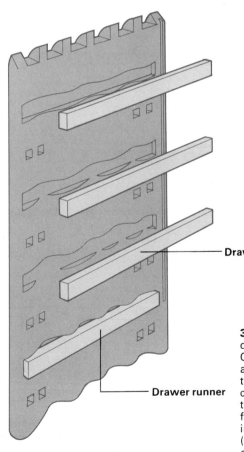

Drawer runner

Drawer runner

2. Make up the four horizontal frames according to the cutting list and detail drawing and assemble them dry to check they are square and identical.

3. Cut the two central vertical dividing members to length. Cut out their stopped tenons at top ends and through tenons on bottom ends. Then cut cross halving joints to take the top three drawer frames. These halvings turn into stopped housings (dadoes) on each side of the centre dividers. Then cut four mortise slots for the tenons of the drawer dividers. The rear vertical member must be grooved to accept the two back panels and notched at its base for the back rail.

4. Dismantle the four horizontal frames and cut their end tenons which will enter the side panel stopped mortises. Cut the long frame members to fit snugly into place on the two centre dividers. Cut mortises in the bottom frame long members to house the centre divider through tenons. Finally, cut stopped tenons at both ends of the back rail, and groove to accept the back panel.

5. Returning to the side panels, carefully chop out the stopped mortises for frame tenons and back rail. Cut, glue and insert the eight drawer runners so that their surfaces are flush with the most intrusive inner folds of the "drapes", thus providing a constant surface against which the drawer sides can run.

113

The chest of drawers 2

Assembly

1. Assemble the frontal sections of the four horizontal frames by gluing the cross members and drawer dividers into the four front members. Plug the four rear horizontal members onto the protruding tenons (all these mortise and tenons remain dry to take up contraction in the event of shrinkage). Then press home both front and rear vertical members.

2. Offer up the frame assembly to the two side panels and dry cramp the whole structure, then check for squareness.

3. Lay the top in position and mark all round for the two sets of dovetails, blind mortises to accept the centre divider top tenons, and grooves for back panels.

4. Dismantle the whole structure and, taking the two side panels, carve their outside faces as previously described.

5. Cut dovetail joints and mitre all four corners then cut all grooves for back panels.

6. Finally re-assemble by gluing all joints save those tenons to remain dry (see **1.** above).

7. Cut the two plywood back panels to size and slide them into position. Do not glue – these should remain dry.

8. Apply glue to dovetail pins and assemble with top. All three front edges of the chest are radiused in the same manner as previously described for the night table.

Drawers

All eight drawers are of conventional design – see also Sam Maloof's drawers for a simplified approach. The only unusual feature being the handles which are a pleasing relief from the common metal, porcelain, or even wooden knobs.

Front panels on all drawers lap their side-panel dovetails so they are invisible from the front when the drawers are closed. Their rear panel dovetails are lapped by the side panels which produces a smoother running drawer and "cleaner" appearance when the drawer has been completely withdrawn from the carcase.

The 6mm (¼in) plywood bottoms slide between grooves in sides and "plug" into the front panels. They are retained by four countersunk screws passing into their rear panels.

1. Refer to Wendell Castle's instructions for carving drawer pulls from drawer fronts – page 110. Alternatively, if attaching separate handle blocks, glue them on now in a roughly pre-shaped form. When carving to finish, be particularly careful not to cut into the front panels' surfaces. Best results may, therefore, be achieved with diminishing grades of sandpaper.

Constructional illustration of chest drawer

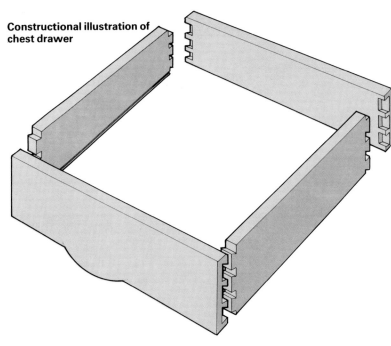

The bed ends ⟨★ ★ ★⟩

Cutting list Mahogany:	Length	Width	Thickness
4 Rails	787mm (31in)	102mm (4in)	38mm (1½in)
2 Fielded centre panels	686mm (27in)	305mm (12in)	38mm (1½in)
Carved panels			
22 Headboard	864mm (34in)	variously tapering	38mm (1½in)
22 Footboard	533mm (21in)	variously tapering	38mm (1½in)

If required: Two rails 127mm (5in) by 32mm (1½in) by length of mattress.

The double bed
The bed can be built to suit most size requirements. For instance; for Queen size, increase mattress dimensions to 1524mm by 2032mm (60in by 80in); and for King size to 1930mm by 2032mm (76in by 80in). Increase the length by extending the mattress rails, increase the width by extending the panels and their top and bottom rails.

115

The bed ends 2

1. First, cut out the four panel cross rails which have 64mm (2½in) by 12mm (½in) tenons at each end. The two top rails have mitred haunches on their tenons to counteract any twisting at the tops of joints where it would really show.

Constructional illustrations of head and foot assemblies

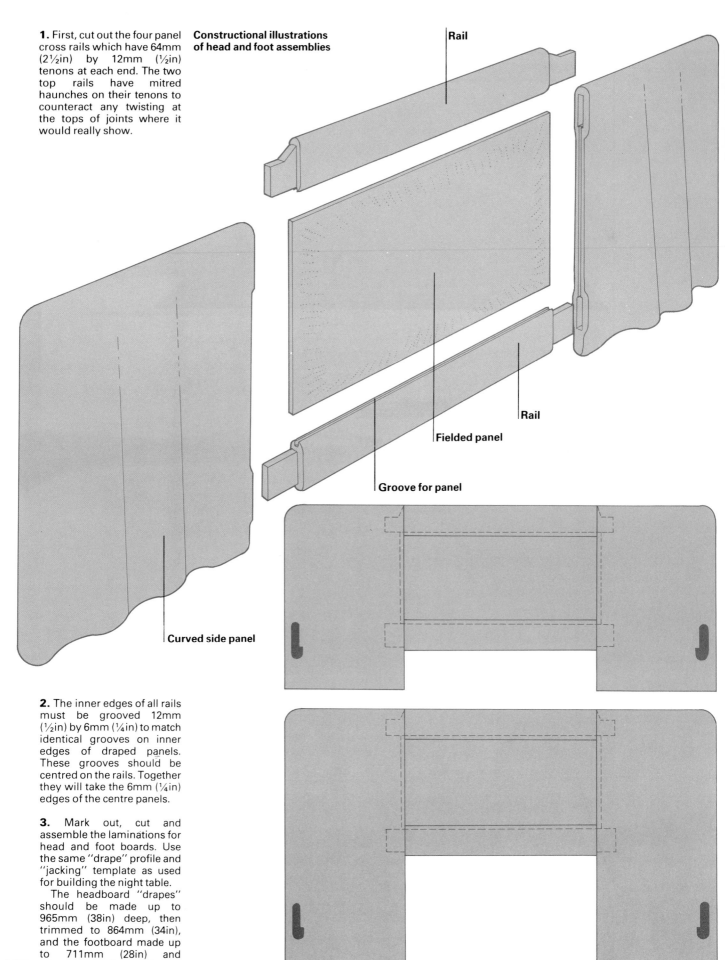

Rail

Rail

Fielded panel

Groove for panel

Curved side panel

2. The inner edges of all rails must be grooved 12mm (½in) by 6mm (¼in) to match identical grooves on inner edges of draped panels. These grooves should be centred on the rails. Together they will take the 6mm (¼in) edges of the centre panels.

3. Mark out, cut and assemble the laminations for head and foot boards. Use the same "drape" profile and "jacking" template as used for building the night table.

The headboard "drapes" should be made up to 965mm (38in) deep, then trimmed to 864mm (34in), and the footboard made up to 711mm (28in) and trimmed to 610mm (24in).

4. Next, glue up the two inner laminations on each of the four "drape" panels (those that accept tenons from panel cross rails and are glued flush together) and cut their mortise slots and panel grooves before assembly with their mating laminations.

5. Dry cramp both head and foot assemblies and radius all inner edges and corners, then dismantle.

**The fielded centre panels
Action hints**
* The centre panels on both boards are fielded from a curved dome centre of 38mm (1½in) thick down to 6mm (¼in) all round. This operation requires a great deal of hand work which can be drastically reduced with the aid of a power router inverted and fitted with a domed cutter over which the panels can be passed (see illustration). The panels can be reduced to a final finish with sandpaper.

* Both boards must be assembled in one operation. When the glue has set, radius all outer edges and finally sandpaper to a smooth finish.

* If the mattress base is a naked metal spring frame, then the two long rails should be cut to cradle and hide both it and the bed rail hooks. Alternatively, the frame could simply be bolted to the hooks but here some device to maintain rigidity and prevent racking would be necessary. A divan base would require another and quite different type of fitting. The mattress and its type of base will determine whatever fitting is most suitable.

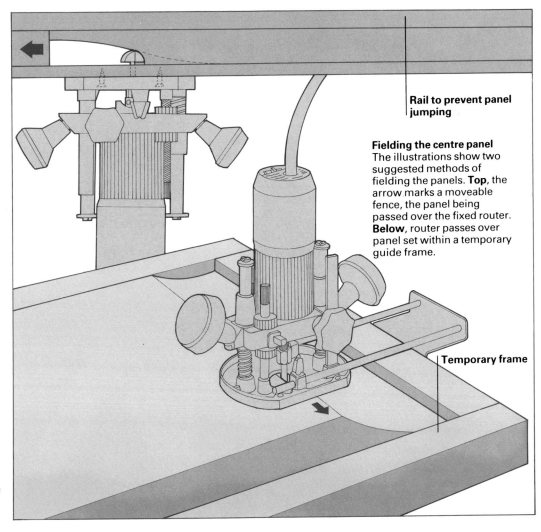

Rail to prevent panel jumping

Fielding the centre panel
The illustrations show two suggested methods of fielding the panels. **Top,** the arrow marks a moveable fence, the panel being passed over the fixed router. **Below,** router passes over panel set within a temporary guide frame.

Temporary frame

117

The garden by Ashley Cartwright

"When I left school I went through the conventional art college system which in England starts with a year's foundation course to enable you to decide in which direction to go. While I was at school I didn't really consider that I would end up as a designer/maker because the idea that I would be a practical person ran contrary to the academic feeling of the school. It was at *Kingston on Thames Art College* that I was guided into furniture design. In retrospect, had I not been steered away from a single-minded concentration on ideas and drawing into the practical side, I would have been very frustrated.

"Prior to my final term at college I applied and was accepted for a place in the Furniture Department of the *Royal College of Art*. The RCA was another even more significant turning point. My college diploma course had involved three-dimensional design in various materials, but now I began to get involved in wood as a subject. This was due to David Pye, who was there at the time – his enthusiasm rubbed off on me. It was there too that I decided not to launch myself into industry but become involved in my *own* work.

"When I finished my time there I applied for a job with John Makepeace

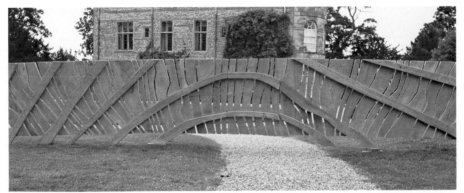

and I was with him for about three years, after which I began to set up my own workshop. With John I spent half my time designing and the other half actually making one-off pieces for private clients, businesses, etc. The process was as follows: the brief would come in that someone wanted a certain piece of work; we would start throwing ideas around and get prices sorted out; sketch designs and costs would then go back to the customer.

"In retrospect, the point that was most useful from my time with John was the practical side. I left with a fair idea of construction, an ability to make things in

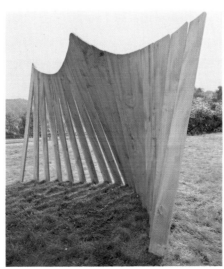

a precise manner, which I certainly didn't have when I left the RCA. There I had the strong intention and desire to design and make, but not enough practical know-how. Also of course, designing in a professional situation, rather than the 'pretend' professional situation which one has at college, is exceptionally useful in preparation for setting up an independent workshop."

Designing your own furniture

"Look at the problems that you (or the client in my case) want to solve. The brief one gives oneself is only the starting point, since clearly how to support something two feet above the ground, for example, may be answered in a variety of different ways.

"It is essential to visit the place where the piece will be. Get the dimensions, the feel, the light quality, the size, the colours

The garden 2

around. Then go away with an open mind.

"Then of course there are personal preferences. One person may prefer soft curved work; others go for angular work. Do you want a round dining table or a square one?

"The wood is another very important factor. I take samples of various timbers to clients. What is most suitable in terms of the quality of the room, the other work that happens to be around, etc? Should it be a certain colour, light tone or dark tone? What about the grain? Should the timber be highly figured? These are all starting points too.

"Function is also a starting point.

"These are all factors from which I let my abstract ideas stem. The fact that one has a specific problem to solve actually helps. If everything is open, it's more tricky just because you *can* do anything.

"I like to marshal the facts without thinking about the job. Then I sit down with my lay-out pad and see what comes along. If you were to look at these pads, you'd see page after page of unrecognisable drawings. *If you think about something directly, it is the worst thing you can do.* I encourage students to approach the job by *not* thinking about it.

I mean, if you think about 'a table' you are already calling up a picture in your mind's eye of a table. It is too difficult to keep away from non-abstract things. But everything is abstract until it is labelled. If you went out into the street and asked what a table looks like, I can be pretty sure that you'd come back in here with a square or rectangle and probably four legs. But that is not what a table is of course. There are a million other ways – or at least one wants to think that there are.

"The ability to draw is not an essential element in good furniture design. Although it is the quickest and most direct method of recording ideas, often details have a way of changing as you react to the material, etc. But the illustration below

did for once happen absolutely according to my full-size drawing. It was as it came; it worked! It also happened to come from an idea uninhibited by someone else's brief; it was an idea I just wanted to realise.

"It is made out of a number of pieces of wood approximately 25mm (1in) wide and glued together on their side to form a surface. What's nice is that you have got a pattern forming from grain and colour changes as the grain moves from one piece to the next across the surface. You cannot attain this same effect by pro-

ducing a flat surface from boards in the normal way. Additionally the depth of each piece was staggered, so across the side of the table there is a variation in thickness as well."

"Ashley's relaxed approach to design, and his very direct approach to making things seem particularly appropriate to this book. Without technical wizardry, the designs are visually and structurally exciting – it's often the way!"
John Makepeace

Introduction to the garden furniture

"I have used two species of Ulmus – English elm and wych elm – for my series of garden furniture, the main difference being in their grain pattern.

"English elm is tough and close-textured – you will notice this particularly when working across the grain. Its twisty cross-grain contributes to its very attractive figure and has the added bonus of being very unlikely to split. The swirling effect of its grain is further enhanced by its reddish-brown colour peppered with small red pip knots. Additionally, English elm is ideally suited to damp conditions. Of course the wood is bound to move in sympathy with prevailing atmospheric humidity, but the design has allowed for this, and there should be no problem in each piece of furniture remaining structurally sound.

"Wych elm, is straighter grained and slightly lighter in colour. I have used it for the structural parts of the various pieces, such as the legs for the small table and small stools. The mild colour difference between the species presents no visual problems since direct sun will soon bleach all the wood to a very interesting grey colour.

"Structurally, and because of its natural earthy appearance, elm is really an ideal choice of timber for use outdoors and is, by comparison with many other hardwoods, inexpensive."

Treating the wood

"You will need to treat the wood against rot and insect attack. Various brand name rot proofers and insect repellants are available from your local hardware store. Increasingly though, local sawmills are providing a retail service for all finishing and fixing requirements, and even tools. You should submerge the wood in a bath of the preservative solution – make one by folding a polythene sheet over a perimeter of house bricks.

Finishes

"I do not recommend a polyurethane (or similar) varnish – the ultraviolet rays of the sun, together with the effect of direct rainfall, will soon have it peeling away leaving a nasty discoloured appearance. After treating the pieces, allow them to dry and finish with linseed oil or some similar natural finish. You can periodically apply further coats to ensure a year-round protected finish."

Tools

"The tools you need will depend on whether or not you plan to prepare and shape the timber yourself. If you make it absolutely clear what it is you want, you will find sawmills happy to do the job. If you want to do your own cutting and do not have access to a band saw, use a jig (saber) saw or mounted circular saw and plane to finish."

The large table ★ ★ ★ ★

Cutting list Elm:	Length	Width	Thickness
4 Table tops, each made up from			
9 strips as – 1		140mm (5½in)	35mm (1⅜in)
2		130mm (5⅛in)	35mm (1⅜in)
2		120mm (4¾in)	35mm (1⅜in)
2		110mm (4¼in)	35mm (1⅜in)
2		115mm (4½in)	35mm (1⅜in)
4 Legs, each made up from 4 boards	1430mm (56¼in)	245mm (9⅝in)	35mm (1⅜in)
Oak:			
1 Base made up from 8 strips as – 4	900mm (35½in)	60mm (2⅜in)	60mm (2⅜in)
4	300mm (11⅞in)	60mm (2⅜in)	60mm (2⅜in)
Marine plywood	340mm (13⅜in)	340mm (13⅜in)	25mm (1in)
Metal – angle iron, 4 underframes each	790mm (31⅛in)	790mm (31⅛in)	32mm (1¼in)

Tools

Jack plane
12mm (½in) mortise chisel
Screwdriver
Electric drill with 12mm (½in)/20mm (¾in) flat bits, 12mm (½in) plug cutter, 6mm (¼in) drill bit, and 12mm (½in) dowel bit
Bradawl
G-cramps
Adjustable spanner
Wire brush
25mm (1in) paint brush
Jig (saber) saw
Cross cut saw

Alternative design suggestions

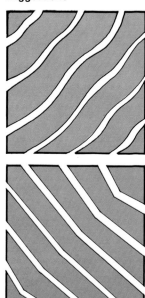

Preparation

1. Make a full-size drawing.

2. The legs are the most demanding feature. It might be useful to make hardboard templates of most parts prior to marking the wood. It might also be worth considering making a full-size mock-up (say in 20mm (¾in) chipboard) of one of the legs in order to produce the correct angles and height from the ground.

The table top

1. The table top is divided into four separate sections. There is no rule as to how you should make up each of these sections provided the eventual result comprises four 860mm (33¾in) square top sections. The large table illustrated was made from 9 strips of wood as detailed in the cutting list. It will be noticed that the corner (shortest) strips are 115mm (4½in) wide rather than 105mm (3¾in) which might have been expected in the progression down from the central 140mm (5½in) strip. As it happens, besides serving its purpose, the corner strips look no wider than their adjacent strips in the finished construction.

Alternative tops you might care to consider include using boards (strips) with wavy, wandering, or curved edges.

2. The strips have been spaced 15mm (⅝in) apart to give the table top a floating appearance.

3. Cartwright suggests that you cut hardboard templates for each of the strips, draw round the templates onto the elm boards and then cut into strips.

Constructional illustration of large garden table

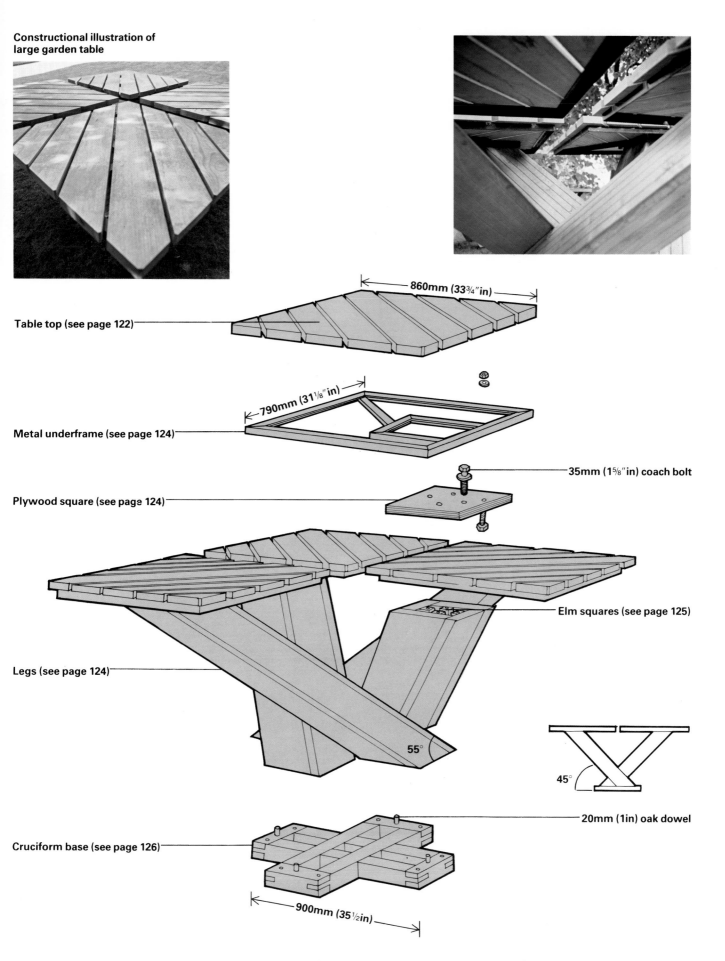

Table top (see page 122)

860mm (33¾"in)

Metal underframe (see page 124)

790mm (31⅛"in)

35mm (1⅝"in) coach bolt

Plywood square (see page 124)

Elm squares (see page 125)

Legs (see page 124)

55°

45°

20mm (1in) oak dowel

Cruciform base (see page 126)

900mm (35½in)

The large table 2

The metal underframe

1. The underframe *must* be made of metal, for strength without bulk – each table top will be supported near one edge of the frame by its corresponding leg. It is by far the best solution. A.C. suggests that you seek out your local blacksmith or any metal worker with access to oxy-acetylene equipment. He will do the job easily and quickly. Each frame cost A.C. about £5.00 ($12.50). Draw the shape full size and make a hard-board template. Take it along to the blacksmith and he will lay the metal on the template and braze it straight away.

Each metal underframe is made out of 32mm (1¼in) angle iron, mitred and brazed at its corners. The inset is 350mm (13¾in) square. The diagonal metal shaft hits the inner square 135mm (5¼in) from corner A as shown in the illustration. Each frame

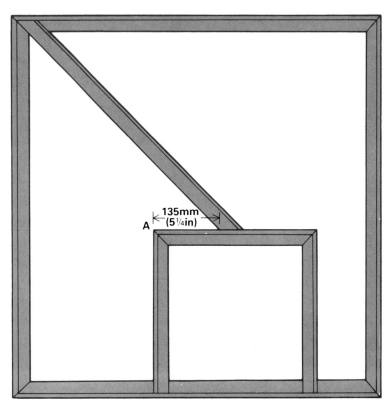

will measure 790mm (31in) square so that each wooden top section will protrude 35mm (1⅜in) beyond its edges.

2. Drill five holes into the inner square of the metal frame to take 35mm (1⅜in) coach bolts – one either side of where the diagonal metal shaft meets the inner square, and one centred on every other side of the inner square. The bolts will eventually attach the frame to a ply-wood square, and thence the leg.

3. Clean the underframe with a wire brush, and prime it with red lead primer, and then paint it first with an undercoat, and, when dry, with a coloured exterior gloss of your choice. Ashley Cartwright wanted it to 'dis-appear' and chose a colour similar to the wood.

The plywood square

1. Cut four squares of 25mm (1in) thick Marine plywood measuring 340mm (13⅜in). Think of each square as a transition between the leg and the table top. It provides a strong base for the framed top. The angled metal frame is L-shaped in cross-section and would provide less stable a construction if fastened directly onto the leg. The ply is also an im-portant factor in minimising any tendency for the legs to twist.

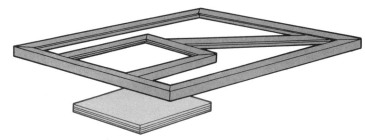

2. In each plywood square drill five holes to correspond with the five 35mm (1⅜in) coach bolt holes which you have already drilled in the inner square of the under-frame. Do not affix the bolts at this stage.

The legs

1. Cut to size and *make sure that the edges and surfaces are absolutely square.* As already suggested, it might be a good idea to make a full-size 20mm (¾in) chipboard model of one leg before attempting to mark out the elm. Whether you choose to or not, you might consider using a hardboard template.

2. Having set the bevel to an angle of 55 degrees against a protractor and cut the tem-plate, draw the template shape onto each prepared board. Remember that the template will have to be reversed to mark two of the boards in each leg.

3. Using the cross cut saw cut the meat of the waste

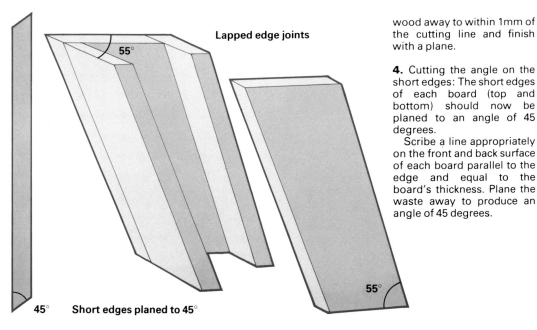

Lapped edge joints

45° **Short edges planed to 45°**

wood away to within 1mm of the cutting line and finish with a plane.

4. Cutting the angle on the short edges: The short edges of each board (top and bottom) should now be planed to an angle of 45 degrees.

Scribe a line appropriately on the front and back surface of each board parallel to the edge and equal to the board's thickness. Plane the waste away to produce an angle of 45 degrees.

5. Cutting the angle on the long edges: The long edges of each board (its side edges) should next be planed to an angle of 55 degrees.

Draw a cross-section through the board, measure the 55 degree angle appropriately and scribe lines down the front and back surfaces parallel to the edge to be planed away and the correct distance away from it.

6. When completed and assembled each leg should present a top horizontal plane 300mm (11¾in) square. Into the long edges, bore holes for 60mm (2¼in) galvanised screws to be countersunk 12mm (½in) below the surface and then plugged.

Action hint
*Notice that Ashley Cartwright has made a virtue of the inevitable lapped edge line down each side of each leg by routing extra grooves equidistant from these lines across the face edge of each leg.

7. Cut 16 pieces of elm 50mm (2in) square (an approximate measurement only), glue and cramp each of them centrally to the top inside surface of each board as shown in the illustration. These will provide additional strength to the construction when the plywood squares are fitted.

Attaching the plywood squares

Each plywood square should protrude approximately 20mm (¾in) over each leg top. Prime and paint each square prior to fixing. Fix each square with 100mm (4in) coach screws.

Attaching the table top strips

1. Lay the strips face down on a flat surface and place the metal underframe face down on top of them. The object is to secure each strip onto the metal frame in three places along each strip's length with 30mm (1¼in) round-headed japanned screws. This will have the effect of minimising any future movement across the strips.

2. Calculate where to bore the holes in the underframe, and when drilled replace the frame in position on the wooden strips marking them for drilling with a bradawl.

3. Drill accordingly and secure all but two strips (marked X on the illustration).

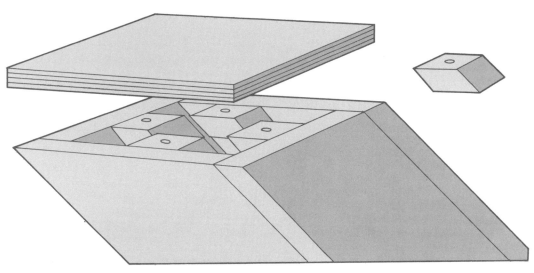

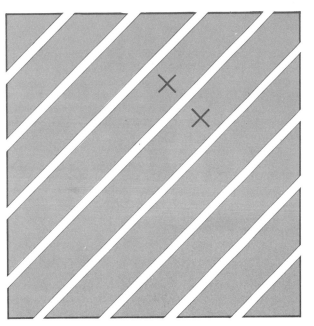

Securing the legs into position

1. Before securing the tops to the plywood squares, assemble the four legs into position. Since the legs lean at 45 degrees you will need assistance to hold the assembly into position as you work.

2. Turn all four legs upside down in position. Secure each adjacent leg with a 75mm (3in) coach bolt and washers.

125

The large table 3

How to establish where to drill the holes for the coach bolts

There are three ways to do this:

1. Mark a line around the face of each leg where it touches the next. The shape will look like this:

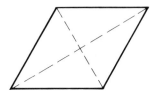

Draw diagonal lines through the centre of the shape. Where they meet, drill the hole.

2. Make a hardboard template of the above shape and apply appropriately to each leg.

3. Establish, by 1. above, where the holes should be drilled in one leg. Tap in a panel pin (finishing nail). Pinch off its head. Set the leg into position with the next and a corresponding pin point will be set.

Once you have drilled the holes, secure the bolts into position and grease thoroughly to prevent rusting.

Securing the frame onto the marine plywood square

1. The two table top strips were left off the frame to enable you to attach the frame to the plywood square. Drill five holes to correspond with the holes already drilled into the inner square of the metal frame, and secure.

2. The heads of the bolts should then be countersunk into the underside of the wooden strips that have yet to be secured to the metal frame.

3. Lastly, secure the strips to the frame.

Making and securing the table base to the structure

1. The cruciform base presents four 300mm (11⅞in) squares projecting from each side of a central 300mm (11⅞in) square. Make the base from well-seasoned oak. It should be 60mm (2⅜in) thick. For maximum strength the corner joints should be lapped as shown in the illustration on page 123.

2. They should have a 12mm (½in) dowel drilled and knocked through the centre of the joint and should be glued, although the corners will remain strong as dry joints.

3. House one section of the base into the other as illustrated. Use the edges of the top section to mark the recesses in the lower section. Cut and chisel.

4. Assemble, glue and cramp.

5. Coat the base with bitumen or creosote.

6. Then set a 20mm (¾in) oak dowel 25mm (1in) long into the centre of each of the four sides. The dowels should be slightly pointed or domed to fit into corresponding holes in the centre of the outer edge of each leg. These dowels act simply as vertical location points for the legs (i.e. they prevent any sideways movement). They are not active in stabilizing the table which will be kept stable by its weight.

7. Bury the base in the lawn (or wet concrete if on a patio) so that the bases of the legs are flush with its surface.

Drill a hole approximately 20mm (¾in) in diameter between the legs to allow for drainage.

The small table and stool ★★

The table top
1. Secure the 4 boards making up the table top 17mm (⅝in) apart with 12mm (½in) dowel set at 55mm (2⅛in) and 235mm (9¼in) from each edge.

Action hint
*The dowel could from a structural point of view be round, and bought in lengths from any supplier. But 12mm (½in) square dowel was used for the small table and stool units and mortised into the wood strips so that the cross-section of the dowel presented a diamond shape.

It is interesting what difference a little extra work can make to the design of these pieces. Light is picked up on one edge of the dowel, shadow falling on the adjacent edge, so highlighting what otherwise would be a fairly plain structural necessity. A further design consideration confirmed that this was the very best solution. The shape of the dowel relates perfectly to the shape of every other component of the table and stools.

2. If the boards are 30mm (1⅛in) thick, mark the end grain of one board thus:

Action hints
*It is not neccessary to score the side of the dowelling to let the glue traverse the wood when inserting the dowel, provided you drill the

dowel hole a few mm longer than the dowel and don't use an excessive amount of glue.
*It is also a very good idea *not* to glue the two middle dowels in each wooden strip. Leave them tight but dry to allow for any movement across the width of the top.

3. Bore the dowel holes at least 30mm (1⅛in) into the boards. Use a mortise bit if you have a drill stand. Alternatively bore the boards with a dowel bit and square the hole with a 12mm (½in) mortise chisel. Great care should be taken to drill these holes square to the boards.

Cutting list Elm:	Length	Width	Thickness
1 Table top made from 4 boards	650mm (25⅝in)	150mm (5⅞in)	30mm (1⅛in)
4 Legs	990mm (39in)	64mm (2½in) square cross-section	

127

The small table and stool 2

The legs
1. Cut the 4 legs to the specifications given, out of one board, setting a bevel to an angle of 75 degrees.

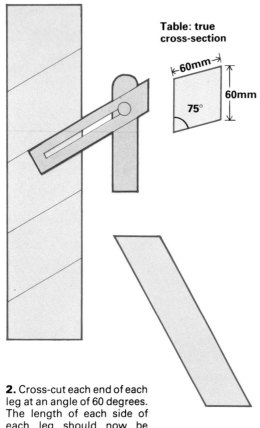

Constructional illustration of small garden table and stool

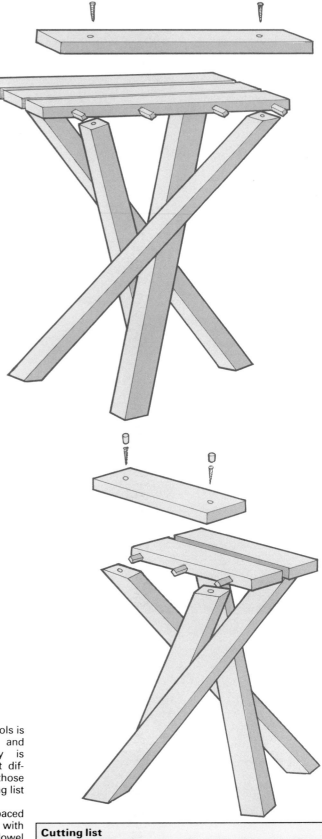

Table: true cross-section

60mm × 60mm, 75°

2. Cross-cut each end of each leg at an angle of 60 degrees. The length of each side of each leg should now be 940mm (37in) to give a 750mm (29½in) distance from ground to table top.

3. Secure each leg to the next with 64mm (2½in) zinc galvanised screws (to prevent rust), countersunk and plugged. As with the large table, in assembling the table legs enlist help to hold the structure together while you mark for drill holes (see section on large table for further assembly points). The holes will be 420mm (16½in) from the base of each leg.

Stool: true cross-section

45mm × 45mm, 75°

Final assembly
1. Having assembled the table top and legs independently, position the top face down on a flat surface. With the legs placed symmetrically on the underside of the top, mark round them with a pencil. Turn the table right way up and re-position the top to your pencil marks.

2. Drill appropriately and secure both parts together with 38mm (1½in) screws, countersink and plug.

The garden stool
The structure of the stools is similar to the table and method of assembly is identical. Measurement differences other than those mentioned on the cutting list are given as follows:

The seat boards are spaced 20mm (¾in) apart, with 12mm (½in) square dowel set 45mm (1¾in) from each edge and one located in the centre.

The final cut length of the legs (600mm (23⅝in)) gives a seat height of 475mm (18¾in).

Cutting list Elm:	Length	Width	Thickness
4 Seats, each made from 3 boards:	325mm (12¾in)	95mm (3¾in)	20mm (¾in)
16 legs, each made from boards:	630mm (24¾in)	50mm (2in)	50mm (2in)

The fence and gate ☒

Once again, consider possible design variations to suit your needs and taste. There is no need as such for the top and bottom edges of the boards to be straight – they could flow like the tops of the screen. There is a real opportunity here to determine not only the eventual height and width of each board (measurements which are bound to depend upon your own needs anyway – a short low fence requires appropriately narrower boards, for example) but also the actual design. Sketch out rough ideas, but leave things flexible where possible allowing the characteristics of the wood itself to determine the shapes.

As can be seen in the photograph, although the boards were cut to shape by the sawmill they were deliberately left unplaned and the band saw marks made their own contribution to the design.

As Cartwright sees it, the structure is an attempt to break away from the rigid formal appearance of most barriers – hedgerows excepted. How far you go with it is up to you, but it is essential that the gate be an integral part of the whole design. He has so arranged his design that the gate is positioned at the point in the fence where the boards are almost upright. There's a practical sense to the thing too, since hinging the gate would be extremely awkward if attempted at an angle. Another design point, keep all hardware simple and unobtrusive, otherwise it will interfere with the rhythm set up within the line of the fence.

The fence and gate 2

Cutting the boards

Draw the general shape of the fence and then play around in cutting specific templates which may be a reaction to grain patterns in the wood, colour changes, irregularities, whatever. The most important point to remember is that each adjacent side edge matches the next – see illustration of three 'matching' boards. If you cut a template with a view to marking a shape onto one board, move it along so that the right-hand contour is marked on the left-hand edge of the board next along to the right. Similarly, the template's other contour will match the shape of the other adjacent board's right-hand edge.

When you have marked the boards, cramp each in turn on a saw horse and use a jig saw to cut the shapes.

Connecting the boards with rails

Connect the boards with rails cut to counteract the general lean of the fence. The rails may form a fairly clean curve or wander – see illustration. Countersink 50mm (2in) galvanised screws to connect the boards to the rails. If you plug the screw holes (and Cartwright thinks you should), it may be an idea not to tap the plugs level with the surface. He left them slightly raised so that when a shadow is cast along the fence they present an agreeable pattern.

Connecting the supporting posts

The supporting posts can lean with the flow of the fence and need not be parallel. There is no special value in structural terms for the posts to be upright. Vertical lines, parallel surfaces, right angles . . . have no real place in the construction as I conceive it. See what you think.

First mark and cut the posts. Then sink them into the ground separately. Bring the fence up to the posts and see where they will connect. Bore holes, countersink, and plug as above.

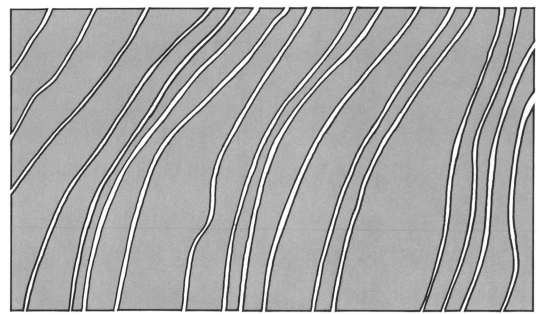

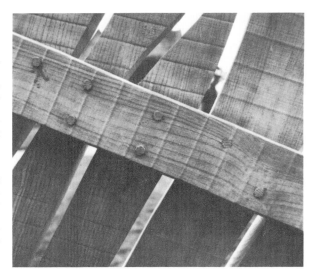

The gate

As mentioned above, the gate should be an integral part of the design of the

fence. Two 100mm (4in) galvanised steel butt hinges will form a visually unobtrusive means to securing the gate. One point – make sure that the edge shapes of fence and gate boards at this juncture allow for the gate to open easily. Finally, the fence rails on the other side of the gate should protrude about 25mm (1in) into the gate opening to act as a stop when the gate closes.

The screen ⊠

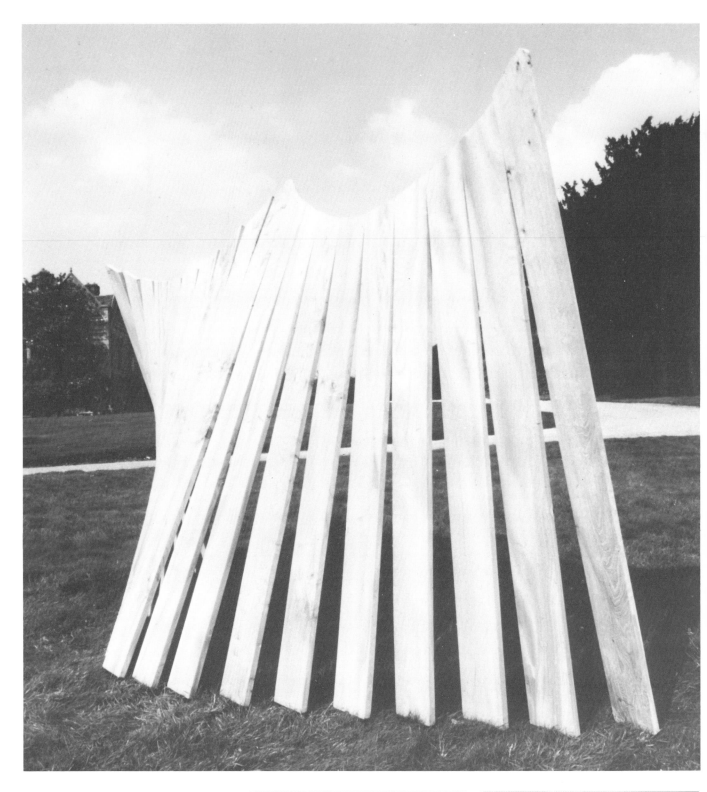

The garden screen

There are many feasible design variations for the garden screen. The overall height could change depending upon your needs or the length of timber you find available. Widths might also vary within a single screen. You may decide to shape the boards down scheir length – there's no practical reason why they should be parallel-sided. Finally, the overall shape is easily changed by varying the relative lengths and the number of the boards used.

Cutting list Elm:	Length	Width
19 boards as:		
2	1823mm (71¾in)	150mm (5⅞in)
2	1722mm (67¾in)	150mm (5⅞in)
2	1640mm (64½in)	150mm (5⅞in)
2	1598mm (62⅞in)	150mm (5⅞in)
2	1577mm (62⅛in)	150mm (5⅞in)

	Length	Width
2	1612mm (63½in)	150mm (5⅞in)
2	1703mm (67in)	150mm (5⅞in)
2	1832mm (72⅛in)	150mm (5⅞in)
2	1974mm (77¾in)	150mm (5⅞in)
1	2046mm (80½in)	150mm (5⅞in)
Threaded steel rod:	2650mm (104⅜in)	10mm (⅜in) diam.

As made, the screen consists of nineteen boards 150mm (5⅞in) wide. The actual lengths are given in the cutting list. The 10mm (⅜in) steel rod is threaded at each end for 76mm (3in). This rod will be threaded through the boards and secured at either end by lock nuts, so you will need these and eighteen nylon washers (one to be placed between each board). Finally, you may decide to buy nineteen 6mm (¼in) rods, 150mm (6in) long, to be let into the base of each board, although 6in nails would do as well.

1. First erect a 3m (10ft) support rail, the top surface of which is 1.5m (4ft 11in) above the ground and parallel to it. This construction can be built from any inexpensive random softwood, indeed anything you have lying around that is suitable.

2. Then cut nineteen straight-edged parallel-sided hardboard templates to the cutting list lengths. The real advantage of using templates here is that you can play around with your own lengths and shapes. Prop the cut templates up against the support rail with each of their bottom edges at varying distances from a base line (marked on the floor) parallel to the 3m rail.

3. Next, with a pencil, mark a gently sweeping curve (Fig. 2) working from the centre board. You might also find it helpful to mark each board one to nineteen. Take them down, then cut to shape. Use the templates to mark cutting lines on the nineteen hardwood boards. Cramp each in turn to saw stools and cut with a jig saw.

4. Assemble the shaped hardwood boards into the position previously held by the hardboard templates on the support rail. Mark a pencil line along the face of the screen using the top of the rail as a guide. Square this mark across the edges of each board and bore a hole (from each side) through the inner seventeen boards to take the 10mm (⅜in) diameter steel rod.

5. Into the bottom edge of each board bore a central hole to take the short rods or 6in nails. The 75mm (3in) of rod left protruding from the

Constructional illustration of screen

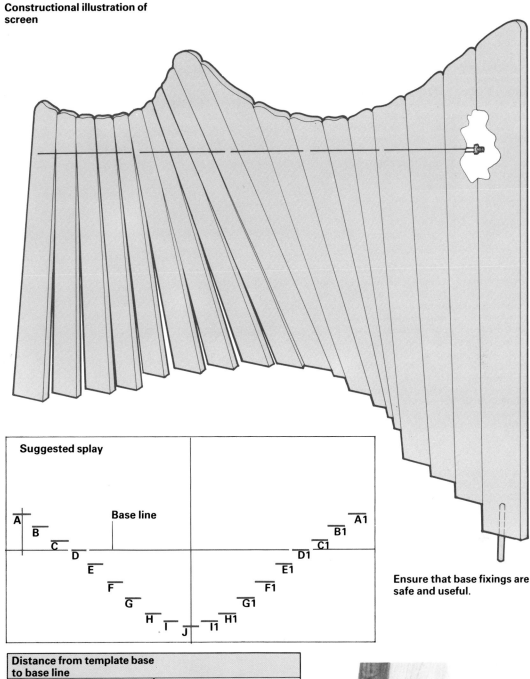

Ensure that base fixings are safe and useful.

Suggested splay

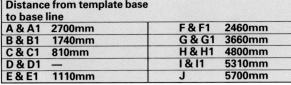

Distance from template base to base line			
A & A1	2700mm	F & F1	2460mm
B & B1	1740mm	G & G1	3660mm
C & C1	810mm	H & H1	4800mm
D & D1	—	I & I1	5310mm
E & E1	1110mm	J	5700mm

base of each board should have its end rounded so that it can be easily pushed into a lawn, but is also safe for storage.

6. Thread the long steel rod through the inner seventeen boards placing a nylon washer between each. Tighten the construction with two lock nuts at either end and countersink a hole on the inner edge of each end board to take the ends of the rod and hide the lock nuts.

Turning project by Richard Raffan ★ ★ ★

"I was born in 1943 in Devon. I left school intending to be an artist, but after two years at Art College and various jobs ended up working for a London wine shipper for about five years. I always wanted to return to the West Country and in January 1970, began turning wood under Douglas Hart at Shinners Bridge in Devon. In July that year I established my own workshops. I chose wood turning on a whim as possibly being quicker to learn than most other craft skills. I assumed that one week's work would tell me if I liked it, and two months if I was going to be any good. The move proved to be an instant success.

"Although the original intention had been to run a small factory with several employees, I realised it was possible to earn enough working alone and without the problems of finding work for others.

"My main interest is in making useful domestic objects – in the main I make bowls, boxes, scoops with plates, lamp bases, cooking implements and such like. I have no catalogue, only a few outlets and usually I find myself with several months' work in hand. Most of what I now know has been learned the hard way, by experience, be it selecting and buying timber or tool-handling techniques.

"For supplies of wood, I maintain close contact with two or three saw mills who often inform me of any log particularly suitable for my purposes. I will buy the log (if I can possibly afford it) once I have satisfied myself that the grain and colour indicate possibilities. I personally like variations of colour and strong, irregular grain patterns, burrs (burls) and the like. Fortunately, the wood I buy is generally regarded as unsuitable by other timber users.

"I approach my work with few preliminary drawings, preferring to work direct with little more than a vague idea as to the final shape in my mind's eye. It is a matter of knowing when to stop and when things look right. I prefer plain shapes, relying on grain for surface interest."

Finished specifications: Putumuju –	Diameter	Height
External measurements	50mm (2in)	75mm (3in)
Internal depth	47mm (1⅞in)	
Lid height	32mm (1¼in)	

Tools
6mm (¼in) gouge
6mm (¼in) square-end scraper
12mm (½in) skew chisel
Parting tool
25mm (1in) and 12mm (½in) round-nosed scrapers
12mm (½in) to 25mm (1in) gouge for roughing out
Garnet or aluminium oxide abrasive paper (80, 100, 180, 220 grits)

Left to right:
Parting tool
Round-nosed scraper
Roughing-out gouge
Square-end scraper
6mm (¼in) gouge
Round-nosed scraper

"It is a great thrill to watch Richard working – like a juggler's performance – speed and perfect control."
John Makepeace

1. Tool rest
2. Face plates
3. Collett chuck
4. Spur
5. Jaw adjusting key
6. Three-jaw chuck
7. Screw chuck
8. Universal 6 in 1 chuck
9. Cup chuck

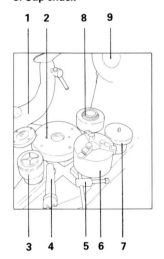

Design points

1. The domed top is more interesting than a flat surface and is also easier to make. Alternative ideas for tops shown right.

2. There is a 'V' groove between lid and base which makes any future change in the box's shape, due to natural movement in the wood, less obvious. It will also help hide the effects of an excessive use of abrasives in finishing (which might make a cylinder oval).

3. The base of the box has been faced off and lightly grooved to confirm the fact.

4. The internal shape of the box is rounded and different from the external shape. This provides tactile interest, greater capacity in the base and strength in the lid.

5. There is a long flange on the base over which the lid fits. Provided both fitting parts have parallel sides, this makes for slight suction when the lid is removed.

6. The box has been made with the grain, end grain being exposed at top and bottom.

7. The size and grain pattern (straight and close) of the box have been chosen deliberately, being good specifications to begin with. Once lid fitting has been mastered, more difficult woods with complicated grain patterns can be approached.

Suggested alternative designs for box tops

Turning project 2

Turning the box

Action hints
* Ensure a good sharp left corner on the square end scraper.
* Grind the round nose scrapers well back on the left to present a longer cutting edge.
* Grind the skew chisel with a very slight curve.
* Turn at 2,000 rpm maximum.

1. Rough square to cylinder shape, leaving spigots at either end to fit your own particular chuck. Richard Raffan uses a three-jaw or collett, but a cup chuck or even a hollow spindle will do as well. Allow 25mm (1in) for parting off over and above the measurements specified for base and lid.

2. Part the material, leaving top and bottom sections with matching grain.

3. Mount the lid section; true up the block with the skew and turn inside. The part which fits onto the base is best cut with the 6mm (¼in) square end scraper, the tool rest at centre height, and should require no more than a two second dab with 220 grit abrasive paper. It is this action of the scraper that demonstrates the importance of having a good sharp corner. Finish the inside of the lid with the round-nosed scraper and then turn as much as possible of the outside shape of the lid. Part off, leaving an extra 2 to 3mm (⅛in).

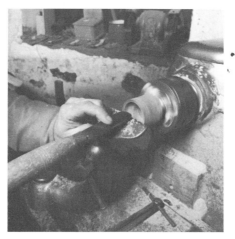

4. Mount the base section; true up the block. The next step is to fit the lid – the key to a successful box and the most difficult operation. The object is to cut a tapering flange so that the end of it fits the lid. Then hollow and finish the inside. Fit the lid gently to the revolving base and the resulting friction mark will indicate the point of exact fit.

Cut the flange from the friction mark, reducing the taper to a near cylinder until the lid fits tightly. Richard Raffan uses the skew chisel either flat as a scraper or its

long sharp point. The skew cutting edge permits greater precision and is less likely to catch. Cut the end grain shoulder (at the bottom of the flange) with the long point of the skew chisel.

5. With the lid fitting tightly onto the base, turn the outside shape of the box, checking with calipers or using the lathe bed and your eye as a guide. Then cut the groove where the lid joins the base.

6. With the long point of the skew chisel, cut the end grain on the lid top in one motion for best results. Finish the outside of the box and remove the lid for final fitting.

7. Two or three quick dabs on the flange with 180 grit should make for a perfect fit, which is neither too tight nor too loose. When trying the lid, proceed slowly and check often as mistakes are difficult to correct.

8. Part off the base, leaving 2 to 3mm (⅛in). Reverse it in the three-jaw chuck or on a wood taper. Turn the base with the skew point. Alternatively, if you do not want to risk the operation at this late stage, cut a small chamfer on the bottom before parting off and finish on a sander. Richard Raffan would never cover a rough base with baize. In his words, not only is it unnecessary on properly finished wood, but it is usually a sign of laziness and incompetence!

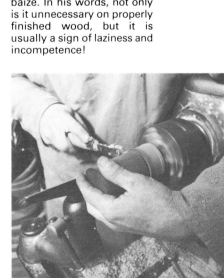

Bob Stocksdale–an individual approach

"Like a musician practising scales, the turner should have his equivalent discipline. Practise the basic cuts over and over again, preferably making something in the process. Make rolling pins or light pull-knobs with a skew chisel, or hollow bowls with a small gouge to get the action right. Above all, experiment to find your own way of doing. Books show starting points, and the right way to turn is that which produces the end product that you want." Richard Raffan

Bob Stocksdale's work is especially interesting in this context. Stocksdale is self-taught and over thirty-five years has earned himself an international reputation as a turner with a completely individual approach in terms of techniques and the form of his finished pieces. One of the keys to his success is the special relationship he nurtures with the wood he uses.

"I have approximately twenty tons of wood in stock at any one time. A lot of it is Californian wood such as black walnut, acacia, and suchlike which I get for practically nothing and use mostly for salad bowl stock."

His special delight, however, is in scouring the world for rarer woods, finding them at auctions, ship repair yards, even in garages and basements where people have hoarded rare woods that they have collected but never used.

"I have several other sources of supply for rare and fancy woods. I buy occasionally in New York, and I have a friend who buys wood for me in London and Le Havre, France. He gets the really exotic woods since England and France have established connections with their former colonies. I have an additional advantage in that I am not interested in buying my wood dry (see Method).

Zebrawood

"What interests me is the beautiful grain that may be present in a particular log. So I prefer to select my own wood if at all possible. It may pay me to go out and take down a tree, but I don't do that very often – in fact sometimes I even get wood that's already cut to fire wood lengths and work them up into bowls.

"Rarely do I make a series of bowls out of one log. It would be too monotonous working up a whole log in that way (although I might make a lot more money doing it). I would rather just work from one project to the next, taking my time to see what I can develop out of a piece of wood to bring out the best grain pattern in it. A lot of time goes into planning the best use of a log so that I can get the best out of it. Usually, when I get a log, I take a cross-section, work that into decorative bowls, and then see what is available in the rest of the log. I never glue up any wood to achieve a larger size object. Every object I make comes from one piece of wood."

With this emphasis on planning (investigating his material in relation to what he can make out of it) comes an individual – and functionally realistic – choice of finishes.

"I have several different methods of finishing my pieces depending upon what they are going to be used for. Salad bowls, for instance, are finished by being soaked in mineral oil for several days until the oil has penetrated right through the wood. Then, when the bowls are washed, the oil comes back up to the surface again. I use that same oil finish on small bread and butter plates and dinner plates too. These things are made to be used. They should not require any care whatsoever. They can simply be washed and drained on the dish rack. You don't even have to dry them. We have a set which has been in daily use for about eight years. They are still very flat and have no tendency to warp.

"My decorative bowls and trays made from dark exotic woods are usually lacquer finished to bring out the grain as well as anything can. I use two coats of gloss lacquer and sand a little before applying a final satin finish lacquer. On lighter woods I may use a tung oil finish – one part tung oil, one part linseed oil, one part turpentine. This is brushed on, left to set for a few minutes, put on the lathe and thoroughly wiped off. Two applications,

on consecutive days, are usually sufficient for that oil finish."

Method

"I have developed my own techniques of turning. I work initially with wet wood. What I do is to rough out the form of the piece from the wet wood, leaving it thick enough to take care of shrinkage. Then I put it in a small drying room (it's about ten feet square with a little heater in it) and leave it there from two weeks to two

months depending upon its size. Smaller bowls dry out quite quickly because they turn down to about 12mm (½in) thick in the first roughing out process. The large bowls are roughed out to a 25mm (1in)/32mm (1¼in) thickness and take proportionately longer to dry. I have experienced few problems in drying because a bowl can dry from the inside as well as the outside and is less likely to crack. If it warps, which sometimes it does, you may have a little problem in remounting it on the lathe – but I have not had any real difficulties. If a bowl dries oval-shaped then I re-set it on the lathe, turn it round again, taking it down quite thin with a final turning. Then I sand it and apply a finish.

"I do practically all my work using 'the gouge method'. I have only three tools – a 25mm (1in) gouge for the roughing out process, a 12mm (½in) gouge for most of my work and the final turning, and a small diamond-point tool for making a shoulder on a base or a little foot on a footed bowl, for example. The less you change tools, the more time you save."
Bob Stocksdale

Top left:
Light brown blackwood acacia. "It is a difficult wood to work because the sanding and tool marks are difficult to remove. This shape is a hard one to do too. When I roughed it out the top of the bowl followed the curvature of the log, as it does now."

Middle top:
Para kingwood, purple in colour. "A friend found this wood in London for me and I think it the most beautiful I have worked . . . Being in the rosewood family, it turns beautifully and is so easy to finish."

Top right:
Hedge maple, a pinkish brown colour drifts cloud-like through the wood.

Right:
Nigerian ebony, black. "This ebony is not real hard, and turns and sands without problems. Cracks can be repaired with epoxy and lampblack."

James Krenov-making your work your own

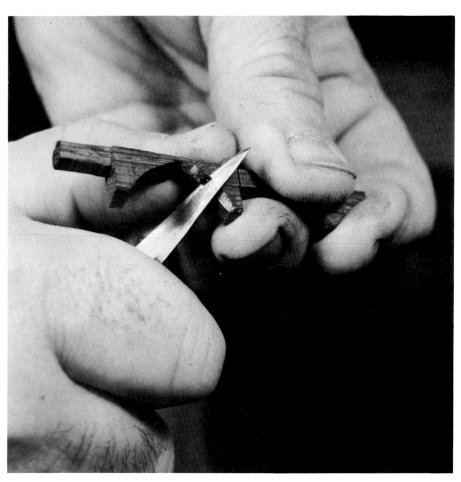

Many amateurs shy away from designing their own pieces of furniture. Some, intimidated by the conformity and unimaginative nature of woodworking as taught to them, assume that intentional individuality of design is the sole province of "gifted" craftsmen. *James Krenov*, through his books, lectures and, above all, his work, has dedicated himself to an approach to craft which lifts the pressure of professional concepts from the woodworker's shoulders, and encourages amateurs to make their work their own by showing how design and craftsmanship are inextricably linked as one process.

"I get letters saying, 'My name is Joe Doakes, and I come from Ohio, and I've got six chickens and two wives, and I've been working with wood for years trying to do something my way. All my friends tell me I'm crazy. Then I read your books and found that you're sort of crazy too! So now I feel better.'

"There's this need for encouragement", says Krenov. "It's not so much a need for someone to pay you for what you've made, as for someone to say, 'That's fine; you've done it; that's something special.' These people need encouragement like they need air."

Why it is important
to make your work your own
"Basically we are apt to talk about two different things when we talk about craft. One is usually craft as a profession, and the other maybe craft as enjoyment. The most important thing for people who go into woodworking for enjoyment is to be happy doing it. But enjoyment as I mean it needs explaining. I read in a British craft magazine somebody asking a very venerable gentleman whether the process, the 'doing', is more important than the result. He said, 'Oh my God, no! The only thing that's important is the *result* of course.' I believe there is another aspect to this, a third and more balanced point. The process, if it is personal enough, and enjoyable in its myriad of discoveries and adventures – will show in the result. So finally there will be not only the result, the piece, but also evidence of how the work was done. This evidence is what I mean by intimacy. It is central."

The intimacy
of the method
"Craft methods are taught so that you can produce the objects you want with the minimum amount of effort and the maximum amount of efficiency. If *you* are original, *it* is original. But all too often originality is something that depends on visual impact, which tends to be a tricky, rather speculative thing. Many students are not satisfied that this is what their craft is about. There's this big question mark . . . Maybe there is another kind of originality – *the fingerprints on the object of the person who made it.*

"In the 'thirties we used to write on walls, *Kilroy Was Here*. Today, a lot of people who admire craft objects are looking for Kilroy, something to counteract the impersonal, hurried and mechan-

ized way most of us live and work. Now, finger prints are very intimate things; yours belong to you and you alone. What's more – they cannot be falsified.

"Finger-prints in craft are, I believe, the intimacy of the method. A closeness to your work that comes from really living with it. Once you accept that, the first thing that changes is your relationship with time. The greatest problem I have in America is helping students get on the right terms with Father Time. We are in a hurry all our lives. But certain things have got to take the time they need. You can't argue with yourself about it and still be happy. And there is a special satisfaction in the deeper experience of living with what you do. One discovers energy-saving harmony. At times it is like the old Greek concept: anyone who moves gracefully accomplishes the best results with the least effort."

Taking the time
it needs
"I won't say hurrying is a problem typical of young people only, but it is very prevalent in current crafts. It is difficult to teach people to take time because even at school level there's competitiveness. The person who has made four pieces in the past year is reckoned to be better than the person who has only made one piece. But is one fine piece worth less than four which may be somewhat less fine?"

Intimacy of the method
dependent on the "what with"
"Intimacy in our craft is very often the difference between having that specially suited tool, and wanting and knowing how to use it, or relying on something else to do the work for you.

"When it comes to details – and they should be many in craftsmanship – there are basically two approaches. The most common one is to turn to the mechanical aids in the shop. What machine can I use that will do most of the work? I need some handles for cabinet doors and I have a well-equipped workshop with the usual handy machines. So, I can cut curvy shapes with a router and then divide the shaped stock into two, or four, handles. Quick and easy. Or turn them on a lathe; yes, why not round knobs? Or handles shaped on the drum (spindle) sander.

"Handles can be done in a quarter of the time I took here (see illustration). But whose handles will they then be – yours, or the machine's? Whose *feel* will there be in such handles? Because feel is what it is about for some of us; aesthetics *and* actual physical feel. So there is this other beginning point, another source of energy; you close your eyes and ask yourself, 'What would I like to take hold of when opening those cabinet doors?' Then, in order to make those handles (or anything you feel strongly for) you simply have to have the right tools. I don't mean generally right, but specifically, intimately right in the sense that you can use them to make the detail you feel for, that you enjoy the doing and get the result you want.

"The details I do, whether main shapes or small parts, are usually asymmetric in some way. Not actually round as when turned – nor stiffly straight. Hopefully they do not have a mechanical message – or a contrived cool. I spent a part of my life working with fine wooden boats, and sailing too. What stayed with me is the experience of the wonderful living lines such boats have (or had), the curves balanced, harmonious, and yet not arcs or circles, or parts of some computerized formula...

"A sail-boat mast may be fairly straight at the dock, but you go out there sailing in the wind and look at it, and it's just beautiful. If you put a straight line on a piece of paper and a line that's just a little bit curved, which one will you take for granted? Of course it depends on how sensitive you are. There's some tension in one line – and that little bit is often more intense in its message than the over-statement, especially the over-emphasis that rests on something mechanical.

"I wanted some handles which felt nice between the fingers, were pleasant to look at. And because I have these lovely knives, I can make them. It's enjoyable work, really.

"Unless you have fine, sensitive tools, you turn to your machines and you buzz something out. But you can't buzz feelings!

"None of this has anything to do with the logic of the profession, it's your own individual logic – the way *you* are put together. Whatever your methods, they must make sense to *you*, so that you're not struggling with what you do. Or with your wishes. Wholeness is the beginning of what works for you. This too is very difficult to teach, but one of the things we can accomplish is to release the pressure of too much and too rigid teaching – most of which says that there is one definite way to do something – that it's got to be a, b, c, d. It just could be a, d ... provided we get it together, and the result is pleasing, or, when one is lucky, even beautiful. Keep in mind always: even though we are but craftsmen – we *do* strive towards beauty and harmony.

"Once you get into this intimacy thing, wood becomes method. Take a sculptor with a marvellous piece of Italian marble, and a block of granite. The way that his head and his feelings work, the things that he conceives in working with that piece of marble won't be the same – hope-fully – as they would be with the granite. The methods he uses will be different; the marble will have something to do with what comes out; there will probably be a delicacy in the marble object. And some-thing else in the one of granite. When you get close enough to wood, when you get emotional about it and are involved in these intimate methods – the heart and fingertip things about wood – then the whole concept of what you are about to do is transformed.

"Besides living in accord with time, learning to see is the most difficult thing – being able to take a piece of wood that is ¾in thick, hold it in your fingers and say, 'I need the ¾in for my construction, but I don't want it to look ¾in;' and to know that you can make an object look hard or soft. I could almost go so far as to say that by choosing a certain wood and then working sensitively with it you can make

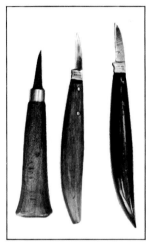

Above, two sets of cabinet handles carved by Krenov. **Illustrated right** is a selection of his knives. Krenov admits that most of the knives on regular sale are awkward to use and do not appear to have been made for someone who carves well. He keeps a wide selection of tools and is forever altering them to suit his needs. So equipped, he feels free to make a personal statement out of a detail which is sensitive to the nature of the whole piece. **Below**, door frames of elm and panels of pearwood creating soft and sharp-cornered effects.

it look masculine or feminine, give it a certain character, and yet keep the re-quired structural sizes. The *eye* will ex-perience something else than just given dimensions."

Learning to see

"Wood grain is part of the graphics of wood. Not just in the usual eye-catching sense, 'Oooh, what a pattern!' but in the sense of what Bob Stocksdale – or any good turner – does with his bowls (see page 138). Grain is part of the shape. Bob gets the shape he wants out of it, but allows the wood a say in it, too. You have got to realise that it isn't just a question of striking patterns and weird shapes, but of subtleties. A little bit of tension, used

right, will turn a rectangle into the begin-ning of an oval. We feel curves – and yet the actual shape, the lines, remain straight. Once we discover its true possi-bilities, wood becomes a marvellously *living* material.

"It's not pure chance that the wood in the frame of one of my cabinets – especially the curved one – evokes a certain feeling as you experience it. If you turned the door parts around, you would 'flatten' the cabinet. So, whatever shape, whatever detail you are working on, you need to have a clear sense about it. That is your hope, your point of orientation. You have to accept the fact that perhaps no one will notice a certain detail; but some-one will *feel* it. There is a difference

James Krenov 2

between merely noticing something – and having a feeling about it. For example, you may approach someone, notice them as you pass, and yet if you're asked what they looked like, you may have difficulty in describing them. Still, you do have a feeling about them. So there doesn't necessarily have to be something showy, a detail that jumps out at you and waves its hand and says, 'Look at me; I'm what makes this piece!' The wholeness of a piece is what matters most. Modesty *is* a virtue.

"When you do this sort of thing, searching as you work, you have to look ahead. How, you might ask yourself, would the cabinet look with glass shelves? Or should the shelves be of wood? Without shelves the cabinet looks one way, with different shelves its character changes. You must try to predict results. What I did was to tape some pieces of thin wood on the inside of the verticals, and looked

at the door before I glued it. Then, when I had decided how it would look with wood shelves, I thought about what might go on the shelves. I decided on a loose bottom shelf because without it, you would only be able to see the top of a small object when the door was closed. Also, by removing the bottom shelf you could have the base of a statuette, for example, out of sight when the door was closed."

What is design in this context?

"Today, design *per se* is basically commercial, a profession. A lot of it is about reaching the most popular market, eighteen to twenty-five year olds whose habits are stereo, TV, living close to the floor. The main concern is: what will people buy? How can it be made in quantity? Among us craftsmen, the word design is often terribly mis-used. And exploited! I like to think that rather than

design pieces, I build them. Very often, I have nothing to go on but a thought and my material. Sometimes I have a little scrap of paper, a sketch. I am not against drawing. But there are too many people, who, though they can draw, cannot see on paper three-dimensionally. They will put in hours in the drawing classes; learn projection; learn to sketch; and to draw perspective. Alas, they too often tend to do nice things on paper, but less nice things in wood!

"A fine craftsman is a good designer, but in retrospect. When you look at things he produces, and experience them, you are apt to say, 'It's good to use; it serves its function; it's interesting. Yes, that's a nice design.' Design, yes. *But in retrospect*. Really good craft is good design, analytically, later on. There is a real danger – a kind of dictatorship – in too much design-worship among us craftsmen."

Far left, cabinet of Tasmanian blackwood showing use of grain to work with fundamental shape and optical experience of the piece. The components of cherrywood cabinet **right** would flatten the piece if turned another way. Note spoke-shaved edges of oak cabinet near left.

The story of a piece of damaged maple

"The boys sent me the maple from the States. The wood is sound, though there are traces of fungus in it. And worm holes. Ah, those are something special! We chain sawed a log of maple, and they sent some pieces over to me. It was partly cracked. But when I opened up one of the planks, there was this combination of dark lines, mysterious brown streaks – and little holes . . .

"I kept the wood against a wall in my workshop. People, sort of wayward displaced persons, find their way to my shop rather often. One day I heard heavy boots on the stairs, and a 'bang, bang' on the door of my shop. In walks this fellow. Just like that, out of nowhere. 'I am with the forest service and I've done a thesis on badgers,' he says. 'Thought I'd drop in . . .' Then he sees these pieces of maple. 'Hey, you know what these little holes are?' 'Yes,' I said, 'someone's been living there, obviously.' 'That's right', he nods. 'But you know, these little creatures – he points to a worm hole – go out and gather the mould culture which later contributes to the fungus and changes the colour of the wood.' And it's true; for every one of those brown streaks, there's a little tiny hole. So this is really ecological wood.

"My only credit is that I didn't spoil what was there. What was nice, I kept, and made a 'box' of. You see, one way of approaching such things is to say, 'I want to make a box which is 14in by 32in by Xin deep.' But the other way is to say to yourself, 'Well, I've got this wonderful piece of wood, and I'll make a box . . . *There's* the most important fact.' Then you can play around

with it and make the best out of what is there. A wall cabinet like this is experienced from various angles and heights. Even though it may have an ideal position – we are trying to make it so that it will not be unpleasant however one views it. Something that is good however you look at it, not just *en face*. So as we

work, during various stages of composing such a simple and yet elusive piece, we use our imagination, looking ahead, trying to envision the final result. We make changes and weigh each carefully. Try – and look again. And though we are eager, we do not hurry so as to endanger the result we hope for."

Adventure in craft

"We have so much exact information about our craft. Some of us get lost in crisp facts. It's all tangential this and diagonal that, and all sorts of figures. I get letters from craftsmen saying, 'Gee, I can't even buy a piece of wood! I can't start working because I don't know the damn humidity of the wood I'm supposed to be using. Help!' I write and tell them to cool it (not the wood, but themselves). All you've got to have are a few points of orientation, stars on a dark night, which help us a lot. Without common sense and the benefits of a few simple experiences we can share – we'd all be lost.

"I admit that for some people the scientific, professional approach may be right. They've been put together that way. They're technicians, the engineers of craft. But I believe they are more interested in finding ways of avoiding work than of doing it. I would like to leave you with a message of the simplicity of our craft. A lot of what it is about is emotion and simple reasoning – living with what you do, from one discovery to the next. And the next. Not for a week or month or a year, but for a long, long time. You want to express something that is your own, that is you, rather than a machine. You are combining *your* logic with the basic rightness in our craft. That rightness is alive, full of discoveries and personal satisfactions. It is there for us, lending adventure to our work. One of the ways to find it is to believe in a natural simplicity that is the essence of most fine craftsmanship."
James Krenov

Books by James Krenov include:
A Cabinetmaker's Notebook
The Fine Art of Cabinetmaking
The Impractical Cabinetmaker
All published by Studio Vista in London and Van Nostrand Reinhold in New York.

Tools and techniques introduction

Sharply defined work clearly requires finely tuned equipment, and care and maintenance of your tools are important whatever your aesthetic objective.

Tools merit the respect a musician holds for his instrument. Care for them and both you and your tools will perform better. In fact, the craftsman in wood has an advantage over the musician in this respect. There is virtually nothing in the workshop which cannot, by your own efforts, be modified to perform better (and they may need to be, since tools which you buy are frequently inferior). Very few musicians would feel competent to do the same for their instruments.

Discovering how to make your tools more efficient springs from an awareness of why they are designed as they are to perform the precise function for which you have bought them. And that, in turn, comes from experience of using them. By studying the action of your plane you'll see how important it is to keep its sole flat (see page 158). Should one of your tools perform badly, look in detail at how it was designed to operate and deduce which aspects of it need to be modified to achieve optimum efficiency. It is worth taking the time.

Buying tools

It is not necessarily a good idea to go out and buy all the tools we recommend here. Buy according to your needs. This policy is one that John Hardy still follows today and has done since Design Workshop was in its infancy.

Here are some rules which you might find useful when assessing tools at point of purchase:

1. Select the right tools for the job. Go into the shop with a clear idea of what it is you want the tools to do for you.

2. Look at the trade mark and choose those manufactured by a reputable company.

3. Assess the quality of their construction: your new saw will have a ring about it, will spring back when bent to one side. It will have a natural tendency to remain straight; it will be a comfortable weight to handle. Your chisel should have a flat blade checked with a straight edge. Look for quality of metal finish and quality of handle. It may be prejudicial to avoid plastic handles, but the tendency to think that if a tool has a wooden handle it has a better blade arose out of an association of plastic handles with a carpentry trade that was never strong on accuracy.

Tackling new techniques

There are a few techniques covered here which are likely to be new to some. When tackling new or demanding techniques, the important thing is to take your time,

look carefully at the task in hand, jot down each step of the process on a piece of paper, select which parts of your wood are best for which parts of the finished piece, and mark accordingly. In thinking about which tools to use, relate their principles of design to the demands of the joint, or whatever it is you want to make, and make the appropriate selection.

Don't rush into the job, eager as you may be to enjoy the finished object. First practise on an odd piece of wood and get the feel of how those particular tools cope with the idiosyncracies of the wood you have chosen. You may discover how they can be coerced into producing the desired result faster than you think. In any event, the time you take will be well spent and you may even find yourself enjoying the preamble to the job. You will certainly enjoy the job itself better, and the eventual result.

"It is very important to keep things going well, so that one does not reach that state of irritation. Then one cannot work well. Even the finest ideas and the best wood and even an initial enthusiasm can't help us once we get bogged down in a lot of small errors that keep accumulating. So at the first sign of difficulty, stop and back up a bit, think not only in terms of detail, but even more in the light of what it is you want to accomplish – and take the time to get on the right track again." James Krenov

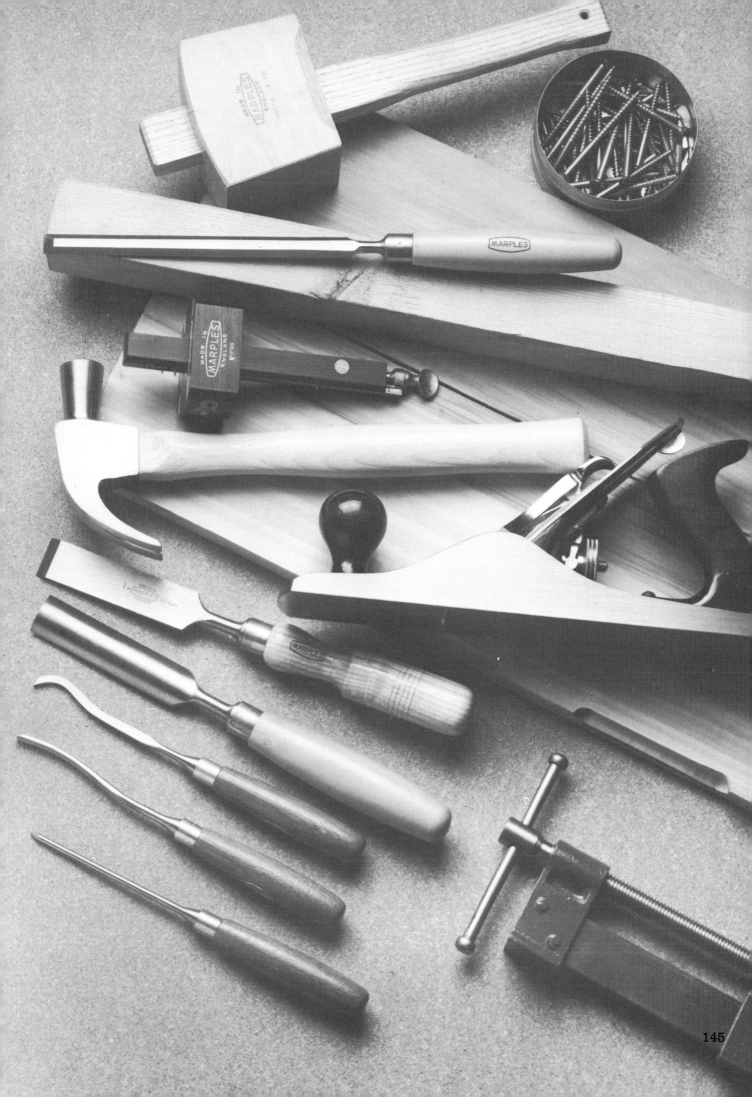

Saws and sawing

There have been hand saws in existence for thousands of years, but it was a long time before engineering developments produced the variety of designs which is available today. Many basic design modifications, now taken for granted, were centuries in the making.

For example, saw teeth were not always 'set', that is made to point alternately to the left and to the right to produce a groove (or 'kerf') fractionally wider than the blade, thus enabling it to clear itself from the wood. Handles were not always positioned at one end of the saw; more common were framed handles whose function was (and still is in the case of the bow saw, a 'relic' of times past) to tension a thin blade within a wooden frame.

Today we have hand saws of many different designs. In the context of this book we have listed relevant hand saws under three general categories: saws for cutting boards in a straight line; saws for cutting shapes; saws for making fine precise cuts for joints. Within these categories, each saw has evolved more subtle peculiarities which reflect its individual purpose; and it is vital that the furniture-maker appreciates the design principles behind them, how each saw operates, and thus which saw to select for a particular job. It follows that it is as important to be able to maintain each saw so that it may continue to serve its specific purpose.

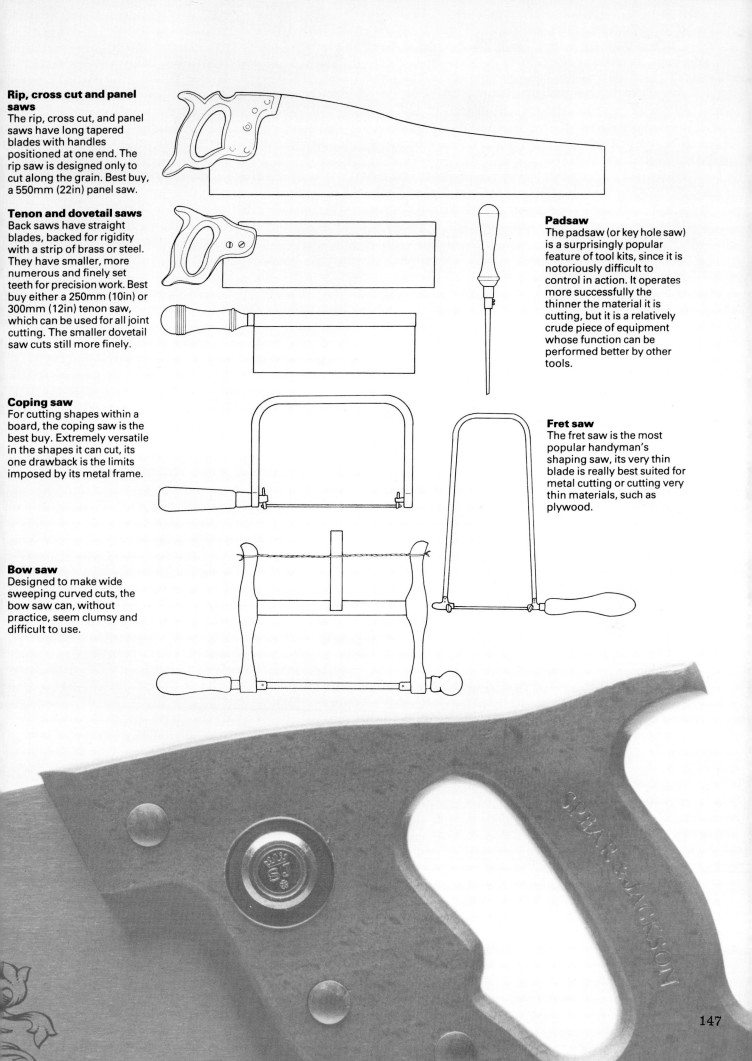

Rip, cross cut and panel saws

The rip, cross cut, and panel saws have long tapered blades with handles positioned at one end. The rip saw is designed only to cut along the grain. Best buy, a 550mm (22in) panel saw.

Tenon and dovetail saws

Back saws have straight blades, backed for rigidity with a strip of brass or steel. They have smaller, more numerous and finely set teeth for precision work. Best buy either a 250mm (10in) or 300mm (12in) tenon saw, which can be used for all joint cutting. The smaller dovetail saw cuts still more finely.

Coping saw

For cutting shapes within a board, the coping saw is the best buy. Extremely versatile in the shapes it can cut, its one drawback is the limits imposed by its metal frame.

Bow saw

Designed to make wide sweeping curved cuts, the bow saw can, without practice, seem clumsy and difficult to use.

Padsaw

The padsaw (or key hole saw) is a surprisingly popular feature of tool kits, since it is notoriously difficult to control in action. It operates more successfully the thinner the material it is cutting, but it is a relatively crude piece of equipment whose function can be performed better by other tools.

Fret saw

The fret saw is the most popular handyman's shaping saw, its very thin blade is really best suited for metal cutting or cutting very thin materials, such as plywood.

Saws and sawing 2

Saws for cutting boards in a straight line

Rip saw

The rip saw is designed for coarse cutting in a straight line along the grain. Unlike any other saw, its teeth points present themselves in an upright position, filed square to the blade, and cut with the action of a series of tiny chisels. This aspect restricts their use to cutting along the grain.

Rip saws have large teeth and wide spaces (or 'gullets') between them, and consequently less teeth points per 25mm (1in) of blade than any other saw. Saw teeth are set to about half their depth, therefore these have a wider 'splay' than in any other saw. This is the reason why the rip saw makes a coarser, wider kerf and more waste dust than any other saw. It is, then, of all saws the most 'rough and ready', but no less important to maintain. It may not be an essential feature of your tool kit, especially if you have a circular power saw or a friendly saw mill or timber merchant willing to cut boards in section for you.

Cross cut saw

The cross cut saw is designed for cutting in a straight line across the grain. It is available with as long a blade as the rip saw, but its teeth are smaller, with more numerous points per 25mm (1in) – 6 to 8 pts per 25mm whereas the rip saw has 5pts – and is consequently fractionally finer set and less coarse in cutting. The main difference, however, is that its teeth are raked (pitched at about 14 degrees from upright) which gives them a knife-point cutting action enabling the tool to cut across the grain without tearing it.

Panel saw

The panel saw is a smaller version of the cross cut saw with 10 teeth points per 25mm (1in). With a finer setting than the cross cut, it has to be the best buy for working in hardwood.

Three points to watch when buying. The very best saws in this category are taper ground to facilitate the blade clearing itself. That means ground on both sides of the blade so that the back tapers to its 'point' while retaining its full thickness along the teeth. Also look out for the position of the handle. It should be set low on the blade's back for balance. Finally, check that it has been correctly tensioned. The blade should not flop or sag when held horizontally.

Action hints

*Supporting the wood.** Distribute the weight of the wood evenly over the saw stool (or stools, depending on board length) and make sure that the wood is at least as far from the ground as the length of your saw.

Distribute the weight evenly when cross cutting

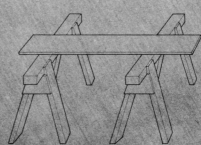

*Controlling the saw.** Grip the saw handle, positioning your index finger down the handle and in line with the blade to prevent any tendency to twist the saw in use. Rest one knee lightly on the board to help secure it to the stool and position your shoulder directly above the work. Place the saw at a low angle to the board and on the waste side of the cutting line, your forearm in line with the blade. Rest your free hand lightly on the end of the board steadying the saw with your thumb.

*Establishing the first cut.** Proceed with one or more downward or upward strokes. It doesn't matter which, the important consideration being not to put pressure on the saw teeth.

*Cutting.** When the saw has reached the back edge of the board, remove your thumb and raise the cutting angle between blade and wood to about 60 degrees for rip sawing or sawing man-made sheets, otherwise to about 45 degrees. Let the saw move easily over the timber – the downward strokes should do the cutting, so relieve the pressure when drawing the saw back up through the wood. Cross your free hand over the front of the saw and lightly grip the un-supported wood.

*Jamming the saw.** Jamming is not

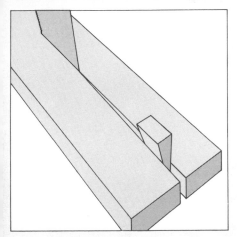

always due to poorly supported wood. Sometimes, particularly if timber has been seasoned too quickly, stress builds up which may be released during the sawing process causing the wood to close in on the saw. Jamming *can* be relieved by gently wedging a piece of wood into the cut, but be sensitive to the possibility of putting the wood under strain which will surely damage your work. Far better to check that the wood is properly supported and back-track.

*Finishing the cut.** One firm sweep of the saw to finish a cut takes experience. So be careful not to exert too much pressure with your supporting hand – it should merely hold the sawn section lightly in its original position – and approach the finish with measured strokes of the saw. Reversing the board, cramping up and finishing the cut from the other end is frequently advised. Just as often it will damage the wood.

* Never put undue pressure on saw teeth; never put wood under strain.

Saws for cutting shapes

Coping saw
For cutting gentle curves, the coping saw has no peer. Its blade, which is very thin with fine teeth, is tensioned within a metal frame. By turning the handle in an anti-clockwise direction and restraining the blade holder, the blade will be loosened, either for replacement or to swivel the existing blade to facilitate cutting practically any shape. The saw's one drawback is that its frame inhibits cutting far from the edge of material.

Action hints
* When the blade is swivelled at an angle, remember to keep your eye in line with the blade and not the frame.
* Set the blade so that the teeth point towards the handle and the saw cuts on the pull stroke.
* Support wood in a vice and use the saw in a vertical position, angling the blade when necessary. Hold the saw with both hands and do not force anything.

Fret saw
The fret saw comes with a wide range of blades suitable for fine cutting of thin material only. The blades, which are thinner than coping saw blades, are tensioned in a deeper frame and can cut curves without adjustment.

Padsaw (key hole saw)
The padsaw is, by virtue of its shape, very difficult to control. It may be useful occasionally for cutting holes within wide surfaced thin material. But if you need to make a cut within a board and the coping saw frame inhibits you, it is a far better idea to bore a series of holes with a brace and chop out the waste with a chisel.

Bow saw
The bow saw blade is tensioned in a traditional wooden frame by means of a tourniquet at the top of the frame. Designed to make wide-sweeping curved cuts, it may at first seem clumsy and difficult to use. Operate it with both hands on the handle to control the direction of the blade and steady the frame. Its blade swivels through 360 degrees.

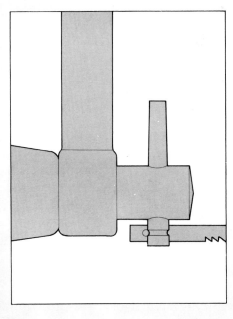

Saws and sawing 3

Tenon and dovetail saw
Both tenon and dovetail saws have straight blades (with cross cut teeth) backed with a strip of brass or steel to add rigidity. The tenon saw is useful for cutting all joints, the smaller dovetail saw with finer set is recommended in a 200mm (8in) size with 18 to 22 points per 25mm (1in). But it is not a good idea to use the dovetail saw indiscriminately. It should be kept exclusively for dovetails or fine mitres, otherwise its precision edge will suffer.

Action hint
*New tenon saws invariably have too much set. Very gently run a fine slip-stone along each side of the teeth with even pressure to produce a cleaner cut.

Bench hook
Use a bench hook when cutting with either saw across the grain. You can make one yourself. It consists of a square-edged parallel-sided board onto each end of which are screwed two square-edged parallel-sided blocks at right angles to the long edges of the board. One block hooks over the edge of the workbench, the other supports the work.

Portable power saws
Two portable power saws – the circular saw and the jig (or saber) saw – can lighten the work load considerably. Both are given detailed consideration in the section on Power Tools pages 170/1.

Care for saws

Any saw you buy is worth looking after. Take the time to oil them occasionally, even those you use least frequently. Do not wait until you detect the first signs of rust.

Tensioning saws

Tensioning is a specialist's job involving hammering out the steel blade from the centre. Send it back to the manufacturer rather than attempt to rectify a buckle, but if you drop a back saw (tenon or dovetail) and it performs badly, gently tap the tool on the workbench.

Preparation of saws

Sharpening and setting your saws yourself is no bad way to discover how and why they are made as they are. You are likely to use them better as a result and your work will benefit. It is also cheaper than sending them to the ironmonger.

The aim is to achieve:
1. Level teeth.
2. Correctly set teeth.
3. Gullets constant in angle and depth.
4. Saw teeth which gleam to their points.

Section illustrates gullet and constant angle of set

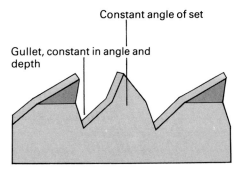

Constant angle of set

Gullet, constant in angle and depth

Saw setting

Buy a saw set which automatically bends each alternate tooth to the correct set. It has a graduated dial which gears the tool to a set appropriate for the number of teeth points per 25mm (1in). The more points per 25mm, the finer the set. It operates like a pair of pliers. Once set, simply fit it over each alternate tooth and squeeze.

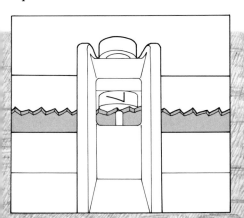

Action hints – sharpening

*Cut two wooden strips or battens to fit snugly round the shape of the handle and along the blade but not covering the teeth. Make a different pair of battens for each individual saw.
*Firmly vice with the teeth uppermost. Additionally you may need to cramp long saws for extra rigidity.
*With a straight-edge discover whether the teeth are level. If necessary 'top' them with a flat file.

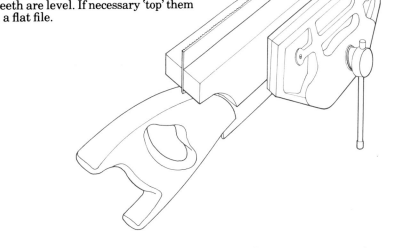

*Choose a triangular saw file twice the height of the saw tooth. (You will need different files for different saws). Grip the file in both hands. When filing a rip saw hold it level to hone the points to a chisel edge and keep the file at right-angles to the blade 'in plan' (i.e. looking from above). For cross cut saws let the near hand bear fractionally downwards to sharpen the teeth to a knife-point shape, and hold the file at an angle 'in plan' of 60 degrees. Always work on the front of the tooth pointing away from you. Make positive strokes with even pressure, an equal number of times across alternate teeth.

Then reverse the saw in the vice and work the remaining teeth. It is vital to be consistent in angle, depth and number of file strokes throughout.

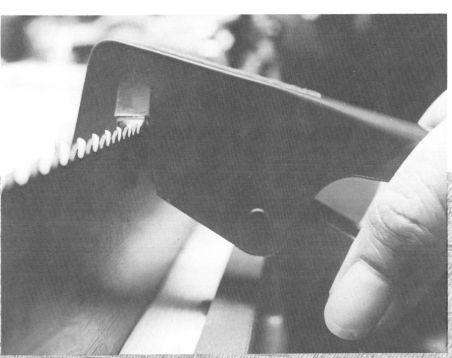

151

Chisels and gouges

There are firmer, bevel-edged, paring, and mortise chisels – and others besides. Since prehistoric times narrow cutting-edged tools have been used for cutting mortises. And the greater sophistication that comes with time has produced a wide range of chisels for every function.

Buy wisely and only as your needs dictate. Sizes are gauged according to blade width, and it is advisable to own a selection of sizes so that wherever possible you can cut 'in one go'.

The firmer chisel
The firmer chisel is the general purpose chisel. It is hardier than any other chisel and when using it to chop out, its stout blade can well stand the strain of a carpenter's mallet. But never use a hammer on wooden-handled chisels.

The 6mm (¼in) and 25mm (1in) are essential for basic work. Building your collection as to your needs will probably mean buying a 12mm (½in) and 18mm (¾in) next.

Bevel-edged and firmer blade cross-sections

The bevel-edged chisel
Similar to the firmer chisel (except that it is bevelled along the top sides of the blade) it is a delicate tool and needs to be handled carefully. Its function is to work in tight restricted areas, such as dovetail housings. It is a more precise tool than the firmer chisel.

The paring chisel
The paring chisel has a longer blade than either the firmer or bevel-edged chisel, and it may or may not be bevel-edged. As its name suggests, this chisel is used to pare long housings.

Action hints
* Chisels must be kept sharp and true. As such they are potentially dangerous tools, so work carefully and store them after use.

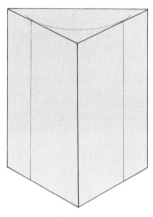

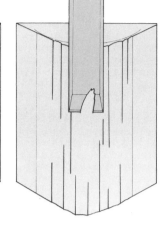

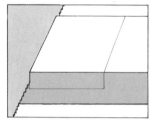

Cutting a through-housing
(see also page 178)
1. Mark out width and depth and saw on the waste side of the width lines down to the depth line.

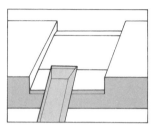

2. Work from either side of the housing, paring a little wood away at a time with the chisel blade inclining in an upward direction. (Only then pare away the middle section.)

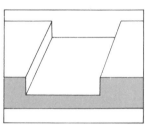

3. Make fine cuts as you reach the base of the housing and check for flatness with a straight edge. Better still, if you own one, finish with a hand router (or old woman's tooth).

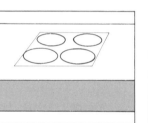

Chopping out a mortise
(see also page 179)
1. Drill a series of holes with a brace and dowel bit to the required depth of the mortise.

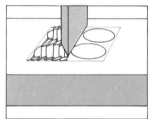

2. Using a firmer chisel, positioned at the centre of the mortise, and at right angles to the wood, make each cut 'in one go' right up to each end line.

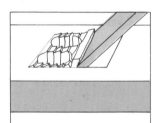

3. Reducing the angle of the chisel from the upright position, lever out the waste. If necessary the sides can be pared, finally, with a bevel-edged chisel.

Rounding corners:
1. Having marked the shape to be cut start with your chisel on the waste side of the line, working very gradually towards the line.

2. Finish with a series of fine paring cuts around the line with a well-honed chisel. Either leave the fine chisel marks or finish with an abrasive, depending upon the finish you want.

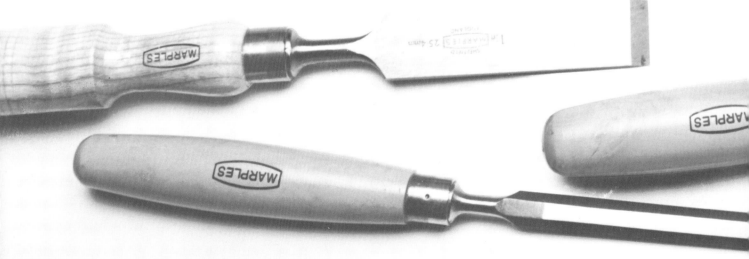

Gouges

You may find it more difficult to buy the gouge of your choice as, generally, there is less demand for gouges than chisels. The steel blades of gouges are curved in cross-section. They are either ground on the inside face, when they produce a cut shaped like the outside surface of the blade, or they are ground on the outside face, when they produce a cut which coincides with the profile of the blade's inside surface.

Sizes range from 6mm (¼in) to 30mm (1¼in). Buy as the need arises, but remember that sizes refer to the width of the blade and not the distance between its points.

The firmer gouge

The firmer gouge is ground on the outside face of the blade, and is used like a carving tool to cut concave shapes. The action is one of entering in and coming out of wood, as you might carve out a bowl or finger pulls for a drawer. The angle at which the blade is honed determines the angle at which it passes through the wood.

The scribing gouge

The scribing gouge is ground on the inside face of the blade, and is more accurate than the firmer gouge. It is used when cutting directionally in a straight line, particularly in precision cabinet work. The blade is ground on its outside face. There is a range of different curved sections for any given blade width.

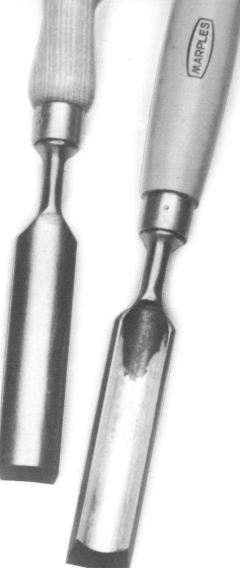

Paring:

1. Secure the piece with a cramp or vice.

2. For **vertical paring**, place your thumb on the top of the chisel handle and steady the blade with the thumb and forefinger of the other hand.

3. For **horizontal paring**, place the handle in the palm of your hand and steady the blade with the thumb and forefinger of the other hand.

4. Go gently. It is difficult to pare across the grain, but of the two possible directions in which you can cut across the grain one will be easier than the other. Discover it by experimenting.

5. Provided you remove a little waste at a time, hand pressure will be sufficient.

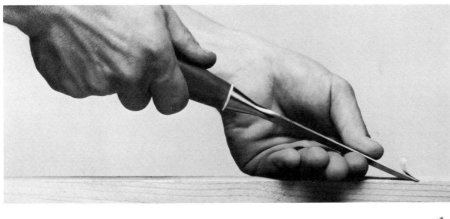

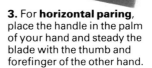

Gouge sizes
Size refers to a measurement straight across the cutting edge.

Carving

It is a good idea to reconcile your choice of carving tools to the type of work you plan to do. Howard Raybould does not rely upon a *complete set*, or even a particularly varied collection of tools. Nor does his carving rely upon traditional techniques. Precision of line and ornamentation is not, as we have seen, his approach to craft. The more relaxed, less rigid and technically demanding approach makes his method especially accessible to the amateur.

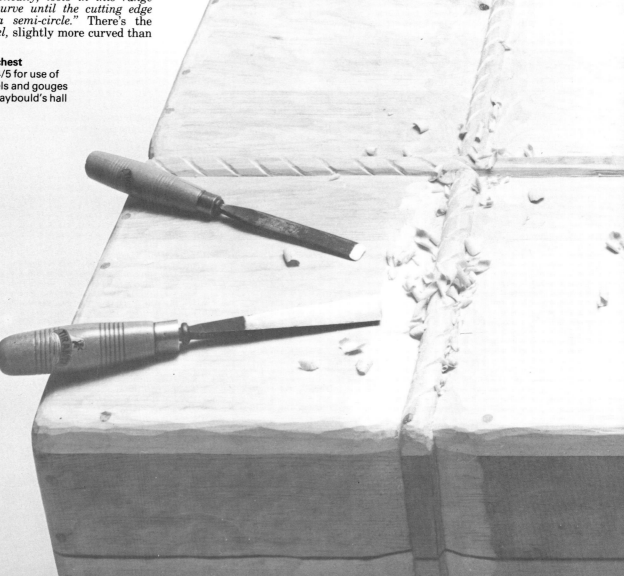

Left:
Curved, skew and straight chisels.
Right:
Two parting tools, straight and curved gouges.

Selection

"Buy general tools first, tools for which you know you will always be able to find a use – tools which will never lie idle, rusting on the shelf."

The flat tool
Most carving tools are gouge shaped, but with a flat carving chisel, *"you can work flat surfaces without forking into the wood. A 12mm (½in) flat tool is a good beginning"*. Carving chisels are ground both sides of the blade, and their grinding and honing angles are (unlike the chisels described on page 152) smoothed together. *"Generally, you use a carving chisel for chopping straight lines."*

From flat to curved
"Characteristically, tools in this range gradually curve until the cutting edge resembles a semi-circle." There's the *curved chisel*, slightly more curved than

the flat chisel and ground only on its convex contour. It is very often used to finish the work of the carving gouge. Then there's the semi-circular *spoon bit chisel* which is useful for finishing the work of the spoon bit gouge. *"If you choose a 'flat', a 'semi-circle' and one in between (of different widths) you'll have a fair scope of purpose. After the semi-circular shaped blades, you get into cross-sections which resemble the Suez Canal – high sides and rounded bottoms. These are veiners – buy one, a small size, say about 3mm (⅛in) across, and explore the possibilities."*

"My feeling is that yes, with a lot of money you could really indulge yourself, but unless you are very careful you might become confused – never really understanding which tool is used for what. You'd do much better to start by buying straight blades. If you start working deeper holes or complicated swirls, then invest in a bent tool. But try to get the most out of the straight blades."

The parting tool
"Finally, I would recommend a parting tool. This might better be described as a 'V'-tool because that's the shape of its

Carving the chest
See pages 44/5 for use of carving chisels and gouges on Howard Raybould's hall chest.

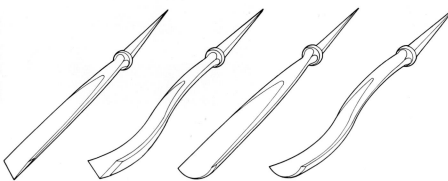

cross-section. But its action is to part like the bow of a ship – and it makes separating one area of wood from another a joy, provided you can keep it sharp! There are basically two 'V' shapes available – one with a tighter opening than the other. Start with the tighter 'V'."

Buying hints
"In a batch of tools not all of them will necessarily be well made. Avoid tools where the blade is too thick, uneven, or lop-sided. Too often parting tools and veiners have too much body, which makes it difficult for the rest of the tool to follow the cutting edge. Also, there's more to grind away."

Handles
Very often blades and handles are sold separately.

"No, you don't drill a hole into the handle and stick the blade in. Even if you drill the hole correctly, the blade will eventually work loose as it tends to be tapered. Also, if the fit is too tight, you might well split the handle as you bang it home.

"The best way, and the way I was taught, is to grip the blade in a vice with the cutting edge downwards and the point uppermost. Use some protection like leather wrapped around the blade, or better still a wooden vice.) Then bang the narrowly holed handle lightly onto the point, and turn until it frees itself. Repeat the process until the handle is about 6mm (¼in) short of the ferrule – then tap the handle home. In effect, the action of banging and twisting free, drills a hole precisely the right size and shape for any blade.

"As for choice of handles, suit yourself. Boxwood handles don't make you a better carver – but you might enjoy them. Remember that hexagonal handles are there to stop the tool rolling off the bench and damaging itself, or worse still ending up in your foot"

Sharpening

"When you go into a shop you may be fortunate in finding that the blades of the tools you are buying only need honing. But very often they need the grindstone first. If a tool does need grinding, don't be impatient. It's easy to burn – and then you'll have to remove that bit which has lost its temper (or was it you?). Green grit, grind stone, or traditional sandstone running through water are all safe.

"If you use an electrically powered grindstone have a can of water at hand to cool the blade before it gets too hot and draws the temper of the steel."
Howard Raybould

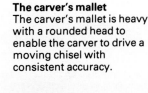

The carver's mallet
The carver's mallet is heavy with a rounded head to enable the carver to drive a moving chisel with consistent accuracy.

Turning

The lathe

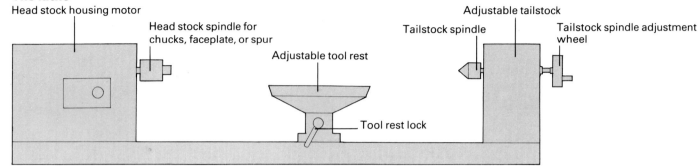

Head stock housing motor

Head stock spindle for chucks, faceplate, or spur

Adjustable tool rest

Adjustable tailstock

Tailstock spindle

Tailstock spindle adjustment wheel

Tool rest lock

This is *the* essential tool for turning wood. Initially, you may prefer to avoid investing hundreds of pounds in a brand new purpose-built model and buy a lathe attachment for your power drill instead (see page 171). Bob Stocksdale began with a home-made lathe powered by an old washing machine motor. See pages 138 and 139.

How it works

The lathe rotates the wood (stock), while hand manipulated tools are applied to its revolving surface to produce the shape. Drive is effected through chuck, face plate or spur centre attached to the head-stock. Various chucks are illustrated on page 135. An adjustable tailstock supports the other end of the work when required.

"The lathe cannot be bedded firmly enough. A tea chest full of concrete does wonders, even when bolted to a small lathe, provided the bearing is solid. All vibration must be eliminated if at all possible. The lathe's centre height should be 51mm (2in) to 76mm (3in) above elbow height. This will save you backache as you bend over the machine to see what's happening. Always ensure that the tool rest is well tightened. An Anglepoise lamp is essential and will help show up unwanted bumps, defects, and abrasive scratches."
Richard Raffan

Turning technique

What follows are the basic principles of wood turning. Three books are recommended for detailed how-to information; see also pages 134/9.

The Craftsman Woodturner by Peter Child. Bell & Sons Ltd., London, 1976. Woodcraft Supply, Mass., U.S.A.

Creative Woodturning by Dale L. Nish. Stobart & Son Ltd., London, 1976. Brigham Young University Press, Utah, U.S.A.

The Practical Woodturner by F. Pain. Evans Bros. Ltd., London, 1957. Drake Publishers Inc., New York, U.S.A.

"Wood is turned either with the grain or across the grain. Either way, wear a mask and goggles (or glasses) for protection of eyes and lungs." Richard Raffan

Turning with the grain

Where the stock is long, and end grain is not to be worked, drive is effected through a spur centre because screws will not hold successfully in end grain.

For small work, say less than 12mm (½in) diameter, fix a three-jaw or collett chuck to the headstock.

The other end of the stock is supported by the tailstock with a revolving centre.

For small jobs involving end grain work, such as egg cups, boxes, etc., use a cup, three-jaw or split ring chuck.

Turning across the grain

When making bowls, platters, etc., where wood grain runs across the surface of the work, cut the stock as round as possible with a band saw or circular saw, and attach it with short screws to a faceplate. The tailstock is not employed. An alternative method of securing the stock is shown below.

The tool rest

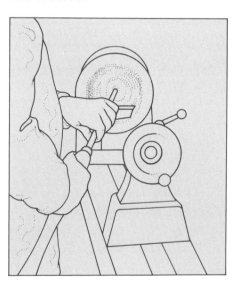

Position the rest 3mm (⅛in) from the work; experiment with rest heights. As a rule of thumb, set it at centre height for bowls. When turning with the grain, position it so that you can successfully shave near the top of the stock surface. Check the work turns clear of the rest.

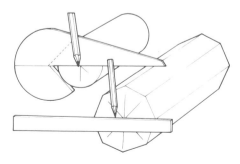

Locating the stock centre

Either use a centre square, pushing the stock into its notch and marking a line against the blade, rotating the tool to make more marks for accuracy; or draw diagonals through a polygon.

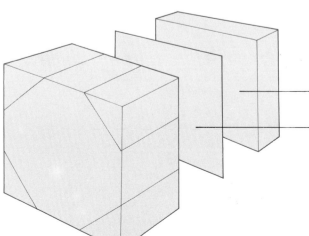

Attaching work to a faceplate

It is possible to attach work without screwing into the stock. Select waste wood thick enough to take the screws.

Glue a thick piece of paper between stock and waste.

Remove the work later by splitting the paper with a chisel.

Tools

There is an important basic distinction between two groups of turning tools – those designed to shave (or cut) and those designed to scrape.

Tools for turning with the grain

A gouge shaves stock from square to round, and cuts coves.

A skew chisel is *the* tool for centre work and produces a smooth cut.

A parting tool is designed primarily to cut work from the waste, i.e. part off, and is made in one size only.

A chisel ground on one side only and with a round nose, produces a scraping action and is used for internal work and hollowing.

Tools for turning across the grain

When roughing out stock for bowls and other work where the grain runs across the surface, use deep-fluted gouges, beginning with a large size and finishing with the small. Grind gouge corners well back to avoid scarring the work.

Scrapers can also be used for final smoothing, but gently so as to avoid pulling out the end grain.

Parting tools and skew chisels are not used at all.

"If you cannot remove wood one way, experiment with another. There is no point struggling 'the right way'. Cut wood as it prefers to be cut."
Richard Raffan

"Have a grindstone close by. Turning tools do a lot of work and need frequent touching up on the stone. I seldom use a slipstone, but when working some timbers I will need to grind every two or three cuts."
Richard Raffan

Finishing

Finishing depends on the wood and the use to which the object is to be put. Mineral oil is commonly used for bowls to be in contact with food. One craftsman reports successful use of Brasso on ebony.

"I use Garnet papers, grits 80, 100, 180, and sometimes 50 grits for really difficult areas and 220 for extra smoothness. I never use synthetic finishes, varnishes or hard wax, preferring a softer mellow look and feel which I obtain with vegetable cooking oil and soft beeswax on top. This is wiped hard with a soft cloth."
Richard Raffan

Left to right:
Parting tool primarily used for cutting work from waste.

Gouge for roughing out, shaving stock from square to round, or cutting coves.

Scraper ground on one side only for internal work and final smoothing.

Skew chisel has a flat blade with an angled cutting edge ground on both sides.

Diamond point chisel ground on one side can be used to cut grooves.

Planes and planing

The jack plane

As an all-purpose bench tool, the modern jack (or fore) plane is worth having. You will find much work for a jack plane 375mm (15in) long. Correctly prepared it will pass smoothly over any hollows in the wood surface.

"A bought plane will hardly ever produce accurate results. It's the body of the plane which determines its precision. Planes are made out of green castings, and they're shifting all the time. Traditionally the castings were left to season until all the strains had been released, and then they would be ground.

"So when you have bought your plane you will have to make adjustments. Grind the sole of the plane on a piece of plate glass covered with carborundum paste. Work through grades of the paste until you have produced a polished surface. Check that the surface is flat with a straight-edge. If you work slowly and carefully enough you can ensure precision."
John Makepeace

Maintenance

When the plane is out of use, the blade should be drawn up inside the body. If it is not to be used for quite some time, dismantle as shown in the illustration and lightly grease the parts to prevent rusting.

Using a plane

As we have seen in the section on preparation of timber (page 32), if you are buying hardwoods you may have to do a lot of planing. And never more than in using a plane is the action of a tool a logical extension of the whole body's movement. So get the feel of your plane. Practise on odd pieces of wood. Make slow easy, smooth movements and notice just how much wood each setting of the blade removes.

Action hints

* *"Calm down, and make one complete stroke in slow motion.*

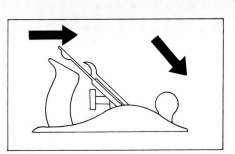

* *"At the start you press the nose (toe) of the plane down, while with the other hand you push more than you press. Actually, you hardly press at all down there; your elbow is down low ... And, because a gradually widening cut starts more easily than a sudden wide one, you should learn the habit of starting your cuts on the diagonal. Let the plane slant 45 degrees at first and gradually straighten it out.*

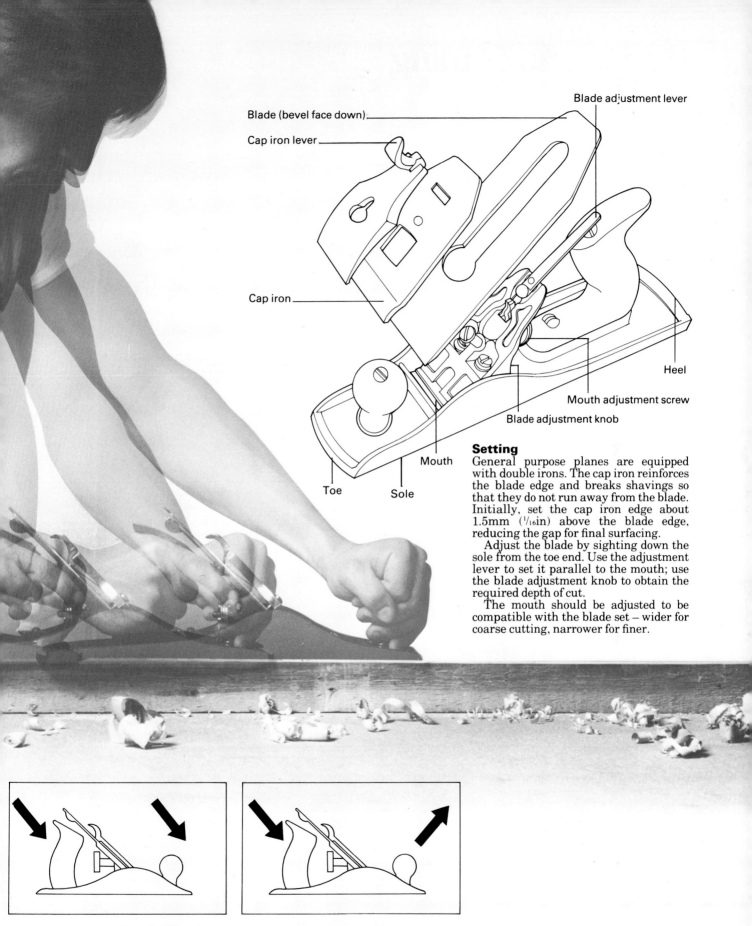

Blade (bevel face down)

Cap iron lever

Cap iron

Blade adjustment lever

Heel

Mouth adjustment screw

Blade adjustment knob

Mouth

Toe

Sole

Setting

General purpose planes are equipped with double irons. The cap iron reinforces the blade edge and breaks shavings so that they do not run away from the blade. Initially, set the cap iron edge about 1.5mm ($^1/_{16}$in) above the blade edge, reducing the gap for final surfacing.

Adjust the blade by sighting down the sole from the toe end. Use the adjustment lever to set it parallel to the mouth; use the blade adjustment knob to obtain the required depth of cut.

The mouth should be adjusted to be compatible with the blade set – wider for coarse cutting, narrower for finer.

*"Along the middle area of each cut, press evenly with both hands; a signal is that your hand and elbow behind the plane want to come up a bit. Your hands and arms are relaxed because the force and pressure are so natural as you lean forward. It's a sort of coasting.

*"You finish your practice cut by lifting your hand from the nose (toe) of the plane and just push-pressing at the back (heel) with the other until the iron has stopped whispering and left the wood, without the plane having tipped forward and jerked. So there are the three stages – start, glide, finish. Press at front, press-and-push, press at back. One smooth motion and even cut." James Krenov

"It is the tool, in the sense that I enjoy planing wood with a true plane more perhaps than any other working . . . planing is something special – like the music of a violin."

Planes and planing 2

The moulding plane
These are far less widely available today than they used to be. Their design is variously appropriate for cutting both convex and concave shapes. Blades and soles of moulding planes are shaped to match the reverse of the moulding which they are designed to produce.

Tongue and groove moulding planes may be sold in pairs – one, whose blade is shaped to cut waste wood away from either side of a tongue simultaneously; the other, whose blade is set to cut a groove to match the tongue.

The plough plane
The plough plane is designed to cut, in one pass, long grooves or rebates up to 12mm (½in) wide.

There is a depth gauge adjustment knob and there is an adjustable fence to ensure a consistent cutting line in relation to the other edge of the board. The plane blade is secured into the body of the plane by means of an in-built clamp which can be screwed tight. Before you make the clamp fast adjust the blade to the required depth.

Plough plane blades cut with the action of a chisel.

The spokeshave
Most spokeshaves consist of two wing-shaped handles, blade, cap iron, and blade adjustment screws which permit an accurate and very fine adjusting set. Some models have a thumb adjusting screw which is more difficult to use.

There are round and flat-faced spoke-shaves designed to plane concave and

Sharpening moulding planes
Tap the notch in the blade wedge with a hammer to release the blade for sharpening. Apply a slipstone to the ground side and a flat stone to the blade back.

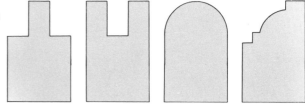

Plough plane shown above grooved work piece

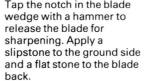

Below:
Cross-section of flat-faced spokeshave

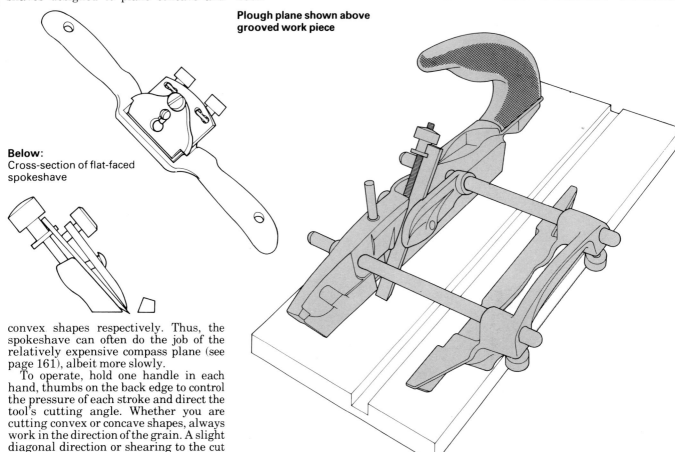

convex shapes respectively. Thus, the spokeshave can often do the job of the relatively expensive compass plane (see page 161), albeit more slowly.

To operate, hold one handle in each hand, thumbs on the back edge to control the pressure of each stroke and direct the tool's cutting angle. Whether you are cutting convex or concave shapes, always work in the direction of the grain. A slight diagonal direction or shearing to the cut can help keep it smooth.

Screwdrivers

The shoulder plane

Shoulder planes are rarely as precise as one would like. Ideally the sole of a shoulder plane is at perfect right angles to each side of its body. Unlike the plough plane blade, this blade is mounted bevel uppermost. It is used to trim shoulders of large joints and cut rebates (rabbets). Its blade extends across the full width of the body to enable it to do so.

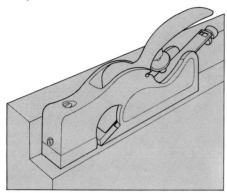

The block plane

The characteristic design of the block plane makes it ideal for chamfering, and planing end grain. It fits snugly into one hand for chamfering edges; place your forefinger on the guide knob at the front of the body of the tool and work on the far end of the board's edge first. It is a recommended tool for softening the edges of the legs of Ashley Cartwright's table and stools, amongst other jobs.

The blade is set bevel uppermost and at a very shallow angle (about 20 degrees). Keep the blade sharp and use both hands to trim end grain – its primary function. You will minimise the possibility of splitting the grain by working the tool from either end of the board (further hints given on page 33).

Some block planes have adjustable mouths to enable you to produce coarser or finer shavings.

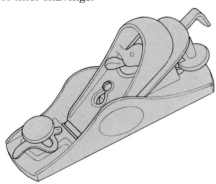

The compass plane

For curved work (the edge of a round table, for instance) the compass plane comes into its own. It has a flexible metal sole, which can be adjusted to any arc to shave both curves and concave edges, in addition to having the more conventional bench plane parts – blade and cap iron. The flexible sole is adjusted by a screw at the top of the plane body which manipulates the sole into shape. It is important to adjust it precisely before commencing, and work it with the grain away from the body.

The cabinet screwdriver

This is the traditional driving tool. Its blade flares at one end to a sometimes tapered tip, and is securely fixed at the other end into a bulbous handle. The handle is designed to fit snugly into the palm of the hand and provide maximum twisting power from wrist to screw.

The spiral ratchet screwdriver

The shaft consists of a chuck, spirally grooved shaft, ratchet and thumb slide leading up to a handle designed to receive pressure from the hand and forearm. Downward, upwards and horizontal pressure is converted into a rotating action by the ratchet and spiral grooves. The thumb slide can be moved to change the direction of rotation. A range of bits and increased speed of working are its two advantages.

Properly ground blades are designed to fit in a perpendicular position into screw slots of the same size. Tool and screw 'become one'.

The bradawl and gimlet

Either can be used to start holes for small screws. The gimlet resembles and works like a corkscrew. The bradawl is worked in half-turn motions by the wrist. Start with the blade across the grain. As a screw will follow a hole started by either tool, care must be taken to hold bradawl or gimlet at right-angles to the surface.

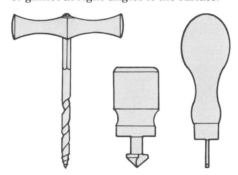

Countersinking

A countersunk hole may be worked with the countersunk tool illustrated, and filled with wood filler, but better still, pelleted. Alternatively, a countersunk hole may be drilled deeper with an appropriate brace or power drill bit, and plugged with wood in a similar fashion to plugging a knot (page 18).

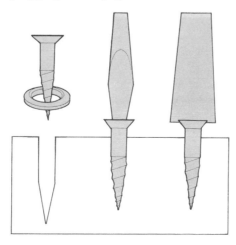

Choosing a bit

Failure to use a blade of the same size as a screw slot will either tear the wood surface or, if the blade is too small, may damage the screw. It may also cause a ratchet blade to slip from the head and damage you.

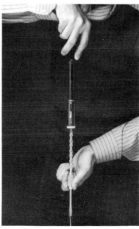

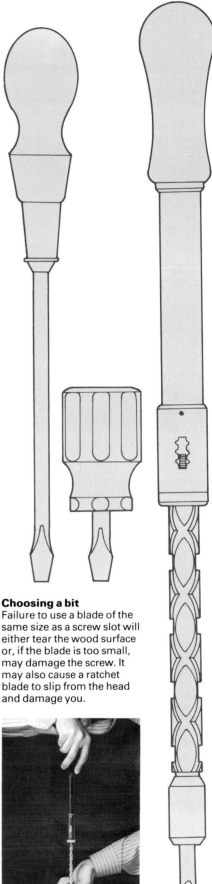

Grinding and honing

It is very important always to work with keen edged blades. Very often, when working with hardwoods whose grain is going in various directions, or when shooting the edges of plywood sheets, blades will need fairly frequent sharpening (or honing). But you should only need to re-grind when a blade edge becomes chipped, when the hollow ground portion of an edge has been flattened by honing, or when the honing angle becomes too thick.

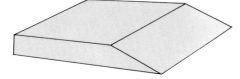

Above, a grinding angle of 25°; **below,** a cutting edge honed to 30°.

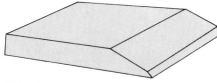

Grinding

Local garages, engineering works, and occasionally ironmongers may provide access to an electric grinder. Alternatively, tool dealers will arrange for tools to be ground elsewhere. But an electric grinder can prove to be more of a necessity than a luxury if you are involved in much cutting work. You can use a hand grinder but it is particularly suitable for touching up your blades – it would take far too long to use a hand grinder for extensive re-grinding.

How to grind

"Probably more tools are ruined during grinding than at any other time," says Robert Foncannon, making the point that a blade that has turned blue on the grindstone from over-heating will never hold an edge. The damage has been done and grinding the blue away merely masks it. The position of the tool rest, a good grinding wheel, and a realisation on your part that the process of grinding metal from your blades is a slow one if you are going to avoid over-heating – these are all important things to bear in mind when setting about your blades with a grinder.

"The tool rest should be positioned so that the blade intersects the wheel at the desired bevel angle. This allows the blade to be fully supported by the tool rest and restricts each cut to exactly the same angle. I grind all my blades to a 25 degrees angle, though others may vary this a degree or so. A 100 grit wheel is best. It will produce a smoother surface than a coarser wheel, thus requiring much less honing."

But, as John Makepeace points out, *"very few manufacturers produce a grinding wheel that's good for woodwork tools. Tell them what you are using it for and that you want a wheel that is fast-cutting and doesn't overheat the edge of the blade. They'll advise you accordingly."*

"Now," continues Foncannon, "lightly apply the blade to the wheel. Keep it flat against the rest and in continuous motion to avoid over-grinding and overheating any single area. Dipping the blade often in water helps prevent overheating, though it is not necessary if the grinding process proceeds slowly enough."

You may find it helpful to make a mark to the ground edge you want to achieve; use your try-square for accuracy.

Honing
The cutting edge angle should be sharpened to 30 to 35 degrees depending on the timber you will be cutting. The higher angle gives a stronger cutting edge which will be more durable for harder timber.

The combination stone
An India combination stone is recommended. It has a medium and fine graded sharpening area. The medium grade is particularly useful if you don't have a grindstone as it cuts more quickly than the fine grade. If you use a grindstone you will only use the medium graded area of the stone occasionally. Besides anything else, working from medium to fine stone can be messy, since before you begin sharpening, the stone must be oiled. Oil may be made from 50 parts clean engine oil and 50 parts paraffin.

Action hints
"How you hold that iron is of great importance. One tendency is to hold it too high up, and not to support it properly ... Try holding the piece way down as low as possible, the finger tips of your fore and index fingers nearly touching the stone. Support the iron a bit higher up with your thumb, ring, and/or little finger. Lightly! You will feel how the tool 'settles' into position on the stone ... after a while this condition will be the only natural one as you work." James Krenov

*The motion which creates friction between blade and stone is important too. There are various theories about this. One is aimed at preserving the stone: Small circular motions will 'belly' the stone. Long to-and-fro strokes are recommended. Another theory advises a round-and-round motion because that is easier to control and makes it easier to maintain the desired honing angle. In practice both have elements of truth.

"One regards the flatness of the stone as vital," says John Makepeace. *"Work in a circular motion and use the perimeter of the stone as much as possible. When you are sharpening smaller blades use areas of the stone which are generally underused. And every so often put a straightedge on the stone and see which areas are getting high. At the end of the day, if the stone gets out of shape, you will have to settle down and grind it with some sand, or fine carborundum powder and paraffin on a piece of plate glass. It's a long and tedious process."*

Re-grinding the stone

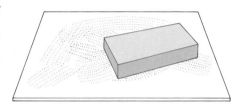

Slipstones
Slipstones are small, shaped stones useful for sharpening gouges or for burnishing any curved surfaces of metal.

Building a burr
The principle of sharpening blades with slipstones or combination stones is the same – hone until a small burr, or wire edge, is built up. Then, alternately, make a few strokes on either side – flat on the stone – until the burr falls off. For outside

Honing to a keen edge.

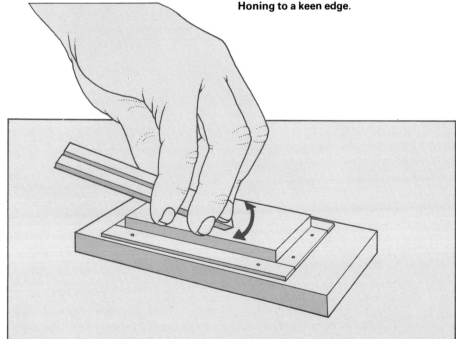

Slipstones – a variety of shapes

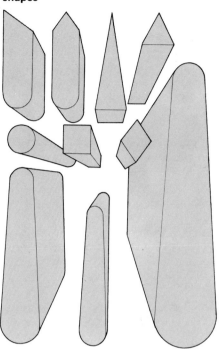

ground gouges, sharpen the angled edge on the stone first and then remove the burr with a slipstone. The reverse is true of inside ground gouges.

Sharpening a cabinet scraper
The cabinet scraper (see page 182) cuts with a serif-shaped burr raise on its edges. First, square the long edges of the tool with a file and take off any resultant burr on the side of an oilstone. The squared edges are then turned over by placing the scraper on a flat surface, its edge overlapping the edge of the surface and drawing a round piece of hardened steel (or the back of a gouge) firmly towards you.

Raising a burr
Cabinet scrapers cut with a burr raised on the cutting edge.

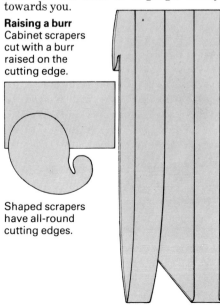

Shaped scrapers have all-round cutting edges.

The resultant burr is now perpendicular to the scraper's edge. Turn the tool on end and reverse the burr with the back of the gouge held at an angle of about 85 degrees to produce a serif-shaped edge.

Driving tools and nails

Hammers
There are all sorts of hammers designed for various different jobs. We recommend you buy only two – the Warrington Pattern Cross Pein and the Claw.

Action hints
Everyone knows how to use a hammer. Or do they? It might seem the simplest of tasks, which makes it all the more devastating when so simple a tool ruins the surface of a workpiece.

* For maximum power, grip the end of the handle.
* Keep your eye on the nail head, nothing else.
* Swinging from the elbow, start by tapping the head with the hammer at right angles to it. Only then begin to strike firmly.
* When the head is just above the surface of the wood, take a nail punch, carefully position it over the nail head and tap it about 1mm ($^{1}/_{32}$in) below the surface.
* Should you, despite the advice, bruise the wood surface, wet the depressed area with a damp cloth and iron out the bruise with an electric iron.
* When extracting nails with a claw, insert a scrap of wood between claw and wood surface. If the nail is particularly long, use progressively thicker scraps for maximum leverage and minimum bruising.
* Occasionally sand the hammer head to help prevent it slipping off a nail head.

* Never strike two hammer faces together. They are case hardened and could shatter.
* It is possible to minimise the likelihood of wood splitting when driving in a nail by making a starter hole with a bradawl and/or nipping the point of a nail with pincers – a sharp point is more likely to tear wood fibres, and so split wood, than a blunt point.

Nails and nailing
There are a great many different types of nail and it can be quite confusing when faced with the choice. Basically you will only need to consider three – the French or common nail, the oval wire nail, and the panel pin – and for most furniture work you can ignore the common nail. Its large unattractive head is unsuitable for indoor furniture, although it may be suitable for less discerning work. Of the three it is also most likely to split wood.

Oval wire nail
The oval wire nail, on the other hand, can be useful. If its oval head is set along the grain it is less likely to split wood.

Panel pin
The panel pin, a smaller thinner nail than the other two, is very useful for cabinet work, fitting mouldings, or for thin sheet material.

These nails come in various sizes. You will probably find the round wire nail available in 20mm to 150mm lengths (¾in to 6in), the oval wire nail in 20mm to 150mm lengths (¾in to 6in), the panel pin in 9mm to 50mm (³⁄₈in to 2in). Choose a nail roughly three times longer than the thickness of the top piece of wood you are joining.

In America, there are three nails which should be considered: the casing nail (available in 1 to 5in lengths), the finishing nail for cabinet work (available in 1 to 4in lengths), and the wire brad nail for light work and mouldings (available in ³⁄₁₆ to 3in lengths), the latter two being most useful. There, sizes are indicated by 'penny' abbreviated as 'd', e.g. 2d=1in, 20d=4in.

Concealing the nail head (1)
When using nails where appearance will be important, it is worth considering ways of disguising the nail head.

An oval wire nail can be driven below the surface with a nail punch and filled. Ideally the ground tip of the nail punch should fit the nail head tightly – otherwise it will be inclined to slip on the nail head and bruise the surface of the wood.

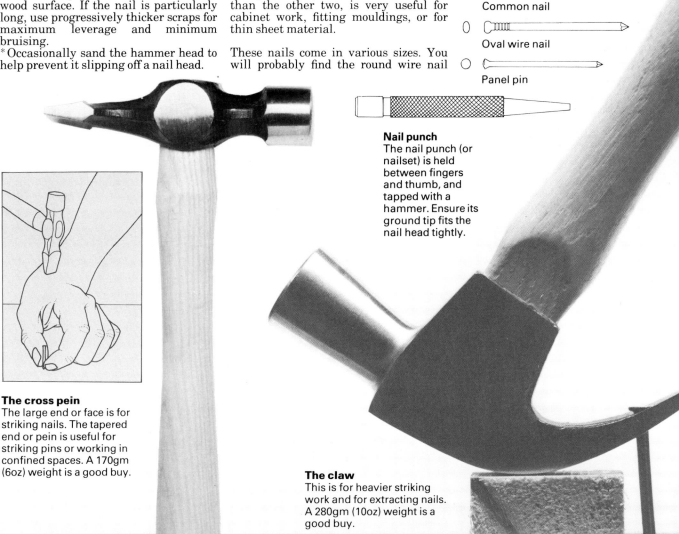

Common nail

Oval wire nail

Panel pin

Nail punch
The nail punch (or nailset) is held between fingers and thumb, and tapped with a hammer. Ensure its ground tip fits the nail head tightly.

The cross pein
The large end or face is for striking nails. The tapered end or pein is useful for striking pins or working in confined spaces. A 170gm (6oz) weight is a good buy.

The claw
This is for heavier striking work and for extracting nails. A 280gm (10oz) weight is a good buy.

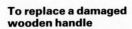

To replace a damaged wooden handle
1. Cut two equally spaced slits about two thirds depth of the hammer head into the new wooden shaft.

2. Drive the head onto the shaft.
3. Alternately, tap wooden wedges into the slits you have made. Make sure of an even spread of the shaft.

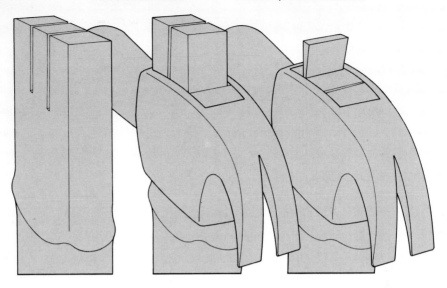

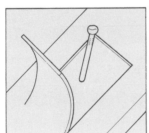

Concealing the nail head (2)
Another method is known as secret or blind nailing. This involves chiseling a sliver of wood, as shown in the illustration, driving the nail into the recess, and finally gluing the sliver back flush with the wood surface.

Carpenter's pincers
Gripping the nail near the wood surface and rocking the tool, lever out the nail in a series of pulls. Use it when a claw hammer is inadequate.

MADE IN
(MARPLES)
ENGLAND
No 7715   4 IN

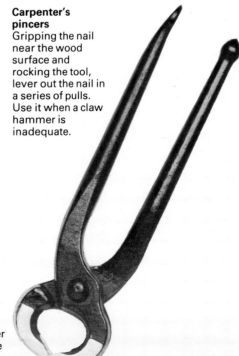

The carpenter's mallet
The carpenter's mallet, with its tapered head designed to enable you to strike the work squarely, is used for tapping joints fast, driving wood handled chisels, or whenever a metal head would damage the surface being struck.

Drills

The hand drill

The hand drill or wheel brace has a capacity for cutting holes up to 8mm (5/16in). Far from being the poor man's power drill, the hand drill can frequently be used in situations where an electric drill is too cumbersome and, since it has an obviously slower action, it is far easier to control.

However, in certain circumstances, you may have to use pressure on the hand drill. When using horizontally, bury its handle into your stomach to stop the tool twisting as you revolve the handle. When drilling in a vertical position with pressure, grip the main handle with one hand and apply pressure with your chest.

As with the brace, it is a good idea to start a hand drill hole with a bradawl, being sure to line up the bradawl accurately, as the drill bit will follow the starting hole.

How to fit hand drill bits

The hand drill chuck comprises three self-centring jaws which can be opened by turning the chuck anti-clockwise. Centre the bit in the jaw opening and turn the chuck clockwise so that the bit is rigid.

The standard brace

The design of the standard brace – its wide-sweeping handle, force-bearing head and alligator jaws – is ideal for the slow powerful cutting of wide-diameter holes. Additionally, the characteristic sweep of the brace handle poses no problems in confined spaces if a rachet is fitted to its chuck (i.e. the rachet dispenses with the need to turn the brace handle a full 360 degrees to effect a similar result).

It is obtainable in a number of sizes – from a 125mm (5in) sweep to a 355mm (14in) sweep – and the 250mm (10in) model is a recommended purchase.

There are a number of bits available, including screwdriver and countersink bits. But the Jennings pattern auger bit is a worthwhile buy as it is designed to clear away the waste wood as it progresses through the hole, and has the added advantage of keeping centred better than most.

Action hints

* The design of the brace is not suitable for starting drill holes. Use a bradawl or gimlet first.
* A try-square placed near the bit may assist accurate vertical drilling.

Pinion

Gear wheel

Drive handle

RECORD

Hand drill bits

The standard drill with its three-jaw chuck, accepting 6mm (¼in) or 8mm (5/16in) drill bits, is designed for fast, controlled drilling of small diameter holes. Bits have parallel round shanks.

Chuck

Self-centring jaws

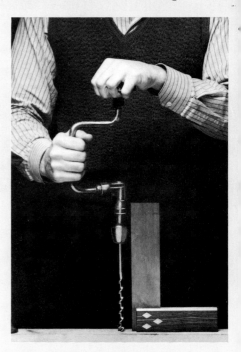

* Press the brace handle against the body when drilling horizontally.
* If you need to drill a precise depth, it is a good idea to wrap a piece of adhesive tape around the bit at the required depth. This is a cheaper alternative to a depth stop attachment which you can buy.
* When drilling a hole right through a board there is a danger of splitting or tearing wood as the bit exits through the back of the board. Drill until the point of the spur just appears on the opposite side. Then turn the wood round and use the small hole as the centre to work from the opposite side. Alternatively, cramp a piece of wood over the position where the hole will appear and drill into it. This will support the grain around the periphery of the hole.

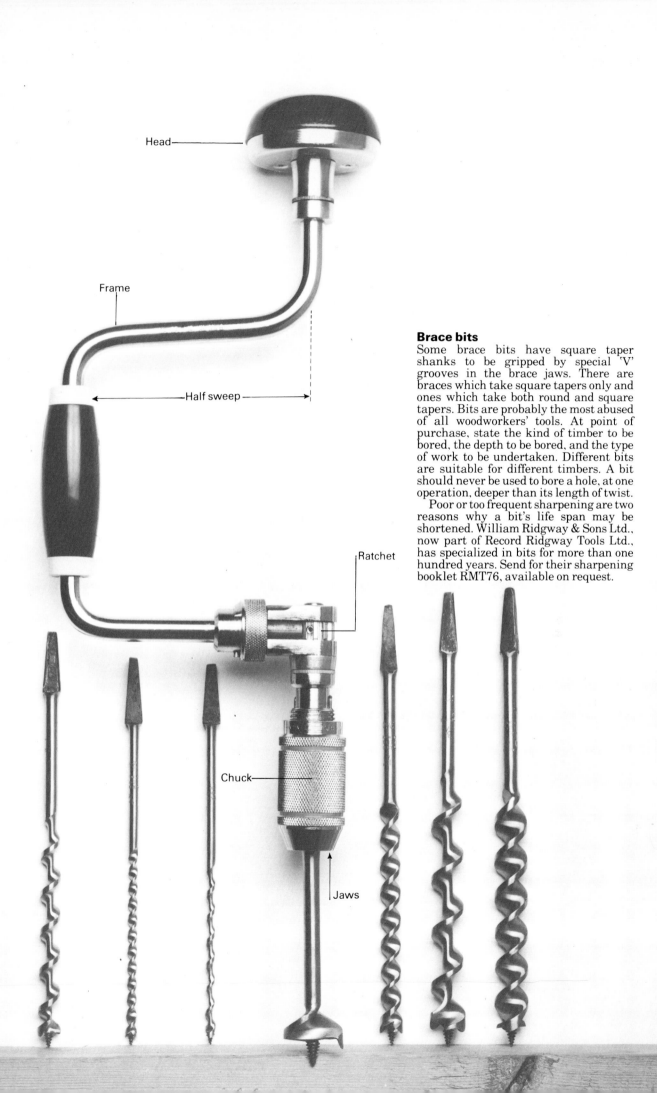

Head

Frame

Half sweep

Ratchet

Chuck

Jaws

Brace bits

Some brace bits have square taper shanks to be gripped by special 'V' grooves in the brace jaws. There are braces which take square tapers only and ones which take both round and square tapers. Bits are probably the most abused of all woodworkers' tools. At point of purchase, state the kind of timber to be bored, the depth to be bored, and the type of work to be undertaken. Different bits are suitable for different timbers. A bit should never be used to bore a hole, at one operation, deeper than its length of twist.

Poor or too frequent sharpening are two reasons why a bit's life span may be shortened. William Ridgway & Sons Ltd., now part of Record Ridgway Tools Ltd., has specialized in bits for more than one hundred years. Send for their sharpening booklet RMT76, available on request.

Power tools

The power drill
This is as common in the amateur's workshop as the washing machine is in the laundry – understandably since it's one of the most versatile power tools on the market. We recommend the pistol grip gun with a chuck capacity of 12mm (½in).

Bits for the power drill
Twist bit. Various sizes from 1.6mm (¹/₁₆in) to 6mm (¼in).
Jennings bit. For larger holes.
Forstner bit. For flat bottomed holes. Withdraw and clean hole frequently. Use only in a drill stand.
Dowel bit. More accurate than the twist bit and less likely to wander.
Spade (or flat) bit. For very large holes up to 32mm (1¼in).
Hole saw (or trepanning) bit. The circular toothed ring acts like a pastry cutter.
Countersink bit. For countersinking a screw head into a wood surface.

Action hints
* You will need to drive your drill at varying speeds. The lower speed is useful, for example, for soft masonry or for large diameter holes in wood. One-speed drills are therefore inferior, but cheaper, smaller and lighter which may in some workshops be more useful.
* Keep the bits sharp at all times for optimum safety and performance.
* There are good electrically powered bit sharpeners on the market.

Power tool safety factors
1. Every manufacturer sells power tools with instructions on how to use them and safety guide lines. Read these very carefully before rushing into action. Similarly, if you are buying attachments for your drill you will find instructions as to how to fit these attachments, so read these carefully too.
2. Read the manufacturer's instructions as to how your tool works until you fully appreciate the logic of its mechanism.
3. Store all power tools well away from children, and ensure that onlookers in the workshop are well out of the way when a tool is in use.
4. Always disconnect tools when not in use, or when changing bits, chucks, blades, etc. It may be especially tempting not to do so if, for example, you are constantly fitting and removing your power drill grinder attachment during an extended period of work.
5. Check that your tools carry the international symbol for double insulation.
6. Never carry your tools around by their cables. Keep your finger away from the trigger when tool not in use.
7. Check cables regularly for signs of wear.
8. Keep cables well out of the way when tools are in use.
9. Never wear necklaces or other loose attire; do wear eye protection.
10. Power drills have chuck keys to loosen their jaws before inserting a bit. Do be careful not to forget to remove the chuck key before starting the motor.
11. Always ensure that your grinder has a wheel guard cover and that the eye shield is in position.

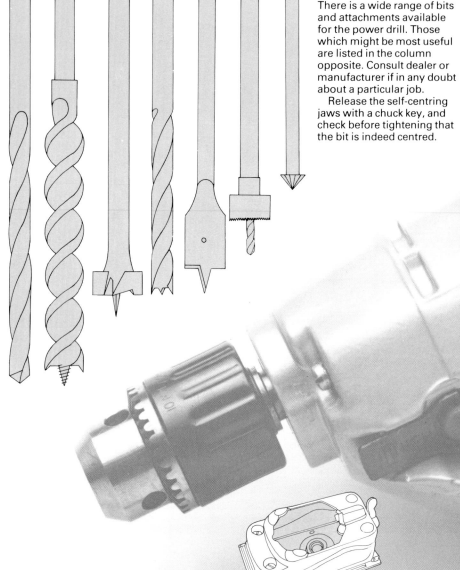

Power sanders
There are various sander drill attachments available on the market – *orbital sanders*, useful for most large, flat surfaces; *disc sanders*, suitable where larger quantities of waste material need to be removed; and *drum sanders*, which can be used to remove waste wood from concave and convex shapes as well as flat surfaces.

Orbital sander attachment
Uncommon in the U.S. where it is more usually an inexpensive, separate tool.

To fit the orbital sander to the drill, remove the chuck from your power drill and replace it with an eccentric drive cam, which you can buy especially to fit the body of the orbital sander. The body of the sander is connected to a large flat pad covered with a sheet of abrasive. The sheet is fixed to the pad by a spring-clip at either end of the pad. This ensures absolute rigidity of the abrasive sheet.

You will need both hands to enable the tool to work efficiently, although you should not need to apply any pressure to it. Its own weight will be sufficient to perform its function, provided you move

Power drill accessories
There is a wide range of bits and attachments available for the power drill. Those which might be most useful are listed in the column opposite. Consult dealer or manufacturer if in any doubt about a particular job.

Release the self-centring jaws with a chuck key, and check before tightening that the bit is indeed centred.

Orbital sander attachment

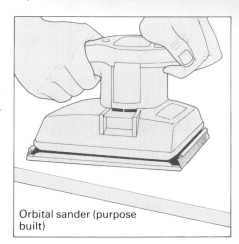

Orbital sander (purpose built)

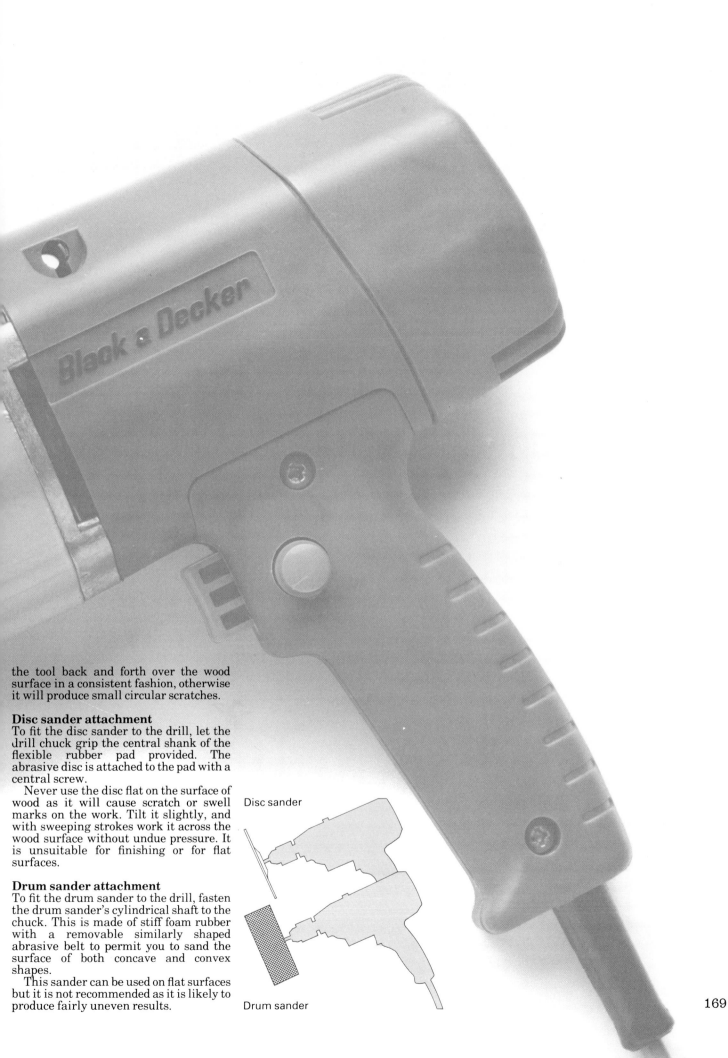

the tool back and forth over the wood surface in a consistent fashion, otherwise it will produce small circular scratches.

Disc sander attachment
To fit the disc sander to the drill, let the drill chuck grip the central shank of the flexible rubber pad provided. The abrasive disc is attached to the pad with a central screw.

Never use the disc flat on the surface of wood as it will cause scratch or swell marks on the work. Tilt it slightly, and with sweeping strokes work it across the wood surface without undue pressure. It is unsuitable for finishing or for flat surfaces.

Drum sander attachment
To fit the drum sander to the drill, fasten the drum sander's cylindrical shaft to the chuck. This is made of stiff foam rubber with a removable similarly shaped abrasive belt to permit you to sand the surface of both concave and convex shapes.

This sander can be used on flat surfaces but it is not recommended as it is likely to produce fairly uneven results.

Disc sander

Drum sander

Power tools 2

Power saws

There are two types of circular saw available. The first may be bought as a self-contained unit or in the U.K. as a drill attachment. It is hand-held and moved manually through the work surface. It comprises a circular blade mounted on a shaft connected to a motor.

There is a guide attachment to the tool which ensures that the cutting angle remains consistent, and there is a blade guard to protect the worker. The other type of circular saw is bench-mounted with its blade pointing upwards so that the work piece is fed into it. A hand-held circular saw can be converted into a bench-mounted model by clamping it to a saw table attachment. Using a bench-mounted saw is particularly useful for cutting angles and joints, as both hands are free.

The hand-held circular saw

The largest model is capable of cutting planks up to 90mm (3½in) thick.

There are various types of saw blade available: a rip blade for cutting along the grain, a cross-cut blade for cutting across the grain, and a combination blade which can cut at any angle to the grain, although great care should be taken when using this angled to the grain.

Action hints

* If the circular saw jams or slows down in action remove the tool from the work piece immediately, and before you turn the motor off.
* Never force the saw along a cut, and before entering the wood make sure that the motor is running at full capacity.
* Because all hand-held circular saw blades cut on the up-stroke (bench-mounted, on the down-stroke) you will find that a shallow setting of the blade will produce a cleaner result.
* If you find that the saw is wandering away from the cutting line do not try to rectify it by bending the saw back towards that line. Remove the saw and cut the section again.
* Always cut on the waste side of the line and when measuring and marking, allow for the thickness of the blade which may vary from blade to blade.

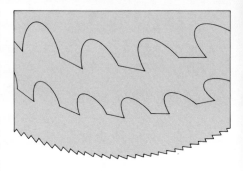

How to change a blade

There are various makes of circular saw and you would be advised to study the manufacturer's instructions very carefully before fitting your chosen blade. However in general, having disconnected the tool, the process is as follows:

1. Fit a spanner onto the bolt holding the blade onto the circular saw.

2. Tap the spanner with a mallet to free the bolt and unscrew it by hand.

3. Remove the washer and blade.

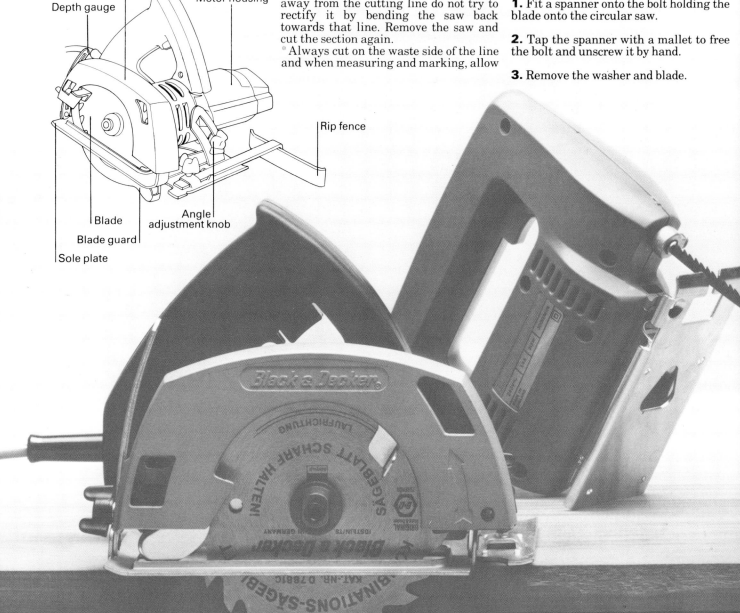

Top plate guard

Motor housing

Depth gauge

Rip fence

Blade

Angle adjustment knob

Blade guard

Sole plate

4. It is important to bear in mind that circular saw blades cutting in an upwards direction should be driven in a counter-clockwise motion. Some makes of blade are arrowed showing you which way the blade should turn, others will simply have the manufacturer's name on one side, and that side should be visible to you once it has been fitted.

5. Replace the blade, washer and bolt precisely as you removed them.

How to set the depth of the cut
Place the tool so that the blade is positioned against the side edge of the work piece; then mark the required depth of the cut on the edge of the work piece and release the depth adjustment knob (see illustration) allowing the blade to swing down so that its lowest point touches the depth line marked on the edge of the work piece. Tighten the depth adjustment knob.

How to set the saw to cut angles
As shown in the illustration there is an angle adjustment knob which clearly provides, on a built-in protracter scale, for any cutting angle up to 45 degrees. Set accordingly. It is advisable to test the angle on a piece of waste wood and check that the angle is true with an adjustable combination try-square.

How to use the fence guide
As seen in the illustration a rip fence is provided with your circular saw. It may be fitted on either side of the saw and is adjustable according to the width of the plank you are cutting. Measure the width you wish to cut from the inside (rather than the outside) of the fence to the blade, and once again allow for the width of the blade itself in making your final marks.

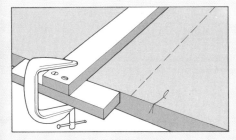

A rip fence can be used only for cutting along the grain. If you are making a cut across the grain you will need to improvise a guide along which the sole plate (see illustration) can run. To ensure that the guide is at right angles to the edge of the board across which you are cutting, the guide will need to be 'T'-shaped – the tip of the 'T' resting against the edge of the board and the vertical section of the 'T' running alongside the sole plate of the gether as shown in the illustration. Run saw. Screw the two pieces of wood to-

the saw through the board making sure that the sole plate is always in contact with the vertical section of the 'T' guide.

To make a mitre-angled cut the principle is the same. Fasten a straight strip of wood to the work piece at the required angle with 'G' cramps.

To cut a series of grooves, set your blade to the required depth and adjust the rip fence so as to make cuts at the required intervals. When you have cut each groove, clear out the waste wood with a chisel. Better still use a groove cutting blade (there is a whole range of specialised blades available) and paring away should not be necessary.

The jig (or saber) saw
This is one of the most useful power saws available to you. Its strength is its versatility. It should be noted that whilst both circular and jig saws are available as attachments to power drills, as such they have inherent disadvantages. Certainly they are cheaper but their potential in terms of power and sturdiness is far less than the purpose built models.

There is a wide variety of blades available to fit your sabre saw. As far as cutting wood is concerned there are coarse blades and various grades of fine blades. The coarse blades are used for cutting large sections of wood and the different grades of finer blades will be variously suitable for\softwoods, hardwoods and man-made boards. Discuss the blades' intended use at point of purchase.

Study the manufacturer's instructions carefully before fitting your blades. One important general rule is to make sure that once fitted, the blade is rigid and well aligned.

The saw is capable of cutting to a depth of about 50mm (2in) in softwoods and 25mm (1in) in hardwoods and man-made sheets.

Cutting in a straight line
The circular saw generally performs this job better than the jig saw. However, it may well be that you choose to buy one rather than the other and the jig saw is certainly more widely useful. Since all these hand-held power saws cut on the up-stroke it is a good idea to lay your work piece finished side down so that any splintering that does occur will not cause trouble later on. Some jig saws come with fitted guide fences, like the circular saw, and in general the rules for straight and mitred-angled cuts are the same as above.

Cutting shapes
This is where the jig saw begins to come into its own. In a sense it is a far more efficient version of the pad saw (see page 147). When using a jig saw to cut along a marked line within a board, bore a hole sufficient to take the width of its blade, so that the outer circumference of the hole is

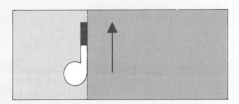

in line with your mark (see illustration).

Most of the drill hole will thus appear on the waste wood section. Feed the blade into the hole and cut along the line.

Action hints
* A vital point, which may appear to be fairly obvious, is always to allow clearance for the jig saw blade beneath the work surface.
* Never *force* the blade to cut a curve – a narrower blade may be the answer, alternatively remove some of the waste wood prior to the curved cut.
* You may read or hear that you can start a cut within a board by tilting the jig saw forward on its shoe, starting the motor and slowly lowering the blade towards the surface. This is an extremely dangerous operation and needs a good deal of practice to perform successfully. Should you attempt it, ensure that you are wearing eye protection.

The band saw
Mention of it is made in the Plans, and if a band saw is outside your investment budget, access to one can cut your work load considerably. Consisting of a looped blade driven round two encased wheels, it is designed for cutting large sections of timber, and cutting curves and angled work.

Other drill attachments

The grinder
We have already seen how important the bench grinder is as a permanent aspect of the workshop. You *can* buy a grinder attachment for your power drill rather than having to buy the more expensive bench grinder. But remember that you will need to set it up every time you want to sharpen something (which is frequently) and this may be inconvenient if you are using the drill for other purposes. Fasten the tool firmly to the bench top.

The lathe
You may find that you are not involved in sufficient turning work to justify the investment of a purpose built model. Clearly, the work of a lathe attachment is restricted by the power of the drill motor itself. However, good work can be produced on a drill-powered lathe. The size of the lathe bed on such an attachment is usually 700mm or 800mm long (approximately 2ft 6in). Remove the drill chuck and fit the lathe to form a composite tool.

Power tools 3

The power router

It is recommended that you buy an electric router. Rapidly becoming available in less expensive models, the power router has largely superceded the far less versatile moulding plane and hand router (essentially a different tool, the hand router is really a block housing a chisel blade – it cuts with a chisel action).

The router may be used to overcome problems associated with the more sophisticated traditional joints. Otherwise it can be handy for cutting grooves (dados) and mouldings. Because of its high operating speed, it has a great advantage of seldom tearing wood.

Attached to the motor is a collet chuck. Over the motor is a sleeve fitted with a depth indicator, two handles, and a base which slides along the surface of the work piece. There is a wide variety of bits available to fit into the collet chuck. Tungsten carbide bits should be bought for anything abrasive – such as chipboard. The illustration on page 173 shows a typical range. It is a good idea when selecting a moulding bit to ensure that it includes a guide pin. This dispenses with the need for a guide fence (see illustration). The guide pin naturally follows the vertical part of the board edge, although light side pressure is needed to avoid burning a board's edge.

There is a choice of machines – some heavier than others. A light machine will probably suffice, although you may need to make more than one pass when cutting deep grooves. The plunge router illustrated and captioned here is fairly new on the market and besides being very competitively priced has the advantage of doubling as a drill.

The router bit cuts with a high speed rotary action. You should keep a firm grip on it as it may tend to twist as it comes into contact with the wood. Keep the tool moving at a consistent rate, but do not force anything.

The router guide fence

As we have said you should buy moulding bits with guide pins. However, if you are cutting grooves in a straight line it is a good idea to cramp a piece of wood onto the work piece to prevent the router wandering. There is a guide fence accessory also available which can be locked into place on the router. This ensures a groove parallel to the edge of your work piece, and works equally well when cutting with or across the grain.

Action hints

* Grind the router bits on a grindstone. You can hone a router bit (following grinding) but because of its shape you will probably need a slipstone.

* Never start work until the motor has reached its maximum speed – it is very quick to do so.

* Relax with your router! Try the tool on a spare piece of wood first and get the feel of it. If it has an adjustable speed (uncommon in hand-held routers) then you will soon grasp, through practice, which speed is the motor's happiest work rate.

The 'plunge-in' router

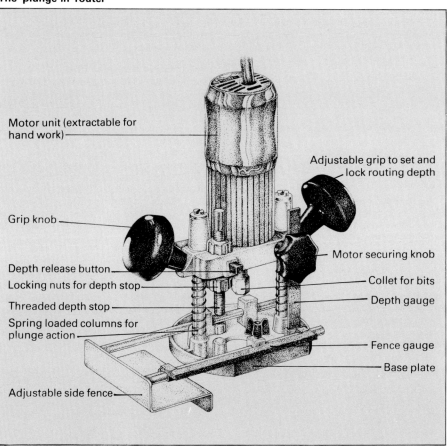

Motor unit (extractable for hand work)

Adjustable grip to set and lock routing depth

Grip knob

Motor securing knob

Depth release button

Collet for bits

Locking nuts for depth stop

Depth gauge

Threaded depth stop

Spring loaded columns for plunge action

Fence gauge

Base plate

Adjustable side fence

Cutting joints with a router

By making good use of the depth gauge and guide fence, a number of joints may readily be cut with a router.

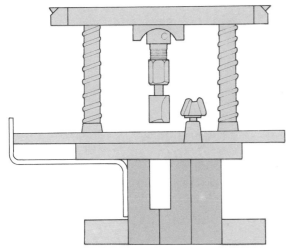

Mortise and tenon

Attach a guide fence to the router base and adjust the depth gauge to the mortise depth you require. Mark out the mortise (see page 178) and, beginning at one end of it, make the first cut up to its centre. Then, by approaching its centre from the other end, you can double check that the mortise sits centrally in the rail. Square off the mortise ends with a chisel.

Before cutting the tenon, mark it out and place that rail between two waste strips of wood in the vice. Ensure that the tenon edge is pointing up and that the ends of the three pieces of wood are absolutely flush and square. The waste pieces are a solid base for the router sole. Set the guide fence and depth gauge to produce a tenon to match the mortise, and make a pass from either side of the tenon.

Tongue and groove

The principle of cutting the groove is much the same as for the tenon. Vise the work piece between two strips of wood to provide a base on which the router can ride, again ensuring that all three pieces are flush and square. Adjust the fence to position the groove correctly in the board edge, and check it by making passes from either side. Cut deep grooves with a series of shallow cuts.

Having cut the groove, use the same depth setting to cut away the wood either side of the tongue. Notice in the illustration that, as before, the router will be cutting partially into the two strips of waste wood.

Dovetail

The dovetail joint, frequently considered one of the more demanding joints, can very simply be cut with a router and dovetail jig.

Plant one board horizontally and the other vertically into the jig as shown in the illustration. The fingers of the jig will guide the router dovetail bit to produce tails and pins of equal size.

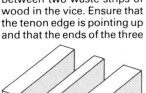

Cutting a tenon
Vice the rail between two strips of waste wood.

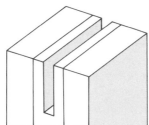

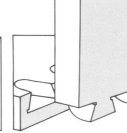

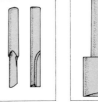
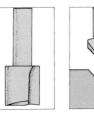

Right to left:
One flute cutter
Two flute cutter
'V' groove cutter
Dovetail cutter
Stair housing cutter
Drill and counterbore
Plug maker
Chamfer cutter
Chamfer cutter with bottom cut
Rebate (rabbet) cutter
Cove cutter
Moulding bit
Radius cutter

When using a guide pin, make light side pressure to avoid burning the board edge.

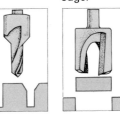

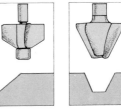

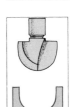

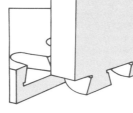
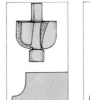

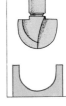

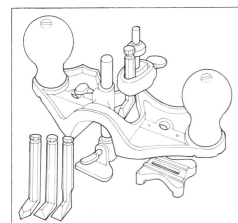

The hand router

The standard hand router consists of a metal frame flanked by two wooden handles. Through the centre of the frame passes a cutter and in front of it an adjustable depth gauge. There is also a detachable fence guide to guide the cutter along edge work. The small detachable sole or shoe is there to support the metal hand router when working through narrow sections of wood.

The hand router is primarily used for cutting grooves (or dadoes) and is usually supplied with 6mm (¼in) and 12mm (½in) chisels and a 'V'-shaped cutter.

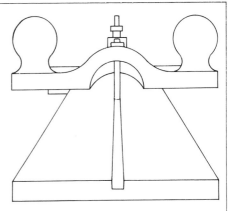

Joints

Which joint to choose

There is a great deal of confusion about wood joints. Why are so many of them so complex? The answer lies in the history of craftsmanship and the complexity of wood itself.

Down the ages, craftsmen have been faced with the perverse nature of wood. Gradually, over a period of time, people came to understand how pieces of wood, cut in certain ways from a tree, would behave. With increasing understanding came the invention of ways to assemble constructions in the most practical fashion.

The origin and evolution of jointing methods also owes much to a lack of reliable adhesives. Animal glues have of course been in use for many centuries, but their particular disadvantage is that they have a short lifespan, being adversely affected by woodworm and other natural agents. So today we have a legacy of jointing methods, some simply designed to fix two pieces of wood together with the addition of a wedge or peg, others, more sophisticated, whose rigidity relies upon the inter-related shape of the two pieces of wood. The dovetail, for example, with its unique interlocking quality was understandably popular in a time when no strong lasting glues were available. The Egyptians used to bind dovetail pins and tails together with rawhide thongs which, when dried, would pull the two pieces of wood securely together.

In practical terms, modern glues have made many complex jointing methods superfluous. The increasing sophistication of man-made sheets, designed to overcome the natural movement of wood in construction, has also contributed to a wider use of simpler jointing methods. But when working in solid wood, the choice of joints must take account of the need to combat the directional problems of wood and problems of hygroscopic movement.

John Hardy, in his designs, has displayed an imaginative use of modern jointing methods because he firmly believes that people should be encouraged to utilise any available modern aid if it facilitates success.

"Why present people with the possibility of failure (or less than a reasonable degree of excellence)? Today we have very strong glues and other fantastic materials. You can build furniture without any joints. The majority of furniture today does not have mortises and tenons, dovetails, etc. We use modern glues or engineering methods. There is an enjoyment here – an enjoyment in using whatever method you can best use to achieve precision."

In the end, your decision to build furniture with the kind of jointing methods John Hardy suggests or with the traditional methods employed by some of the other craftsmen, will reflect your own individual approach to craft. John Hardy's attitude reflects the nature of his business as well as a personal philosophy

about craft. Others argue that the amateur, blessed with time in a non-competitive situation, should be encouraged above all to experiment with traditional methods.

"You are going into it to enjoy it, and you are not going to give up after a year. You are not going to let it become a drag by not realising the number of different ways that you can join two pieces of wood together, and saying to yourself every time you begin to construct a dovetail joint, 'Aw, do I have to do that again!' You begin to realise how you can play around with that joint in an infinite number of ways.

"For example, dovetails do not let go in the middle of the joint; a box or case usually breaks at one corner, or edge. So why not make the tails assymetric for a change. Space the pins closer together towards each outside edge – and further apart along the middle area. When done right, this combines the logic of needed strength with a rhythm in the joint that tells us a person did it – someone who cared, and used a bit of sensible imagination. No machine can do that for you! But you do have to care, be curious and take your time."
James Krenov

Joints can thus become a design decision, a means to develop an individual logic towards your work. The choice is yours. Although the primary consideration must remain the function of the joint itself, as in every other facet of furniture-making, function cannot be divorced from visual and structural considerations. A junction between two pieces of wood can theoretically be made in a variety of different ways.

Here are just some of the ways in which a flat frame or two pieces of wood can be successfully jointed to form a corner. They demonstrate that the choice of joint for a particular job *is* a design decision. We cannot be bound by a textbook solution to construction; there is no *one* correct way. Function, structural requirements, the nature of the material, visual appearance must all be carefully

considered. The important thing is to look, investigate the possibilities and when you have decided what you want to do, either write it down or sketch it on a piece of paper.

"Even in the most disciplined work we can include a flexibility, a human element that is at once sound – and enriching."
James Krenov

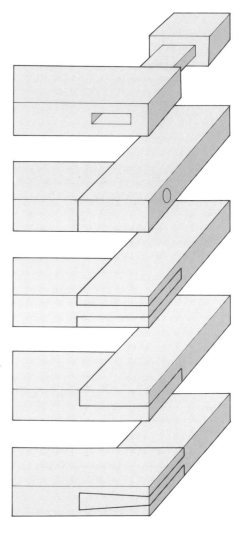

Measuring and marking tools

Included here are some tools which have been alluded to in the section on surface preparation and cutting to length (pages 32 and 33). Others are specifically designed to enable you to cut joints accurately. Makeshift measuring and marking tools are the surest means to disaster especially when cutting joints.

Squares and bevels

Engineer's try-square

The Engineer's try-square is set at a constant 90 degree angle and made entirely of metal. Because the sides of the tool are parallel, it presents a right-angle

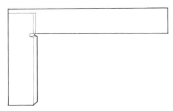

on the outside edge too. It is preferable to the wooden stocked try-square whose accuracy may be affected by movement in the wood. Besides using the tool to mark 90 degree angles, it can be used to check that a piece of wood has been planed square.

Adjustable combination square

The adjustable combination square consists of a 350mm (12in) steel rule along which runs a movable head which can be locked in position by a nut, at any point along its length. It incorporates a con-

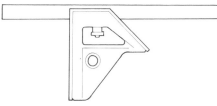

stant 90 degree angle on one side of the head and a 45 degree angle (particularly useful when marking out mitre joints) on the other side. Additionally, there is a spirit level built into the head which can be used to check planed work in both a horizontal and vertical position. The steel rule is also useful for checking the depth of a mortise.

Sliding or 'T' bevel

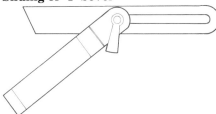

The sliding or 'T' bevel consists of a parallel-sided steel blade and sliding stock. A locking nut is included to set the tool at any angle against a protractor. It is particularly useful when work involves marking out a number of angles of the same size.

Gauges

Marking gauge

The marking gauge comprises a column of wood fed through a movable wooden stock, and a screw to fix the stock in the required position along the column length. At one end of the column is a fixed marking pin. The stock is, in effect, a

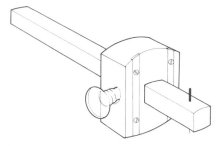

guide fence which enables you to mark a line parallel to the edge of a board. It can also be a very useful tool to find the centre of a rail. Make two pin marks from either side of the rail with the same gauge setting. Should the two points not fall in the same place, adjust the stock by tapping the column gently on the workbench and repeat the process until they do.

Cutting gauge

The cutting gauge is similar to the marking gauge, its difference being that instead of a marking pin it has a flat

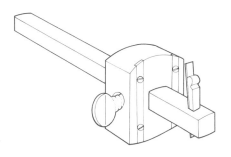

cutting blade. As such it is less likely to tear wood when marking across the grain.

Mortise gauge

The mortise gauge is also similar to the marking gauge except that it has two marking pins, one fixed and one adjust-

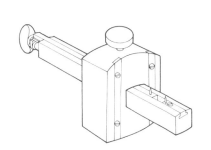

able, for marking out both sides of a mortise. Many mortise gauges have another fixed pin on the underside of the column so that they can also be used as a marking gauge.

Rules and straight-edges

Flexible steel tape

The flexible steel tape is spring mounted into a metal case. Occasionally a lock is affixed to the case to hold the tape at the required measure. The tape is marked with both metric and imperial measures. Its tendency to kink or twist does not make for accurate measurements, but in marking out large sections of timber (where absolute accuracy may be less important) it is a useful acquisition. Its flexibility recommends it for measuring curved shapes.

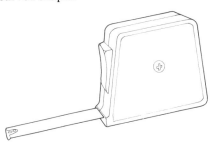

Straight-edge

The straight-edge is a steel tool used for checking the flatness of surfaces. Place it on edge on the wood surface and turn it through 180 degrees. The wood surface is not flat if daylight appears between the surface and the tool at any point. One side of a straight-edge is bevelled to enable you to mark or cut in a straight line.

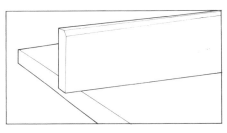

Engineer's steel rule

The Engineer's steel rule is a thin rigid steel rule with both metric and imperial measures and is an extremely accurate measuring tool. It can also be used as a straight edge.

The marking knife

Designed specifically to mark timber for

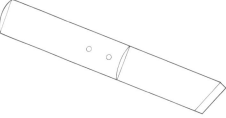

cutting, the blade has a bevel on one side only so that the flat edge can run accurately along the side of a straight-edge, try-square, etc. Since the resultant mark will be square on the finished side and bevelled on the waste side, the marking knife provides an ideally accurate line for a saw.

Joints 2

Joints with screws or nails

"The strength of a joint is its strength at its weakest point." John Makepeace

Screws or nails are invariably insufficient alone – glue should be used. And screws are preferable to nails because their threads increase holding power.

If you do use nails, blunt their points and use a bradawl to start the hole. They are then less likely to split the wood.

For furniture joints, you will frequently want to hide nail heads (page 165) and countersink screws (page 161).

Simple as it may seem, ignoring the correct process of joining two pieces of wood together with screws creates all too frequent problems.

Butt or edge joints
In theory, the simplest joints are butt joints. In practice, they require a great deal of care to achieve long lasting results. To begin with, it is essential to follow the guidance given on surface preparation (page 32) and exercise a great deal of care in planing edges.

Stability is of paramount importance when joining pieces together to form wide boards, and consideration of the juxtaposition of neighbouring pieces will help

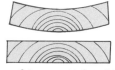

you achieve this essential stability.

Because of the tendency for annual rings to straighten, the board will cup as shown in the above illustration. You can achieve a greater chance of the board remaining flat if the pieces are so placed that their annual rings alternate as shown below. Always bear this principle in mind when deciding upon the position

of pieces in such a construction.

In the past, edge joints were bonded with animal glues. Their quick gel pro-

Action hints – screw joints
* First ensure that both pieces are square to each other. Checking that you have planed the surface square can be carried out with the Engineer's try-square.
* Drill a hole in the top piece of wood (the piece which will take the screwhead) large enough to allow the screw shank to

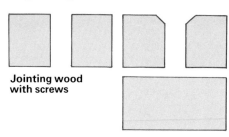

Jointing wood with screws

perties were exploited, and cramping (to provide extra bonding pressure) was unnecessary. Today animal glues are difficult to obtain – this method of jointing, known as rub jointing, has consequently lost popularity. It is also fairly difficult to perform. If you do have access to a hot glue pot, however, here's how:

Rub jointing

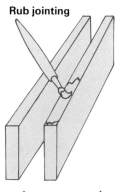

A very good mating surface is essential. Speed is the keyword, as animal glues gel as soon as they get cold. Coat both surfaces thinly and bring them together with a short rubbing motion in the direction of the length of the pieces. The action expels excess glue and creates a suction between the two edges, which, together with the glue's gel properties, binds the joint together. Lean the

turn easily.
* Drill a countersink hole in the top piece.
* Place the two rails in position and with a bradawl, mark the position for the drill hole in the bottom rail.
* When you drill the hole in the bottom piece, make it slightly shallower than the length of the screw it will house.

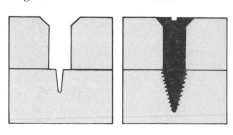

assembled pieces against battens, propped against a wall, until set.

Modern glues require cramp pressure for butt joints. To provide this pressure sash cramps are indispensable. If the finished width area comprises two boards, it is possible to use only one sash (bar or pipe) cramp to bind them together.

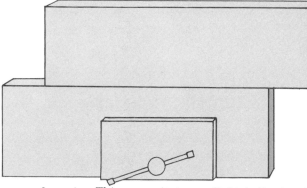

This necessitates a slight hollowing in the length of the planed edge, which should cramp out quite easily.

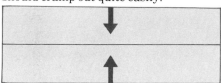

Tongue and groove joints
Further strength and more positive location can be achieved by the addition of a loose tongue. True tongue and grooving, the fixed tongue type used in matchboarding, is more involved unless you have a router (page 172).

The extra bonus of an increased glue surface further strengthens the joint, but the proportion of the tongue is important

– it should not exceed one third of the thickness of the board. On very thick timber (anything over 40mm (1½in) thick) it is a good idea to use two tongues.

Plywood is suitable for loose tongues. The tongue should be an easy fit in the groove, and the grain of the outer plys should run across its length as shown in the illustration. The grooves can be cut either with a plough plane or a router.

With the router, the grooves can be stopped so that they do not appear on the end grain – you have to plane through when using the plough plane. Mention has also been made on page 160 of the less readily available, tongue and groove planes which are sold in pairs. The most efficient way to ensure matching tongue and grooves is to use a router and the same setting to cut both.

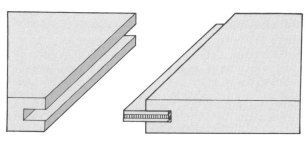

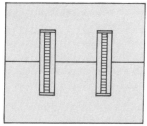

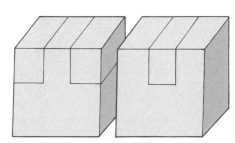

Dowels and edge joints

Any form of reinforcement is beneficial to edge joints, and if tongues cannot be included due to a lack of the correct equipment, dowels can be used instead. Dowels, like tongues, will also improve

Chamfer and score the dowel

the location of each board to the next.

Care in marking out is essential. Place the two pieces of wood together and mark lines across their edges with a try-square. The spacing of dowels for edge joints should be 150mm (6in) starting 75mm (3in) from the end. Find the centre of each edge with a marking gauge and pinpoint the centre points of the dowel holes.

The diameter of the dowel should not exceed one third of the thickness of the board. Bore the holes with a brace and dowel bit, making sure that the brace is square to the surface (page 167). A metal cutting twist drill or hand-held power drill would be unsuitable since they are more difficult to centre on a mark unless the latter is secured in a drill stand.

The depth of the dowel hole is not critical – a rough guide being to drill to a

Mark dowel positions with try-square and marking gauge

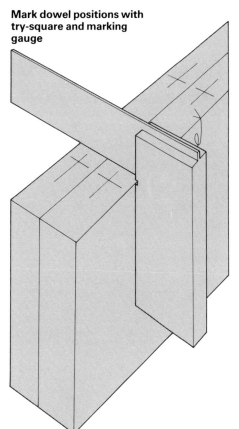

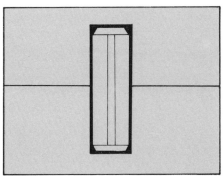

depth equivalent to the thickness of the wood. Cut dowels slightly shorter than the depth of the hole, and run a saw cut along the length to allow excess glue to escape from the hole. Work quickly to prevent the glue setting before the joint is assembled. Run glue into the holes and coat the surfaces of the joint. Assemble the joint and cramp up, finally checking that the finished surface is flat with a straight-edge. Wipe away any surplus glue with a damp cloth. Care exercised during the operation can economise effort when further surface planing is carried out. A dry run, however, is inadvisable when using dowelled edge joints as the joint may be difficult to take apart.

Book-matching

This technique is a worthwhile design consideration when making wide surface areas by edge-jointing narrower pieces of wood. Book-matching means resawing a plank through its depth – thus 'opening it up'. The result can be sensational. You may, for example, have a quarter-sawn plank whose grain and colour features catch your eye, yet it is too narrow to provide the surface width you require. If it is thick enough, it can be resawn. Although this *can* be done by hand using a rip saw, it is best done on a power band saw (a relatively expensive workshop tool) so as not to waste much thickness (in sawdust) which in turn will destroy the closeness of the match. It is a good idea, should you have such a decorative plank, to take it along to the sawmill and get them to open it up for you. It is a fast and inexpensive operation. But, however you plan to cut the board, do not assume that the shades of colour and grain pattern will remain the same as they are on the surface of the board. Krenov explains: *"If the rings are nearly vertical and the colouring calm, book-matching is less complicated . . . With the rings flat or nearly so, the matching becomes perilous. The patterns and shadings in the two halves balance only when first opened – after that they 'leave' one another causing disharmony."*

Book-matched English oak
"The English brown oak was taken from a thick plank which included the root-end of the log. When re-sawn and opened, it revealed this treasure."
James Krenov

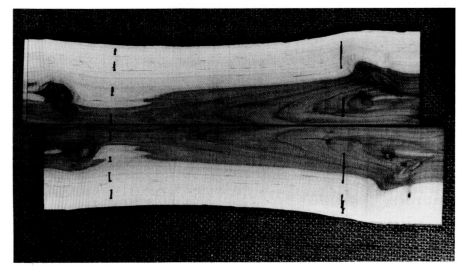

Book-matched apple wood
"On one side, the pattern matches (balances); on the other, it is quite disharmonious. Even a saw kerf can occasion a change of pattern." James Krenov

Joints 3

Housing joints

A housing (dado) is a channel cut across the grain. This definition distinguishes a housing from a groove, which is a channel cut with the grain.

Typically, housing joints are used to support shelves in a bookcase or partitions in a box. But whatever the use, housing joints can be relied upon to provide good load-bearing strength.

square-edged batten can be cramped against the line to provide a guide fence for the saw.

Remove the waste with a mortise or bevel-edged chisel, providing motive power with a mallet. Work in from each edge of the housing to prevent bursting out the grain at the ends of the housing. A long paring chisel can also be used.

Cutting channels
From left to right:
Groove
Through housing
Stopped housing
Batton as saw guide
Stopped shoulder
Cutting a housing

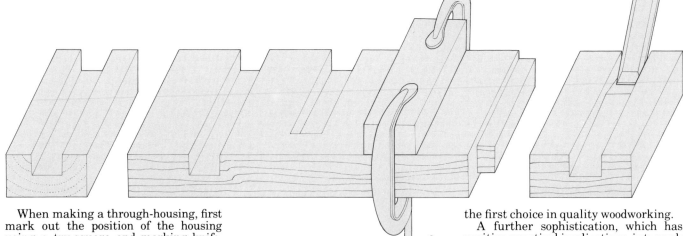

When making a through-housing, first mark out the position of the housing using a try-square and marking knife. Bear in mind that the piece which will eventually fit into the housing will later be 'finished' (i.e. cleaned up with a plane) and thus be thinner. So make an allowance for the loss in thickness and width of the shelf, partition, etc., when marking out the housing.

Next, mark out the depth of the housing with a marking gauge on both face and opposite edges. The depth of the housing should not exceed one third of the thickness of the housing board.

You can cut a housing with a router or with a tenon saw. If using a tenon saw, a

Always cut across the fibres before removing the waste.

A stopped housing does not show on the face edge. It can be cut with a router, but the stopped end will have to be squared with a chisel. If cutting with a tenon saw, first remove a small section at the front of the housing with a chisel. The slot enables the toe of the saw to work unimpeded. Thereafter, the stopped housing can be treated like a through housing. For aesthetic reasons, the stopped housing is

the first choice in quality woodworking.

A further sophistication, which has positive practical implications, is to work a shoulder on the end of the piece fitting into the housing as shown in the illustration. The advantages are a positive control over the length of the shelf, and a facility for cleaning up surfaces without affecting the quality of fit.

The shoulder is cut across the grain. Mark out the squared end of the shelf with a cutting gauge. Cut across the grain with a tenon saw (again on wide pieces use a batten as a guide fence for the saw). Remove the waste with a shoulder plane (but cut the corner away first to prevent wood splitting).

Mortise and tenon joints

This is the joint normally associated with frames and constructions using posts (legs) and rails. It is a joint of considerable strength with very positive location. Before the advent of efficient modern glues, mortise and tenon joints relied upon pegs or wedges to hold them fast.

The principle for cutting a mortise and tenon follows. The description is applied to the making of a joint for a flat frame which consists of rails and stiles (a typical

door frame) with stopped mortise. In frame construction the tenon should be one third the thickness of the rail. In post and rail construction, the rail will probably be thinner than the post but the tenon should still be one third the thickness of the rail. The width of the tenon should be two thirds the width of the rail.

Marking out

First mark out the position of the mortise using a pencil and try-square. Allow the

stile some extra length so that the end projects beyond the rail. This is called the horn and its value will be appreciated later in the process of cutting the mortise. Mark out both stiles together to ensure accurate duplication of measurements. Follow this by marking out the shoulders using a marking knife and try-square. With more than one rail mark them out together.

Select a chisel the width of the mortise and set the points of a mortise gauge to

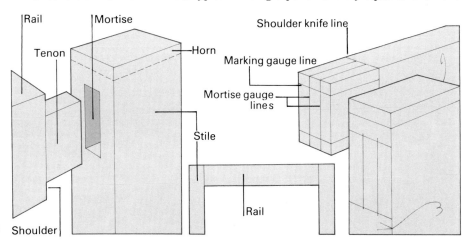

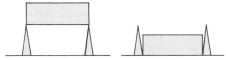

Setting gauge spurs to width.
Left, correct. Right, incorrect.

the width of the chisel. Working with the stock of the gauge against the face side, mark the three surfaces of the tenon. With the same setting, mark the face of the mortise. Next gauge the width of the tenon using a marking gauge. This width should be two thirds of the rail width.

Removing mortise waste

The waste from a mortise can be removed in two ways by hand. Either 1. chop it out with a mortise chisel and mallet, or 2. bore out the waste and clean up with a chisel. Method 2 is described on page 152.

Method 1. Cramp the stile onto the bench top so that the force of the mallet is absorbed by one of the legs of the bench. Do not hold in the vice. Place the chisel across the grain in the middle of the mortise and strike with a mallet. Make a second cut adjacent to the first to form a 'V' slot. Subsequent cuts will push the chippings into the space created by the 'V' slot. Work from the centre to the ends of the mortise levering the waste out as you go along. The amount you are able to

Method 1

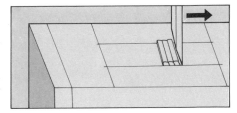

remove will depend on the density and uniformity of grain and the skill gained by practice. Go slowly at first. Do not cut right up to the ends of the mortise at this stage – leave a few millimetres so that the levering action of the chisel does not damage the final corners. It may be necessary to make a number of cuts until

Method 2

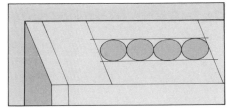

the desired depth has been achieved. The depth should be about two thirds the depth of the stile. Once this is done, the final cuts can be made back to the pencil lines. At this point the value of the horn can be appreciated; it helps to prevent the lever action of the chisel from bursting out the end grain.

Sawing the tenon

The tenon is sawn in four stages:
1. Hold the rail in the vice so that it leans away from you and saw down from the

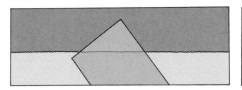

uppermost corner to the shoulder line. The saw cut should just touch the gauge line on the waste side.

2. Turn the wood round and repeat this process from the other corner. This is done because it is only possible to see two

sets of lines at any one time; the third set of lines is on the edge away from you. It is advisable only to work to the lines you can see.

3. The angled saw cuts provide a guide for the saw when the next stage is cut with the rail upright in the vice.

4. The fourth stage is to remove the cheeks of the tenon by holding the rail against a bench hook (see page 150) and

sawing slightly away from the shoulder line. Although it is possible to saw right up to the shoulder line, for really crisp shoulders it is better to saw away from

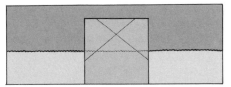

the line and pare back to the line with a sharp bevel-edged chisel.

This can be done either by vertical paring on the bench or by horizontal paring in the vice. Either way, the crisp knife line forms a positive entry for the cutting edge of the chisel.

Through-tenons with wedges

Through-tenons are used when ultimate strength is required or when the stile is too narrow for a stopped tenon to give adequate strength. Wedges are included to lock the joint. They can also be employed as a decorative element in the

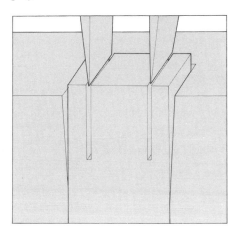

placement of the wedges the mortise is slightly tapered. The amount of taper is one third of the thickness of the tenon.

2. Saw cuts are made down the tenon to finish short of the shoulder. These should be about half the tenon thickness from the edge. Cut the wedges from a piece of wood exactly the same thickness as the tenon. Calculate the taper carefully. Then before sawing the wedges mark them out – wedges that are too thin will not spread the tenon sufficiently and the dovetailing effect be lost. Do not be content simply to whittle them out of any

available piece of scrap, and always make a few more wedges than you need in case some break. Wedges broken in the tenon can usually be extracted with pliers. If spare wedges are not available the glue could become useless before new wedges can be cut.

Gluing

Stopped tenons are quite simple to glue using cramping blocks to prevent damage from the cramp shoes. Wedged tenons provide a complication. Be sure to put glue on the wedges and tap them evenly with alternate blows of the hammer.

design especially when a contrasting wood is used.

1. The mortise is marked out on both face edge and opposite edge, making sure that the mortise gauge is always worked from the face side. The waste is then chopped out working from both ends until the cuts meet in the middle. To allow for the dis-

Other tenons illustrated include twin, double and haunched.

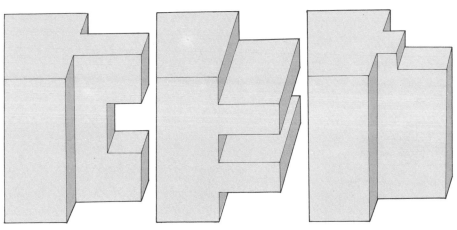

179

Joints 4

Dovetails

It may be a fact that dovetails are difficult to cut and frequently draw an exclamation of wonder from the less experienced. But many craftsmen would argue that a well cut mortise and tenon is as difficult.

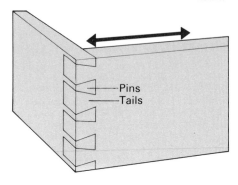

Pins
Tails

Marking out the pins

There are various schools of thought on the correct procedure for cutting through dovetails. Robert Ingham chooses to cut

Dovetail template
Gradient 1:8

Spacing dovetails
Use a ruler to space dovetails, or a piece of wood with equal spaces marked on it.

Cutting the pins

With the timber held upright and low in the vice, saw down on the waste side of the line – the pencil line should just show on the corners of the pins. To get into the rhythm of sawing, saw all pin slopes in one direction first. Once you have sawn across the top of the pin, concentrate on the vertical cutting line, taking great care not to cut below the shoulder line –

With its positive location, interlocking action, and maximised glueing area, the joint possesses great strength. Once you have understood its principle, there remains the cleanness of the saw cut and an awareness of the resultant kerf. Prepare your tools and yourself well, for generally dovetails appear in such positions (for example, the front of a drawer) as to advertise your success or failure.

1. Check the kerf. If it is ragged, the saw may need sharpening or the set may be excessive.

2. Reduce the set to a bare minimum by gently running a fine slipstone along the sides of the saw. Light, even pressure to each side of the teeth will reduce the set.

the pins first. This is the only way that lapped and secret dovetails can be cut so it seems logical to use the same approach for through dovetails. Also, if the pins are

stop just short of it. The waste can now be removed with a coping saw or, in the case of very fine pins, a fret saw. Because the coping saw produces a fairly rough cut, work up to 1mm away from the line, then pare away.

Paring back to the shoulder lines requires particular care. It is best to work in from both sides with a bevel-edged chisel,

3. After each pair of strokes with the stone check the action of the saw. An uneven set will cause the saw to pull to one side. Do not rush this operation or it could result in a saw with no set at all and possibly a visit to the saw doctor.

The through dovetail

The most common form of this most decorative of joints is the through dovetail. The proportions of pins to tails can be a personal decision, but their delicacy or robustness must also reflect the function of the joint and its structural qualities as well as its aesthetic qualities. A joint is strongest when a force or load is applied against the taper of the tails. When designing it, also consider how the piece will be assembled and avoid the necessity of too many points of cramp pressure.

delicate, it is easier to mark around them to produce the tails.

Careful preparation of the ends of the pieces of wood is essential. If four pieces are being jointed together to form a carcase or box structure, mark out lengths in pairs to ensure consistency. Next, mark out the shoulder lines either with a try-square and marking knife or with a cutting gauge. Set the line slightly less than the thickness of the wood from the end. (It may be necessary to prepare the wood initially so that it is about half a millimetre thicker than the finished size. This can be planed away after the joint has been glued. By doing this, you can avoid using complex cramping blocks.)

Having decided upon proportions and number of pins, mark them out on the end grain with a dovetail template and sharp HB pencil. Ready-made templates are hard to find so you may have to make your own. Then square the pins down to the shoulder line on the outside face. Check that the pencil remains sharp. Before cutting, mark the waste wood to reduce the risk of removing the wrong pieces.

making a vertical paring action. Do not try to undercut the shoulders. When paring from the first side slant the chisel so that the tool clears the line on the opposite side. The cutting gauge or knife line provides a positive location for the final cut from the first side. Turn the wood over and repeat the process, being sure to stop short of the corners already produced.

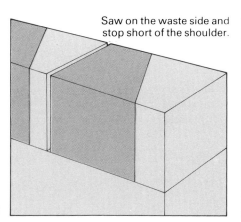

Saw on the waste side and stop short of the shoulder.

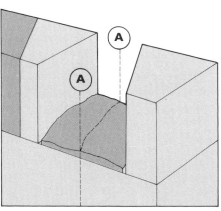

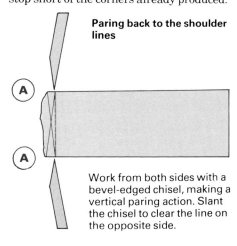

Paring back to the shoulder lines

Work from both sides with a bevel-edged chisel, making a vertical paring action. Slant the chisel to clear the line on the opposite side.

Marking the tails
The pins are now used as a template for marking out the tails. Place them in position ensuring that they are facing the right way. With a sharp pencil transfer their profiles to the tail piece. With a try-square continue the angled lines of the tails from the face on to the end of the piece of wood.

The lapped dovetail
Most commonly associated with drawer construction, it reached its peak of perfection during the Victorian era when the pins were often so delicate as to be only the thickness of a saw cut at their thinnest point.

Marking out the pins
Square up the ends, mark the shoulder lines as before, but slightly less than the thickness of the piece for the tails. Next, mark a line on the end grain to the depth of the pins, and with a pencil, mark out the pins' profile on the end grain. Finally square the marks onto the inside face down to the shoulder line.

Cutting the pins
Place the wood vertically in the vice and saw on the waste side of the line stopping at shoulder line and end grain gauge line. Next cramp the wood onto your bench so that the joint is near its edge. Chop across the grain with chisel and mallet and remove the waste to the depth of this cut with a horizontal paring action. Because the saw cuts were angled you may need a 5mm (³/₁₆in) chisel to clean out the corners.

Mitre joints
These are very often used for picture frames. The angle at which they meet must be exactly half the angle of the complete joint. A mirror or picture frame with 90 degree corners means that the mitre cut at each corner will be 45 degrees. The process of cutting mitres is as follows:

1. Wooden mitre boxes are available with slots to cut both 90 degree and 45 degree angles. They soon become useless through use, or inaccurate due to wood movement. There are metal boxes on the market, but it is a good idea to use the adjustable combination square to mark angles, then cut the wood with a tenon saw, and finally plane using a mitre shooting board. This operates on the same principle as the regular shooting board (page 33) but has a 45 degree angle stop.

Removing the waste from the tails
Place the wood upright in the vice. You will need to tilt the saw to follow the angled lines, although some people find it easier to tilt the wood and keep the saw upright. As when cutting the pins, aim the saw cut to leave the pencil lines just showing. Remove the waste with a coping saw and pare back to the cutting gauge or

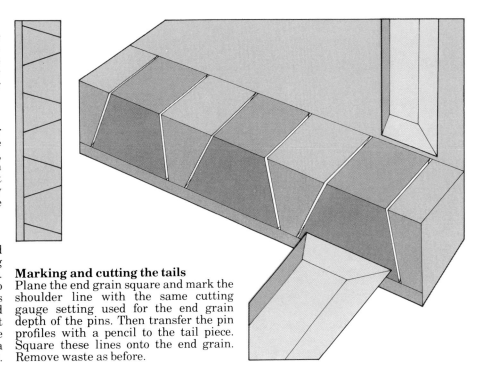

Marking and cutting the tails
Plane the end grain square and mark the shoulder line with the same cutting gauge setting used for the end grain depth of the pins. Then transfer the pin profiles with a pencil to the tail piece. Square these lines onto the end grain. Remove waste as before.

2. Glue all four joints (in making a frame) and cramp with the traditional corner cramping device pictured here. By turning the tourniquet rod the four corners are pulled together from a central point.

Mitre cramp

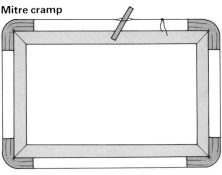

knife line. Assemble the two pieces using a block of wood under the hammer to prevent damaging the tails. Only moderate force should be needed to tap the joint home.

When the glue has set, clean up the joint with a smoothing plane, working in from the ends towards the centre of the pieces to avoid end grain splitting.

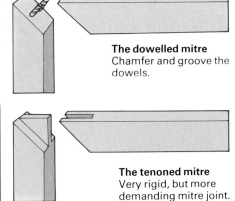

The dowelled mitre
Chamfer and groove the dowels.

The tenoned mitre
Very rigid, but more demanding mitre joint.

Cramps (or Clamps)
'G' or 'C' cramp
Open jaw capacities vary from 18mm (¾in) models to 305mm (12in) models made in steel. Through the top of the metal frame is threaded a metal screw on the bottom of which is set a ball joint shoe designed to hold fast any shape to the base of the cramp. In all operations protect the wood surface by attaching a wood block to the shoe.

Sash cramp (bar or pipe)
This is designed to hold boards together when building up a large flat surface.

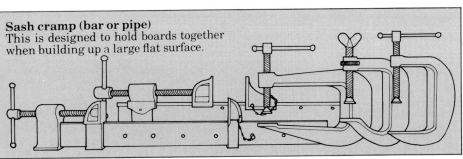

Finishing

Abrasive papers

Different woods; different methods
It is true to say that some timbers cut better than others and are thus more susceptible to a finish with cutting tools alone. Ash, elm, pearwood are just three of many capable of fine, clean, sometimes lustrous finishes using either chisel, spokeshave, or plane. Other more stubborn timbers require perforce the abrasive action of sandpaper to shape and finish them.

A design decision
"*The very nature of sandpaper tends to press forth shapes, to knead them, rather than outline, or underline them as well-used cutting tools do.*" James Krenov alludes to the characteristic action of abrasive papers as opposed to the clear, fine, definite shapes left by finely tuned, well-honed cutting tools. He also makes the point that cutting tools give the user an opportunity to get closer to the material he is using – every cut is in that sense a more clearly defined direct process between craftsman and wood than sanding is. The essence of Krenov's work is this directness – he will invariably leave his personal imprint on a piece, say in the shape of a beautiful carved handle on a cabinet door. Somehow the handle feels absolutely 'right' to the touch and evidences the care and skill with which it has been made. This approach and end result are in contrast to the flowing shapes that are characteristic of Wendell Castle's work. To judge between them is to miss the point. The intentions are different, the action of tools and sandpaper is different, the personalities of the craftsmen are different. But each factor is in balance for each of the craftsmen. The point is that decisions of this nature reflect individual approaches to working with wood, tell us something about the craftsman, and result in startlingly different appearances.

Types of abrasive paper
Sandpaper as such is no longer available. It is now a general term used to describe all abrasive papers – be they made with granules of glass, emery (for metal), garnet, or silicone-carbide (used damp to remove paint from metal or wood). Garnet paper is suitable for finishing all types of timber and is available in finer grades than, say, glasspaper. A fine finish, of course, can only be achieved with a finely graded paper.

Action hints
* Keep the paper dry.
* Always work with the grain, otherwise you will scratch the wood surface – marks will show through liquid finishes.
* Clogged papers are ineffective. Tap the paper free of dust occasionally.
* Wrap the paper around a block of softwood or cork – shape the block to work mouldings. This will prevent the paper following surface indentations, besides being easier to handle.

The cabinet scraper
Its name belies its true action. The

cabinet scraper does not just scrape, it cuts. Like the plane, it is a traditional part of the cabinet maker's tool kit, and its success depends upon how well it has been prepared for use. Once dull, the scraper *will* scrape rather than cut. See how to sharpen the scraper on page 163. Be sure not to leave scratch marks on the surface of the tool when sharpening it – these will tear wood fibres and produce an effect akin to that of coarse-graded sandpaper through liquid finishes. Properly sharpened, the scraper will produce fine shavings of wood. Hold the scraper in both hands, your thumbs applying pressure on the centre of the tool for forward motions – your fingers apply pressure on the back of the tool when drawing it back towards the body. The scraper should be held at an angle of 120 degrees to the wood surface when pushing forward – reverse the angle when drawing the tool back towards the body. Work cautiously with it in a to-and-fro motion to avoid ruining the finest edges of your work.

The Surform
Files are not designed for working wood. A rasp is, but it has been superceded by

Light, easily worked finish.

the Surform – a tool which enables you to separate areas of wood one from another. Some craftsmen feel strongly that files should only be used for sharpening saws or shaping metal castings, whereas

Wendell Castle recommends second cut and bastard cut files for shaped work.

The general purpose Surform is light and easy to work. When worked along the grain, its sharp cutting edges literally separate and lift wood from the work surface, passing it as shavings through its holes. If you work the tool across the grain, it will work faster but produce a rougher finish – the action tears wood fibre and denies you the really beautiful finish which a correctly used Surform characteristically produces.

Liquid finishes
Today, most wood finishes are surface finishes. Traditionally, finishes were designed, like French polish, to be rubbed into the pores of wood over a long period of time. French polishing is a specialist craft. The best mirror-like finishes come only after long periods of time and numerous thin coats of polish. Such a finish is neither water nor heat resistant.

We apply finishes for the following reasons:

1. To seal the wood pores and minimise movement in the wood.

2. To protect wood surfaces from permanent marks, scratches, etc.

3. To enhance the natural beauty of wood.

"*We go through terrible traumas over the selection of suitable finishes. Of course, it would be marvellous if those who commissioned furniture had time to wax and oil the furniture which we make for them. Unfortunately most of them lead very busy lives where they need relatively easy maintenance and this has led us to*

use synthetic resins extensively over the last few years."
John Makepeace

"The point about wood, is that it is nice all the way through. The Victorians never understood this, and that is why their very highly finished Victorian cabinets are so repulsive – there's just no homogeneity to them. As far as I am concerned it is vital that nothing is done to the surface of the object which makes it different from the wood below the surface."
Richard La Trobe Bateman

Function and aesthetics

"Finishing is a headache. And I'll tell you why it's a headache – wood is like blotting paper. The thing that one likes most of all about it is its nakedness – the stuff of wood. Yet it's that aspect which is blotting paper. If you are going to use the finished piece as a utilitarian object, you cannot leave it as blotting paper. So there's a conflict between the aesthetic quality to which we all respond, and the fact that we are going to use it. You just cannot have something made of blotting paper and hope that it won't soak up the moisture. That's the problem, and everyone has his own way of solving it."
Richard La Trobe Bateman

Types of finish

"Recently we have been thinking more about the uses of waxes and oils. Whilst beeswax water marks very easily and oil tends to dull the wood, both are relatively easy to apply. The oil seems to give a much more resistant finish, and can be made good locally without finishing the whole piece. It seems to me that the oils available in Britain are not as good as those in Scandinavia and America. The ones used there give a much richer result."
John Makepeace

Wax
* Easy to work into wood and to renew from time to time.
* Best mixture is one of pure beeswax and turpentine – 1 lb of beeswax to ½ pint of turpentine.
* Good moisture resistance, but no resistance to heat or scratches.
* Wax is great to apply and really does enhance the natural beauty of wood.

Oils
Linseed oil
* There are two sorts of linseed oil, raw and boiled. Either is a good inexpensive finish and fairly stain resistant, but does not seal wood against variations in atmospheric humidity and subsequent movement.
* Remember, if considering using linseed oil on light-coloured timber that it will tend to discolour it.
* Boiled linseed oil dries more quickly than raw oil. A drying agent, such as Terebine or Japan drier, can be used to hasten the process.
* Work into the grain with a brush or cloth allowing the first to dry completely before applying the second. Wax polish for extra sheen.

Teak oil
* Teak oil is essentially different from linseed oil in that it comes under the category of 'sealer finishes'. It seals the wood against humidity variations and provides a hard-wearing durable finish.
* Two or three coats will be needed. As with all sealers, do not apply during humid conditions. Abrase with fine wire wool between coats, and use a light coat to finish.

Colour stains
There are three sorts of stain which change the colour of wood. Always test on an odd piece of wood from the same plank as the object, before applying.

Water stain
The problem with water is that it tends to raise wood grain when applied. So, apply at least two coats and sand the grain down in between coats, or wet the wood first to raise the grain, and sand before applying the colour stain. Water stains are available in a wide range of brilliant warm-toned colours.

Oil stain
Easier to apply and comes in ready-mixed colours. Fairly fast to dry.

Spirit stain
Again available in a range of colours, which are more cool-toned and transparent than water stains. Ready-mixed colours are not as available as they used to be. It really does dry fast and is thus better applied with a spray gun. *"It is very difficult to get an even tone with spirit on a large area or complicated shape because it dries so quickly. So I tend to use it only for smallish objects."* Fred Baier

Polyurethane
As coloured paint or transparent varnish, polyurethane products are sealers against humidity variations and very tough. But Fred Baier gives a word of advice – *"I have heard that you should not use anything prefixed by poly-, particularly outdoors, because it is susceptible to ultra violet – the sunlight breaks it down. So I steer clear of polyurethane and PVA except for jigs and glue blocks."*

* Tough, heat resistant, and not vulnerable to water or spirit marks.
* Available in gloss and matt finishes.
* Apply as other sealers, wire woolling between coats.
* Transparent varnish will darken the wood slightly.

Cellulose lacquers
* The toughest and most resistant finishes.
* Available as clear or coloured, very often used coloured for children's toys.
* Dries very fast. Wire wool between coats, of which at least three should be applied.
* It is not easy to apply by hand. It is advisable to spray for best results.

Veneering
Veneering by hand is a difficult and slow process. Traditionally, animal glues were used – the process exploited their quick-geling properties. Today, as modern synthetic glues have superceded animal glues, veneers have to be held in place with cauls until the adhesive has set. Impact adhesives can be used though extreme care must be exercised when coating the surfaces to be joined – thixotropic impact adhesives spread most evenly, but are really only practical for small surfaces. For more permanent results, PVA and resin glues are recommended.

1. Select or prepare a ground board. Man-made boards present good flat surfaces which require no further treatment before applying the glue. They are ideal grounds for veneer.

2. Make cauls from thick slabs of chipboard. If necessary, build up the thickness by bonding two 20mm (¾in) chipboard thicknesses together with an impact adhesive.

3. Glue the ground piece. Sandwich it and the two veneer sheets between the cauls, using sheets of paper or polythene to prevent the veneer sticking to the cauls.

4. Cramp up with 'G' cramps around the edges of the cauls. On wide boards (over 305mm (12in) wide) it may be difficult to squeeze the glue out from the centre of the board, so use curved spreader bars at 153mm (6in) intervals along the length of the cauls. The natural spring in these bars imparts pressure to the centre of the board. Leave the work in cramps for at least twenty-four hours (as a lot of moisture is trapped in the wood). When it is taken out of the cramps, expose both surfaces of the veneered board to the air so that it dries out evenly.

5. The dry surfaces may be cleaned up with a cabinet scraper, but take care not to cut through the veneer.

Action hints
* Veneering flat boards is most easily handled prior to construction.
* To ensure future stability, both surfaces of the ground board must be veneered. A less expensive veneer may be used on the reverse side as a balancer.
* To stabilise the board, the grain of both surface veneers must run in the same direction.

Edge jointing veneers
Many exotic veneers come from narrow stock. It may be necessary to edge joint veneers to achieve the required width. To do this, trap the two pieces to be jointed between boards held flat on the bench and skim the edges with a finely set, long-soled plane. The resulting butt joint is held together with gummed strip.

Edge treatment of boards
Lip with solid wood before or after veneering. If the lipping is applied before veneering, it gives the appearance of solid wood. But, rather than approach veneering as if it were a means to disguise 'inferior' surfaces, use the process, wherever possible, to make a positive statement.

Index 1

Index 2

Glossary

Log	Useful part of the felled tree.
Butt or boule	Lower section of trunk near stump.
Bast	The inner bark.
Sapwood	Layer of wood beneath the bast.
Heartwood	Dead sapwood, the stiff backbone of the tree.
Burr or burl	Growths usually at the trunk's base, which often display exceptional figure.
Quarter-sawn	Description of method of cutting planks from a log as near as possible to the natural lines of cleavage (radially) so as to expose figure most advantageously.
Plain-sawn	Description of method of cutting planks tangentially from a log (through and through).
Grain	The lay or arrangement of wood fibres.
Straight grain	Wood fibres running parallel to length of tree or plank.
Cross grain	Where wood fibres deviate from the parallel.
Wavy grain	Irregular patterns formed by wood fibres.
Interlocked grain	Direction of grain reversing through the wood.
End grain	That grain which is produced by cutting across the face of a plank.
Texture	The size and arrangement of wood cells. Fine or close textured wood has smaller cell pores and generally gives itself to a finer finish. Uniform texture refers to the similarity in cellular formation through the seasonal growth areas of the wood.
Figure	The decorative markings occasioned by wood's structural characteristics.
Movement	Term used to refer to wood's natural disposition to swell and shrink in sympathy with the humidity of its surrounding atmosphere.
Face side	Usually the surface of a piece of wood selected for its best qualities to show in the finished piece, and from which all other measurements are taken. Traditionally marked with a loop.
Face edge	A true edge in relation to the face side traditionally marked by a line continued from the end of the face side loop.
Chamfer	An angled corner of a piece of wood.
Arris	A sharp corner or edge formed by the meeting of two surfaces.
Groove	A channel cut in the direction of the grain.
Housing or dado	A channel cut across the grain.
Mortise	Part of a joint normally associated with frames and constructions using posts and rails. It is a rectangular hole cut into a post (or leg) to accept a rail tenon.
Tenon	The end of a rail cut to shape so as to fit into a mortise. The width of the tenon should be ⅔ the width of the rail.
Book-matching	Re-sawing a plank through its depth.
Rebate or rabbet	A rectangular recess cut into the edge of a board.
Bevel	The angled edge of a board or tool (the bevel edged chisel).

Our special thanks to the Norman Beverton Workshops for building the following pieces for the book: The workbench, saw horse, chest and mirror frame (carved by Martin Atcherley), bench, cook's counter, dresser, dining chair, table, sideboard, study chair and shelving (finished by Fred Baier), night stand, dressing table, chest of drawers and bed ends.

Photograph credits

Pages 6,7	Shaun Skelly/Daily Telegraph
10,11	Robert Estall
18	Richard Starr/Fine Woodworking
21	John Makepeace
42	Howard Raybould
64	Richard La Trobe Bateman
80, 81, 83	Jonathan Pollack
90	Ian Dobbie
99, 100, 101	Fred Baier
105	Wendell Castle
120	Ashley Cartwright
138, 139	Lee Friedlander, Bob Stocksdale
9, 140–143	Bengt Carlén
140, 174	Martin Atcherley

For invaluable assistance with our photography, we would like to thank Dennis Gray, Mr. Wharton of Buck and Ryan Ltd. London, John Sainsbury, Record Ridgeway Tools Ltd. Sheffield, Mr. Philips of Trend Machinery and Cutting Tools Ltd. Watford, William Mallinson and Sons Ltd. London, The Building Research Establishment Princes Risborough, and Black and Decker Tools Ltd.